PAUPERLAND

JEREMY SEABROOK

Pauperland

Poverty and the Poor in Britain

HURST & COMPANY, LONDON

First published in the United Kingdom in 2013 by
C. Hurst & Co. (Publishers) Ltd.,
41 Great Russell Street, London, WC1B 3PL
© Jeremy Seabrook, 2013
All rights reserved.
Printed in the United Kingdom

The right of Jeremy Seabrook to be identified as the author
of this publication is asserted by her in accordance with the
Copyright, Designs and Patents Act, 1988.

A Cataloguing-in-Publication data record for this book is
available from the British Library.

ISBN: 978-1-84904-273-4

www.hurstpublishers.com

CONTENTS

ACKNOWLEDGEMENTS

Although this book is the result of many years' involvement with poor people, it has also been nourished by the work of many writers on the nature and development of poverty. Among those whose publications have been informative and stimulating, Sir Frederic Eden's *The State of the Poor*, in 1797, has provided the most comprehensive history of the poor up to the middle of the eighteenth century; and it provided a framework for the history of poverty. Dorothy Marshall's *The Poor in the Eighteenth Century* is a rich store of insights into the late pre-industrial era, while the *Report of the Poor Law Commission* of 1834 must be one of the most profoundly ideological documents ever to have been produced by government. It embodied the tenets and values of political economy with an exuberance and enthusiasm that have had a long and vibrant afterlife. In the modern era, Gertrude Himmelfarb's *The Idea of Poverty* is a scholarly and sophisticated effort to demonstrate that capitalism is the sole remedy for all the ills it sought to address, as well as the multiple evils it created. Peter Townsend's *Poverty* is an extraordinarily detailed account of what it meant to be poor in the second half of the twentieth century, but most significant of all is R. H. Tawney's *Religion and the Rise of Capitalism*, which chronicles the changing moral status of poverty and wealth.

I would like to acknowledge the help and suggestions of Kamini Adhikari, Barry Davis, Trevor Blackwell and, especially, Ivan Ruff. I have also gained much from Mukul Sharma, Charu Gupta, Bharat Dogra, Sugata Srinivasaraju, Rosy, and Dr Sanjeev Jain. I have been given some financial help by the Network for Social Change, and am grateful to Amanda Sebastyen. I would like to recognise the continuing support of the Institute of Race Relations, especially A. Sivanandan, Jenny Bourne and Hazel Walters.

Jeremy Seabrook   London, July 2013

PREFACE

This book reflects on poverty and poor people. It looks at constancy and change in how people experience want. It is not a history of poverty, nor is it part of an extensive academic literature on the poor. I have simply wondered how poverty has managed to survive both rigorous punishment of the poor and the accumulation of the most spectacular riches the world has ever seen. It consists of a series of questions, to which any answers I suggest are only tentative and provisional. How did sufficiency cease to represent enough? Why have distinctions between the 'bashful' poor and the 'aggressive' poor, the respectable and the rough, been so difficult to sustain? Why did the proportion of poor people increase with the growing wealth of Britain? Is the desire for more really an expression of human nature, or does it tell us more about the nature of capitalism? How did poverty cease to be a 'natural' condition and become a cause for shame? And when did wealth stop being a temptation to which it was foolish to succumb? What is the fate of limitless accumulation in a finite world?

Far from the least of these questions is where do the attitudes which animate popular resentment of the poor come from? The utterances of contemporary politicians, commentators and observers are never without precedent. The remedies and policies advocated by today's government, think-tanks and policy reviews have all been rehearsed for centuries. It is a rarely remarked upon irony that, given the waste and extravagance of the contemporary world, the one thing that is perpetually recycled is our own history, nowhere more so than in the repetition of ancient strictures upon the poor. Ideas that are flourished as novelty by conservatives and radicals alike are usually found to have been slumbering within a torpid consciousness which cannot wait to forget the past, in order to rediscover it and propose its failed responses as the latest expedient for dealing with poverty. For this reason, a good proportion of this book is devoted to historical precedents, legislation and attitudes which illuminate, not so much how far we have come in the increase of wealth—for that is indisputable—but how short a road we have travelled in our reactions to the poor and excluded.

INTRODUCTION

The history of the poor is a history of attitudes towards the poor, since the voices of poor people have generally gone unheard. What can be seen, dimly, in the clouded mirror of legislation affecting the poor, is the responses of those in power which mutated considerably according to the degree of menace they posed to the ruling classes, or the level of charity which these same ruling classes adopted towards them. Even when the poor do express themselves, what they say is almost always interpreted or re-interpreted, not only by their enemies, but also by their friends—the latter usually have some ideological axe to grind, and they enlist the poor for purposes other than their improvement: this is as true of the mob which clamoured for 'King and Country' in the eighteenth century, as it was of an impoverished working class, called by its Marxist mentors to carry out an historic 'destiny' of changing the world.

The English language is particularly rich in terms for 'poverty'; the word itself conceals a multitude of meanings, and does not distinguish the diversity of ways in which it is possible to be poor. 'Poverty' covers the destitution of refugees and victims of natural catastrophes; it is used to describe the condition of marginal farmers, the evictees of development, slum living in the settlements of Dhaka or Kinshasa, the privations of ravaged housing schemes in rich societies; but also the elective frugality of certain religious orders and the restraint of people trying to resist over-consumption. The synonyms for poverty, however, tell the story of how it has changed over time, which is the subject of this book. 'Want' and 'need' (in the singular, because in the plural they have quite different connotations) suggest an absence of basic sustenance, people on the edge of survival. The words evoke ruined harvests, lean seasons and grudging earth; a penury that has been the fate of most peoples through recorded time. To this, 'misery' adds, perhaps, a psychological dimension: it suggests the unhappiness that comes from knowing that this state is not inevitable.

This early idea of poverty has pervaded all its successors. Even when the threat to life has been lifted from societies that can ensure sufficiency, memories of great hungers and migrations haunt the imagination; a menace that still hovers over landless people, indigenous populations and those whose ancestral lands have been degraded, or confiscated for mining and infrastructural development.

Subsistence is a much misunderstood word. Originally a philosophical term meaning 'that which has continued existence', it came in the seventeenth century to denote livelihood, and hence, survival. It is now—erroneously—applied to generalised poverty in developing countries; it means self-provisioning, usually from the land, a form of independence long vanished from the 'developed' world. Because of its association with self-reliance, it is anathema to the evangelists of permanent economic growth, who use it as an index of absolute dereliction.

In passing from a fragile subsistence into a cash economy and then into industrial life, the words for poverty change. Instead of poverty being the common lot, people are 'stricken' or 'afflicted' by it; and the figure of the 'pauper' emerges (verb to pauperise, *to make poor*), spectral, skinny, rapacious. Urban, industrial impoverishment differs from its rural predecessor in that it implies lack of monetary resources to buy the necessities of life. It suggests mendicancy, people abandoned by the supports of kinship and incapable, through physical or mental impairment, of selling their labour.

Until the eighteenth century, 'indigence' was felt to be the natural condition of humanity, from which labour—or the charity of others—was the sole relief. More recently, indigence has become a synonym for genteel poverty, suggesting the downward mobility of the 'distressed'.

The poverties of industrial society are also distinguished by class. 'Immiseration' (*verelendung*) was the word used by Marx in his prediction of the growing impoverishment of the working class; a highly specialised usage, rendered obsolete by the failure of his prophecy. The fears of the working poor were different from the poverty of a sinking middle class, those 'ruined' by speculation or peculation. 'Insolvency' implies temporary embarrassment; those 'in straitened circumstances' have known better times; to be 'impecunious' or 'in difficulties' are euphemisms for those provisionally unable to pay importunate creditors. People 'of limited means' suggest a practice of careful husbandry, distinct from the reckless and improvident.

'Scarcity' remains. This features prominently in modern economics, and the words 'scarce resources' are constantly on the lips of those for whom sufficiency is no longer enough; and who lament the obligations of 'austerity', in a world where global GDP in 2011 reached over $70 trillion. 'Scarcity', in this context, is a result, not of scanty provisions but of a failure of distributive justice; it assimilates even the most artificially-maintained poverties to natural desolation.

Hidden in this lexicon of poverty is a growing contrivance in maintaining the poor in the condition to which everyone else—except themselves—has become accustomed. With mass prosperity, the language of poverty mutated once more. The most common word for poverty today is 'deprivation', a revealing term for the contemporary state of being poor. For 'deprivation' means having something withheld or taken away. To deprive is an active verb; it is what some people do to others. The deprived, as in deprived children, deprived neighbourhoods, deprived families—focus of the charitable exaltations of celebrities and philanthropists—are not the wanting in any state of nature, chance or inadvertence, but are victims of wholly remediable injustice. Their survival in a world of plenty says that modern poverty is an artefact, an expedient that serves ideological rather than humanitarian purposes. If the poor of the modern world have been artfully dispossessed, they must remain so, in order that the necessity for continuing—indeed indefinite—accumulation should not be called into question. Nothing could be more damaging to capitalism than that people should declare themselves content with what they have; a danger, no doubt slender, but one to be averted at all costs.

We use words casually, unaware of the assumptions they contain or the moral charge they bear. But we can see in the changing vocabulary the journey of humanity from a poverty created by nature, into poverties manipulated by ruling castes and hierarchies, and thence into the managed penury of 'advanced' industrial society.

There is another twist in the poverty which accompanies our prodigious capacity to produce. A global iconography of plenty is calculated to make everyone—even the most favoured—feel subjectively, if not poor, at least prey to insufficiency, since few can afford every purchase they desire. In this way, poverty has become once more the 'natural' condition of the majority of humankind; only this poverty has no cure, since it no longer refers to an absence of the necessities of life; but is, rather, an aspect of perpetual economic expansion, an imperative which, paradoxically, impoverishes us all, and not only now, but for the foreseeable future.

Such a wide and highly-charged vocabulary makes it difficult to detach responses towards the poor from the actual experience of being poor. Since poor people are never in power, whatever is being done to them, for them—on their behalf, or in their name—is carried out without consulting them. It has become almost impossible to detach moral judgements from policy, and dispassionate description from polemics.

Since the first industrial era, what Adam Smith called the 'opulence' of the people has grown constantly, although at the same time, the gulf between rich and poor has widened. This puzzled observers in the late eighteenth and early nineteenth centuries—and continues to do so—and gave considerable impetus to the assumption, already several centuries old, that poverty must be caused by the wilful perversity of the poor.

In recent years, the wealth of industrial society has also conjured unfamiliar poverties out of the abundance that has been an object of universal admiration. And instead of the achievement of plenty being welcomed with satisfaction or contentment, it is accompanied by a complaint of enduring insufficiency; to which the obvious—and overused—response of 'rising expectations' is an incomplete answer. For those rising expectations do not necessarily have their origin in the dissatisfaction of the people but are, rather, a reflection of the systematic need of industrial society for permanent growth and expansion. To succeed in making people accept responsibility for the imperatives of an economic system is a strange accomplishment; is it the desire for more an inherent human yearning, or an attribute of an impersonal economic process? Whatever the answer, this has invaded the popular psyche, and serves to propel, from within, the economic machine.

There is a paradox at the heart of this universe of increasing wealth, or at least the version of it originating in Western Europe. A feeling of perpetual inadequacy comes with rising disposable income; with the result that what we cannot afford takes on a more powerful lustre than anything we have already acquired. In this context, poverty, both as concept and experience, takes on a new urgency

INTRODUCTION

This book explores how this has come about, and asks whether the constraints of planetary resources will compel an alteration in what has become, in the rich countries, a 'normal' way of life, and for those who have not yet achieved it, a compelling aspiration. Since growth and expansion in perpetuity are impossible, can the transition to a more modest way of living be accomplished peaceably, or will it occur only as a consequence of some great catastrophe?

This is not the work of fortune tellers or the highly successful merchants of apocalypse, who always flourish at times of global uncertainty. If we are armed with insight into how we got here, there is a greater chance of finding a non-violent way to conserve, or perhaps even more importantly, to survive.

I

HOW THE WORLD REMAINS POOR

'Mankind, it seems, hates nothing so much as its own prosperity. Menaced with an access of riches that would lighten its toil, it makes haste to redouble its labours and to pour away the precious stuff, which might deprive of plausibility the complaint that it is poor.'

These words of R. H. Tawney in *Religion and the Rise of Capitalism*, referred to the increased wealth of Europe in the sixteenth century, wealth squandered on warfare.[1] Tawney's observation has not been invalidated by posterity. For the modern world has learned, with the help of wealth such as it had never seen, a poverty so profound and immitigable, that no one can foresee an end to it. A feeling of impoverishment gnaws away, not only at those surviving on the edge of subsistence, but also at people who, in a more innocent time, might have been called rich.

How such a condition has come about is rarely debated; perhaps because of its central importance to what we commonly understand as 'our way of life'. An experience of insufficiency is natural when permanent economic growth takes priority over everything else. In the presence of limitless expansion, everyone feels under-rewarded, deprived or robbed of the recognition they think they deserve; none more so than the already wealthy, since they measure riches, not against what they have,

[1] Tawney, R. H., *Religion and the Rise of Capitalism*, London: Pelican Books, 1961.

but against the multitude of treasures, material and spiritual, they do not yet possess. Our 'worth' is assessed in relation, not to any known human satisfaction, but rather to the power of production of an economy which is, in theory, boundless. Who could expect to fulfil desires prompted by this profane version of the infinite?

This is why it is vain to protest at greed, to rail at the super-rich, to censure the excesses of those who administer themselves exorbitant rewards, since their work is considered vital for the alleviation of a nearly universal sense of privation. The income of bankers is often described as 'compensation'; as though they were the victims of some terrible calamity, for which no reparation can ever suffice.

If people feel diminished and powerless, pitifully remunerated, constantly unrecognised, this is because capitalism is the keeper of a dangerous, but highly profitable, secret—it knows how to promote a sense of universal neediness, to set up a wanting without end, a cult and culture of desire which must not be thwarted. Human longing, formerly expressed, sometimes contained, often held captive, by the consolations of religion, is now simply another business opportunity; and because even the wealthiest can gain only a fraction of the plenitude of a global market, they become frustrated by what they do not have. This does not, of course, prevent them from flourishing what they do have in the company of those who have less; but they persist in pining for all that remains, tantalisingly, just beyond the reach of their outstretched hands and overstretched means.

So it has come about that no one can now define the meaning of 'enough'. Confronting this riddle, we are all poor. Great philanthropists are poor—imagine all the good works foregone for the want of a few billions more? Bankers are poor, since the solace of their millions still fails to satisfy their mysterious cravings. Russian oligarchs are poor, since, having appropriated the assets of the state, they must go into exile to protect themselves from the envious and vengeful. The great landowners of Britain are poor, under the responsibility of maintaining their estates and transmitting them to posterity. Chief executives are poor, for how can money cure the ulcers, heart conditions and health ruined in monastic dedication to the doctrines of wealth creationism? Showbusiness and sporting celebrities are poor, since noone fully acknowledges the extent of their talent or the burn-out of living and loving in the fast lane? Even footballers are poor, because the period of their agility is brief and their careers are soon abridged by time. Professional women and men are poor, overtaken, both in salary and social prestige, by more showy occupations. Bricklayers, carpenters and plumbers are poor, since they fight constantly to keep up the living standards to which their skills entitle them. Carers and service personnel are poor, because their contribution to society is undervalued. Domestic servants, cleaners and retail workers are poor, since their presence is scarcely acknowledged by those who employ them. Beggars are poor. The homeless are poor. Alcoholics and those enslaved to addictions are poor. Under the universal flail of poverty, governments are poor, compelled to cut public expenditure with heavy hearts, a course of action they can contemplate only in the superior light of the national interest.

Robert Skidelsky and Edward Skidelsky in *How Much is Enough?*[2], argue that capitalism was 'founded on a Faustian pact'. The devils of avarice and usury were given free rein, on the understanding that, having lifted humanity out of poverty, they would quit the scene for good. A paradise of plenty would ensue, with all men free to live as only the happy few had lived.

The promise that all wants may be fulfilled by economic magic has robbed humanity of the very power that wealth was expected to bestow: an awareness of what would constitute a secure sustenance. The objective of almost everyone is to acquire a greater share of the wealth of the world. This is a relatively recent development, since the poor have traditionally scarcely dared even to dream of subsistence. It is also a major contributor to social peace, since what could be a greater source of unity between all classes and conditions of people than their unity in a shared desire to relieve their common affliction? The riots in England of August 2011 disturbed this carefully crafted equilibrium, for it strained the ideological harmony between rich and poor, who make common cause against a shared feeling of insufficiency. The rioters were presented by the government as examples of 'pure criminality', since to succumb to the proposition that they were caused by 'deprivation' would shatter the joint project of a people dedicated to a constant increase in their 'purchasing power', not in theory, but in the practice and experience of daily life.

How easily whatever disposable income we have slips through our fingers, and what a pitiful shortage it represents of what is necessary for

---

[2] Skidelsky, Robert and Skidelsky, Edward, *How Much is Enough?*, London: Allen Lane, 2012.

a half-decent life. When economic consciousness crowds out its social and moral equivalents, the consequences are unlikely to be benign. Individuals cannot be blamed for reflecting the dominant ideology of the age. Economic necessity has been assimilated and now appears as more or less identical with human needs. The people have adopted as their own the requirement of the economy for permanent growth: its impersonality has been 'humanised', and we tenderly articulate its iron compulsions, as though these were an expression of our deepest longings.

The rehabilitation of the rich is a major consequence of these developments; and is the principal reason why bankers have gone largely unpunished for their role in the crisis of the early twenty-first century. Their lack of humility shows they are keenly aware of their indispensability to the sorcery of wealth generation. They are untouchable, and they live in a world of their own, which is not this one, for it is a place of myth; a fortress where billion-dollar decisions are made, fortunes are created and rivals vanquished by a single stroke of the keyboard. They occupy the crystal spheres, a modern version of the Fates or Norns, engineers of human destiny, gods endowed with human jealousies: at the first hint of punitive measures against them, they threaten to retreat to the Olympus or Asgard of tax-havens, taking with them the secret of the holy substance without which we are nothing.

Despite the lament of the people—all the people—that they are on the brink of pauperism, poverty is not the most urgent problem in the world. The source of the mischief of contrived scarcities lies with wealth, or rather, with a reductive idea of riches, elevated into mentor and guide, become oppressor and tyrant.

Long before the poor became a social and economic problem, wealth was seen as the principal enemy of humankind through its power to imperil our immortal soul, the seductive light with which it drew people on to perdition. Perhaps this is why we throw away, or consume heedlessly, the vast productive power of the globe which is so much greater than the modest wealth of the sixteenth century: in order to sustain the gratifying fiction of enduring poverty; a poverty which affects those who live in plenty no less than people scavenging for survival.

Tawney wrote of a world 'which turned the desire for pecuniary gain from a perilous, if natural, frailty, into the idol of philosophers and the mainspring of society'. His cautionary chronicling of how old religious vices were transformed into economic virtues seems to have been lost to the world. And a profound truth—that a lack of the means of sustenance makes the life of an individual not worth living, has blinded us to an even greater falsehood, namely, that well-being grows in proportion to the accumulation of wealth. The cost of this misperception is to condemn humanity to an impoverishment without cure. For poverty is now securely institutionalised. In Britain, anyone with an income of less than 60 per cent of the median is deemed poor. Such calculations guarantee the immortality of misery and hence, the necessity into the most distant of futures, for further economic expansion.

2

THE PERILS OF WEALTH

Mutable moralities

There has always been tension between rich and poor and their respective fates; and although the former have been in control for much of our history, their supremacy has rarely gone unchallenged for prolonged periods. The poor, whether as children of God, peasant insurrectionaries, sturdy beggars, an assertive industrial working class or a feared 'underclass', have given constant cause for concern to the wealthy and the powerful; and history has been influenced by the need to accommodate them, whether they are in the majority, or, as in today's rich societies, reduced to minority status. The relationship has been close, tempestuous, often acrimonious; but the avoidance of violent revolution in Britain suggests that harmony has been maintained by a recognition that both rich and poor have their place in the scheme of things; that wealth may show itself as generous abundance as well as oppressive arrogance, and poverty as stoical frugality as well as rancorous envy.

Our present preoccupation with the 'treatment' of poverty indicates that it is thought of as a sickness, contagious at that. This is not new. The traditional need to 'relieve' poverty shows it has often been seen as an affliction or malady. 'Relief' was, however, only temporary. Rarely has a cure been seriously proposed.

This draws attention from the pathologies of wealth, which are inseparable from the apparently intractable 'problem' of poverty. Everyone knows the world is rich, and capable of answering the basic needs of everyone in it, needs the Chilean economist Manfred Max-Neef says are 'finite, few and classifiable, the same in all cultures and in all historical periods'.[1] Justifications for why these remain unmet for so many people (by no means all those officially classified as 'poor') offer great opportunities to theorists, economists, philosophers, social scientists, prophets and commentators, who have rarely failed to console the rich and powerful for the obduracy of a poverty, the reduction of which is one of the few areas in which they are not displeased to admit their lack of influence.

The first premise of these heroic apologetics is based upon the great informing myth of capitalism, that everyone can be rich, and indeed wants to become so. This desire is ascribed to something universal, called 'human nature', which, in this context, assumes a predatory and savage character; its capacity for altruism, idealism and compassion suppressed. This has less to do with the nature of humanity than with the nature of capitalism; the conflation of the two creates a mischievous ambivalence. Human nature is a kind of beast of burden, hitched to the chariot of wealth, which it drives with an unflagging energy and insatiable wants; and upon which sits power, omnipresent and sanctified, riding in fierce, uncontested majesty.

But wealth has not always been an undisputed object of reverence. In early Christianity, the sin of avarice was an attack upon riches, or rather on the abuse or misuse of them. In the third century of the Christian era, Clement of Alexandria described avarice as a morbid condition, a state of unfulfilled passions which sets the sinner on fire with yearning, and even worse, destroys his rational understanding of the need for moderation.[2] Wealth was not necessarily evil in itself, since if it were so, how could the scriptures have taught that the rich could earn salvation through almsgiving, a ransom which amply justified their material good fortune? Excessive desire for wealth was wrong, particularly if gained at the expense of the necessities of the poor. These admonitions had a long and tenacious life; and if they died, they did so of natural causes among the esoteric calculations of political arithmetic.

---

[1] Max-Neef, Manfred A., *Human Scale Development, Application and Further Development*, New York: The Apex Press, 1991.

[2] Newhauser, Richard, *The Early History of Greed*, Cambridge: Cambridge University Press, 2000.

The sinfulness of usury was transmitted to Christianity from Judaism and classical Antiquity. Aristotle believed money was barren: it could not breed, since it was not a living thing. This idea pervaded early Christianity, in particular the Eastern church. St John Chrysostom, in one of his homilies in the third century, said 'Do you not see how God allows us all things in common? For if He permitted there to be poor people in the midst of prosperity, this, too, was for the encouragement of the rich, so that by giving alms to the indigent, the wealthy might be able to strip the sin from themselves.'[3]

In the medieval world, economic activity was not an end in itself. It was, as in most cultures, embedded in a wider scheme of behaviour and system of morality. It was subordinated to the supreme end of salvation. Tawney quotes Heinrich von Langenstein, a medieval Schoolman, who wrote, 'He who has enough to satisfy his wants, and nevertheless ceaselessly labours to acquire riches, either in order to obtain a higher social position, or that subsequently he may have enough to live without labour, or that his sons may become men of wealth and importance—all such are incited by a damnable avarice, sensuality and pride.'[4] The asceticism of early Christianity, the voluntary poverty of mendicant orders, the poor sanctified by a scripture which promised they would inherit the earth, made of wealth an object of suspicion, as well as of desire. The prodigious riches of the Church, its vast accumulation and extensive economic activity made St Bernard lament in the twelfth century, 'The Church is resplendent in her walls, beggarly in her poor. She clothes her stones in gold and leaves her sons naked.' But poverty was not a matter for perplexity, since it was the condition of the vast majority of humankind; and relief of poverty, however imperfectly accomplished, a sacred duty of the rich.

The preoccupation of the Church with the dangers of wealth should not be taken too seriously. The feudal system depended upon rigid hierarchies of overlordship and servitude, and it was necessary to sustain these pyramids of privilege, a task in which the Church was no sleeping partner. But if people did not live up to professed values—and when do they?—this does not mean such values were not devoutly embraced, and the practices they suggested were not, at least intermittently, and by some believers, earnestly striven for. The tenacity of the idea of the just price,

<hr>

[3] St John Chrysostom, Homily 77 on the Gospel of St John, third century.
[4] Tawney, *Religion and the Rise of Capitalism*, London: Pelican Books, 1961.

usurious lending, the fair wage, suggests that, even as economics freed itself from religious and ecclesiastical control, a sense of economic righteousness was for centuries a serious obstacle to that exuberance which, by the nineteenth century, had burst forth in celebration of the self-regulating market.

After the long struggle by wealth for official emancipation, the idea of *turpe lucrum* remained despite now being shorn of religious associations; ill-gotten gains were still, in theory, stigmatised; money could be dirty and wealth tainted; while 'brass' and 'muck' were long associated, not entirely negatively, in the minds of the pragmatic representatives of British enterprise. Of course, these ancient prejudices have long been overcome; and wealth, through the subtle alchemy of economic reason, has been cleansed of its impurities, and now stands as the supreme enabler of humanity.

Just as wealth has not always been venerated, neither has poverty always been a source of shame: frugality, restraint, even the present-day bogey of 'austerity', have been not terrors to flee but ideals to strive for. Confronted in our age of stupendous luxury, by the stubborn poverties we are all familiar with, perhaps it is time to elevate once more the virtues of a temperate sobriety, since this might call into question a wealth now perceived as an unalloyed good, and an object of universal admiration. For wealth commands many of the rites and observances formerly associated with religion, a development which raises questions about the nature of 'secular' societies.

To rationalists of the eighteenth century it seemed that ancient superstitions were an encumbrance to the making of wealth. They did not, however, in spite of shedding unreason in practical affairs, abandon the idea of the 'invisible hand', of Providence, of edicts of nature, or other manifestations of the elusive laws of God. Faith is like poverty in this respect—it finds its way into human purposes by stealth, sometimes apparently in disguise, and unrecognised for what it is. The spiritual ghost never completely deserted the economic machine; and it has been one of the marvels of modernity that archaic beliefs and outworn values have, not merely lain dormant, sheltered by what appear to be purely material processes, but have been summoned once more to inform contemporary ideologies with irrationality, magical thinking and quasi-religious ideas of the sacred.

THE PERILS OF WEALTH

Secular societies and their faith

The contention that Western societies are secular, like the claims that their urgent economic energies are deployed solely for material ends, is misleading. This is recognised by the orthodox adherents of other religions, who see things less tortuously. The sometimes violent reaction to the declared secularism of the West is a response not so much to its godlessness as to its hypocrisy, to a pretence of materialism, which is nonetheless surrounded by the ceremony and ritual of religion. If the West were truly materialistic, it would show a greater respect for the material world on which its prosperity is based. As it is, the abuse of the fabric of the planet required by the pursuit of wealth suggests a semi-mystical quest to discover what lies on the other side of human destructiveness. This project is perceived by many pious people, including some Christians, as a violation, not only of religion, but also of the security of the only habitat we have.

The dedication of the West to the creation of wealth requires an act of faith on the part of its votaries, no less stringent and arbitrary than the commitment required by all religions, as well as by other cults, dogmas and heresies which have, throughout history, demanded their tribute of human sacrifice. Western ideology—the more powerful for its denial that any such thing exists—is based upon a belief in limitlessness. This, according to the same system of belief, corresponds uniquely and universally to the unlimited desires of humanity: capitalism alone understands the art of marrying these boundless wants with a permanent capacity to answer them; and what is more, possesses the mysterious power to transform these chaotic desires into public good. As soon as any social system engages itself with the desire of humanity for transcendence, it trespasses upon the realm of religions, all of which have taught restraint and continence. It yields to what the ancient world—and the early Christians—called *pleonexia*, a morbid desire for possession.

Any dealings with the infinite, the universal and perpetuity are clearly not of this world. That these should be accounted the stuff of material endeavour is seen by other religions as sacrilege. Faith in infinite economic growth in a finite world is not a more refined belief—or superstition—than any other. The ideology may appear justified, even sanctified, by a tangible productive power, but this does not make it any more worthy of faith than the miracles of other religions.

So when economic missionaries go forth (and the International Monetary Fund, Asian Development Bank and World Bank do maintain 'missions' in countries that extend hospitality to them) to impart secrets of wealth-creation, they recommend not only deregulation of the economy, but also the deregulation of desire, opening up the brimming reservoirs of human longing. Seemingly technocratic recommendations tread on the terrain of faiths, which have preached temperance, self-discipline and sufficiency. This should come as no surprise, since the doctrines of capitalism once violated ground sacred to the Christian faith, before a majority of Christians had become wise enough to learn that avarice, envy and greed were the motors of human nature. The development of capitalism was sustained by these somewhat contorted sacred roots, even if these have now withered, exhausted, perhaps, by the extraordinary harvest it has yielded.

The virtues of thrift and avoidance of excess retained a serviceable link with religious teaching (especially for the poor who had few temptations to anything else), until these were swept away by more urgent economic necessities of consumerism. If we too, in the West, have become caught up in compulsions at odds with our own religious tradition, at least these have evolved from within—a consequence of Reformation, Protestantism, Puritanism and an industrial revolution—and were not brought from elsewhere by imperial entities who claimed mastery of the Earth.

Exhortations to temperance and the curbing of appetite and desire, characterised Islam, Hinduism, Buddhism, Jainism, and the animism of indigenous people everywhere, who made sacred the forests, streams and earth that sustained them and their descendants. When these values are vanquished by a nominally secular creed, this is experienced as an assault on their profoundest beliefs and practices. It is felt as a perversion of human purposes and a violation of the sanctity of creation. The 'creation of wealth' appears, not as the conquest by industrial society of nature, but as a profanation of it.

The triumph in our time of belief in the semi-mystical power of wealth is tempered by pious warnings that the economy exists for humanity, and not humanity for the economy. But spiritual warnings against the perils of wealth have rarely prevented its possessors from being venerated. A Christianity that believed it was easier for a camel to pass through the eye of a needle than for a rich man to enter the kingdom of heaven, had its saints of voluntary poverty, although the Church amassed wealth which was the envy of secular princes and monarchs. Of the medieval world, Tawney observes, 'The Church was an immense vested interest, implicated to the hilt in the economic fabric, especially on the side of agriculture and land tenure. ...The persecution of the Spiritual Franciscans, who dared, in defiance of the bull of John XXII (*Quorumdam exigit*), to maintain St Francis' rule as to evangelical poverty, suggests that doctrines impugning the sanctity of wealth resembled too closely the teaching of Christ to be acceptable to the princes of the Christian church.'[5]

This did not inhibit the social teaching of the Church well beyond the Middle Ages from continuing to warn against usury and against the appetite for acquisition. Wealth was not a just reward for labour; trade and commerce were justified only if the merchant received the equivalent of the labourer's reward. The medieval theorist condemned as sinful what would later become essential for accumulation—competition, enterprise and profit; and so it remained, until Calvinism threw a sheen of righteousness over a moderate interest on money given as a loan.

The economic doctrines of the Church sought to regulate economic transactions between individuals—the small craftsman and the labourer were to be safeguarded against the usurer and the engrosser. With the rise in trade and impersonal large-scale economic activity, the teachings of the Church became obsolete; the mercantile classes assumed independent power; economic and spiritual activity were regarded as separate spheres; and religion was banished to the private cloister of personal conscience.

However often religions reiterated that the last shall be first and the first last, wealth has always been the basis and symbol of ruling powers, and has rarely failed to receive the blessing of spiritual elites. Rulers constructed palaces and assembled armies, embellished their monuments and celebrated their own glory; usually with the compulsory labour of slaves, serfs, captives, bondmen and human chattels; and they built their ziggurats and minarets, towers, cathedrals and spires towards heaven, reaching out to supernatural powers to support their continuing supremacy. And gods universally smiled on those favoured by temporal success; warnings on the dangers of wealth were destined for those least likely to succumb to them.

---

[5] Tawney, *Religion and the Rise of Capitalism*, op. cit.

The maintenance of power by a minority depended upon the acquiescence of the poor in social hierarchies in which those at the apex were endowed with gifts of exceptional courage, prowess and a natural ability to govern. Castes, social class, rank, station and degree have had both spiritual and military power at their disposal to preserve this beneficent order of things. The magnificence of these arrangements is accompanied by disquiet: disaffection, rebellion, disloyalty are always possible, since, the rich cannot know the mind of the poor, and suspect them of harbouring a secret desire to reverse the natural order of things. But power has rarely developed an imaginative understanding of its inferiors, and vague apprehensions underlie even the moments of the greatest self-confidence of ruling lineages, whose fate is always, eventually, to be toppled and replaced, less often by the poor than by rivals, conquerors or those more cunning than they.

The taming of the dangerous poor

That the poor might unite and dispossess the lawful holders of position and wealth is always present, as historic risings show; and although these have usually been put down with great savagery, a subterranean resentment and dissatisfaction persists. A literal version of scripture reinforces a faith which elevated the poor and the meek. If this undermined the powerful, and did not appear in this world, it might do so in the next; in recognition of this, the powerful sometimes tempered the harshness with which they treated lesser beings.

And the poor were always represented as inferior. The image of harmony in medieval society was that of the human body, an organism which depended on the various functions, higher and lower, for its survival—those who governed, thought, prayed, fought, bought and sold, and tilled the earth. These classes were impermeable, for without a clear division of purposes the whole could not perform its necessary labour.

Power also saw those beneath them as children, or assimilated them to animals, brutes, beasts of the field, or later, simply as the abstraction of 'labour'. Their merging with dumb creatures helps to account for their long historical silence. The rich have claimed an inherited superiority, 'breeding' or pedigree, always by the appointment of some higher authority. Privilege has been the custodian of culture and civilisation, of leisure and learning; further evidence that the place they hold is in trust from Him Who bestows it, to guide those of lower estate.

Christianity was particularly prone to self-subversion from within its own doctrines; peasant uprisings were justified by the same scripture which upheld their rulers. During the German Peasants' War of the early sixteenth century, a programme of twelve articles demanded the abolition of serfdom, 'For men to hold us as their own property... is pitiable enough, considering that Christ has delivered and redeemed us all, the lowly as well as the great, without exception, by the shedding of His precious blood. Accordingly it is consistent with Scripture that we should be free.'[6] In Britain, the Peasants' Revolt foreshadowed the Civil War; the presence of levellers, diggers and other dissenters nourished the discomfort of those unable to acknowledge the lowly place assigned to them by Providence.

The 'threat' from religious justifications for disturbances to the social order receded, as the holiness of worldly rulers drained from their displays of power. 'The poor', as a secular menace to society, accompanied the dissolution of feudalism. Migratory, unattached, begging, the mass of poor were enfranchised from feudalism; the fear they provoked reflected the resentment by their betters of those liberated by the decay of order. This appears in punishment of the able-bodied poor from the time of the Tudors; a revulsion that has informed all legislation touching the poor ever since.

This anxiety was not misplaced; in the eighteenth century the French Revolution demonstrated again the fragility of hierarchical structures, which seemed to the rulers of Britain to threaten their own stability, as the agricultural order was being undermined by an economic revolution. The shock of events in France, although quickly dispelled, was ineffaceable; each subsequent moment of rebellion in Europe was seen by the governing classes as a threat to their legitimacy. The urban population, combinations of workers, were seen as ruinous to settled interests. Dorset agricultural labourers the 'Tolpuddle Martyrs' were transported to Australia in 1834 in the panic following the 'Swing' riots, agrarian incendiarism and unrest of 1830. In the 1830s and 1840s, the Chartists, despite their modest political demands (enfranchisement of all adult males, equal electoral districts, abolition of the requirement that MPs be property-owners, annual elections and a secret ballot), were seen in the

[6] Engels, Friedrich, *The Peasant War in Germany*, New York: International Publishers, 1966.

same light. When their petition was presented for the third time in April 1848 a mass meeting was called on Kennington Common to form a procession which would convey the petititon to Parliament. The military presence was unprecedented, although no violence occurred, and the crowds dispersed.

The poor drew a new dignity from their role in industrialism. The congested cities and great assemblies of workers under a single roof, as well as facilitating the spread of contagious diseases, also enabled a con-tagion of ideas of collective action, strikes and organisation against injus-tice and their conditions of labour.

The Industrial Revolution altered the threat to wealth and power; the new poor, embodied in the industrial labourer, gave fresh grounds for apprehension. A new kind of human being emerged, unfamiliar, not only to employers and rulers, but also a stranger to itself. The menace was amorphous: people huddled into industrial cities like Manchester and Leeds, where life expectancy was below twenty years, were believed to be susceptible to agitators and demagogues, and to saboteurs and criminals. Despite early socialists, including Robert Owen, who believed that changing the social environment would transform the character of the people, only Karl Marx's great myth of the proletariat enabled people to act consciously in their own interests against those who, shorn of the primitive magic of their station, were reduced to exploiters and oppres-sors. Although the appeal of Marxism was limited in Britain, his story of the unstoppable power of the workers, gave conviction to and strength-ened the pragmatic programmes of British socialism and trade unions.

The Russian Revolution appeared to vindicate Marx's savage prophe-cies. It created even greater anxiety, since it occurred with the first great twentieth-century bloodletting in Europe. Its initial success, and the panic, both in Germany and in England, in the aftermath of the war, seemed to portend the end of institutions which had endured for centu-ries. This apocalyptic moment was destined to be outdone two decades later, by the rise of Fascism and the Second World War. The defeat of Fascism only eased the triumph of Communism; and with the subse-quent dissolution of European empires, a worldwide commitment to some form of socialism was inevitable, a process that reached a climax with the revolution in China.

Throughout these upheavals, the people, however they were known— as masses, workers or the common people—had to be conciliated and appeased. Throughout the nineteenth century and up to 1945, they emerged slowly from the rough shape as 'labouring poor'. As the franchise was extended, they acquired a greater 'stake in society'; their working and living environment became less harsh by a balance between their collective power and the prudent adaptability of governments: factory acts, laws abridging the labour of children, sanitation reform, compulsory education, regulation of housing conditions and urban planning. Their growing self-confidence expressed itself in parties of labour and trades unions; and if these perturbed traditionalists, they proved remarkably well-behaved, less anxious to overturn order than to claim for those they represented a share of the wealth they created. They proved worthy of the gains their organisation and their numerical strength had won them. When in 1945, the welfare state was established, it seemed they had become full partners in a society which had, at first, fiercely resisted their inclusion in benefits reserved for the rich and, later, the middle classes. It was believed in the 1940s, in one of those persistently scriptural metaphors, that 'the lion had lain down with the lamb'; although which of these two represented labour, and which capital, was not spelled out; for reasons which posterity has made clearer.

It appeared the agreement between capital and labour was permanent. It was, after all, nothing more than what the eighteenth century traditionalist Edmund Burke, had expressed. 'In the case of the farmer and the labourer, their interests are always the same ... It is in the interest of the farmer, that his work should be done with effect and celerity; and that cannot be, unless the labourer is well fed, and otherwise found with such necessities of animal life...as may keep the body in full forces and the mind gay and cheerful.'[7] It echoed the temper of Victorian critics of the 'two nations', and was in keeping with the peaceable 'solutions' proposed by reformers, writers and politicians.

That the interests of workers and employers were identical was apparently institutionalised in 1945. It seemed that the gulf between rich and poor would be bridged, the dignity of labour no longer disputable and political equality established. The weak would be protected, those who fell by the wayside lifted up, and the hard-working rewarded. Of course, the rancour of centuries was never completely allayed; but it was reduced to murmurings about the effects on character of feather-bedding by the

---

[7] Burke, Edmund, *Thoughts and Details on Scarcity*, 1795.

23

welfare state. Some alleged that the unreconstructed of a primitive industrialism used their new bathrooms to store coal, and wasted money on things a newly penurious middle class could no longer afford. But resentment was muted; and was not reciprocated by those made secure for the first time.

If only such moments could last. If only societies could know a serene stasis. If only the poor had been simply an excluded remnant, and could all have been assimilated into a soon-to-be universal well-being. If only the give-and-take, the sharing of hardship in wartime could have been sustained in easier times. If only sufficiency had been enough.

Rehabilitating the rich

It seems, in retrospect, naïve to have believed that wealth would acquiesce in its own demotion, and accept as equal those it had treated sometimes with compassion, often with contumely, and always as inferiors. Capital, nimble and opportunistic, more far-seeing than its opponents, was busy in the time of ostensible tranquillity. Its task, after disasters in Europe, the shattered faith in capitalism and the disintegration of the European empires, was to reinvigorate the rich and powerful. Their reputation had been compromised by failure to prevent two devastating wars in thirty years. They appeared inept, belligerent and greedy. A restoration was required.

The lustre of wealth was refurbished in two ways. One was the conversion of the rich: no longer idle and leisured, they became serious, responsible, devoted to the reconstruction of the fortunes of Britain after the imperial collapse. Privilege relieved the workers of their burden of labour, since it promoted itself after the Second World War as a tireless entrepreneur, assuming an heroic work from which the labouring classes were delivered by a sudden access of affluence. The well-to-do exhausted themselves, rushing to and from transcontinental boardrooms, inflicted upon themselves heart conditions and permanent digestive disorders as a result of rigid work schedules, jetting between capital cities to make decisions on global investments, their turbo-charged lives preoccupied with the latest financial instruments and investment vehicles; vigilant for fortunes to be made from collapsing companies and neglected ventures, the pickings to be had after killings, and not always figurative, on futures, invisibles or other intangible objects of profit. Without rest or vacation from promoting this must-have product, financing that takeover, stripping those assets, moving in and out of commodities as though gold, artworks or oil were gauzily permeable, theirs was a task of modernising, updating, picking the technologies of tomorrow that change forever the way we think, buy, eat, live and, of course, fight against the enemies of our peaceable desire to control life on earth. To these heroes of labour new cohorts of people were recruited, devoted to amusing, entertaining and informing the people. Stars and singers, performers, TV celebrities and actors, footballers and musicians, also criss-crossed the globe, exporting creative industries, from busy TV studio to film-set, producing soap-operas and serials about ordinary people as well as privilege, dramas about hospitals, doctors, lawyers and schools, bringing the world to our screens, making us full participants in the ampler life that beckoned to a destiny other than the restricted round of factory, pub, sooty chapel and a miserable week at the seaside, where people took their own food, writing their name in indelible ink on fresh eggs, so as not to be palmed off with inferior produce; gone the wedding in the community hall and the funeral cortege in rank cemetery grass, in favour of extravagant ceremonies and celebrations that befitted our new status as somebodies. Mobility, glamour, fashion, luxury and a life of pampered self-regard—all this made possible by the models of leisure and ease who paraded before our eyes, damaged in their devotion to duty by addictions to alcohol and drugs, tempestuous loves and stormy divorces, depressions and exaltations; with the result that we eventually transcended sombre social determinants, escaped into the sanctum of a private life, until then the preserve of wealth. The rich inspired mass culture, and in doing so, shed all association with the showy arrogance of their forebears.

Many of the newly rich—whose wealth blended in wholesome alloy with old money—were recruited from the former poor or working class. One day a shop girl in Stoke or a porter in a Glasgow hospital, the next top of the charts; the superstar wasting his time in a factory in Leeds or as a council worker in Crawley, and now the object of adulation of weeping girls at the airport and the mob at the stage door. The talent repressed and intelligence choked by poverty and labour flowered in this propitious climate; and money no longer spoke with upper class accents, but proudly announced its regional origins. At the same time, the professions opened, ripe fruit for the children of merit, just as the shores of the Mediterranean were open to all to take advantage of sea and sun. The ideology of

Lady Luck, the winning ticket, the stroke of fortune was also on the rise once more. Those who had 'come up from nowhere' were only too happy at their elevation to the ranks of people who, having presumably emerged from somewhere, recognised their ability and talent. They had no desire to rock any boats which had been raised by the tide; they occupied Jacobean mansions and Georgian town-houses, sprawling villas with swimming pools and private entertainment centres, to which they repaired when their busy lives permitted, sacrificing personal lives, regretting their broken marriage and scattered children, bingeing and then returning to the rehabilitation clinic, depression and disorders that came from giving yet more of themselves to an insatiable public. Such self-immolation and disregard of their own interests in commitment to heroic acts of consumption were the reward of their high calling—personal jets, yachts, the jewels and fast cars, mansions and hideaways on remote islands, poolside parties, overdoses, suicide, the early death of those who had lived in the fast lane.

While this spectacular work of recuperation was taking place, labour itself, source of industrial wealth, the nameless poor of the ages, who had worked and died in a vain hope of better tomorrows, was being disgraced. The economy—that euphemism for capitalism—was expunging the basis on which Britain had proclaimed itself workshop of the world; and the people who had made the wares, mined the coal, produced the energy, woven the cloth, made the steel and machinery, were being divested of their function, as manufacturing industry dismantled itself and fled to where labour was cheaper than the prohibitive commodity it had become in its homeland. Instead of the poor scrambling for the cast-offs of the rich, privilege now donned a livery of labour to advertise its essential importance in the world.

The erasure of industry in Britain began soon after the war. Among the first to go were textiles and footwear: the shoe factories in my home town of Northampton began to close in the 1950s, as imports from Portugal or Italy took their place; immigrants from south Asia appeared in the textile centres of Yorkshire and Lancashire from the mid-fifties, wafted into Bury and Bolton, Keighley and Huddersfield, to live in attics and cellars and plot a takeover of labour which the people of those towns had already repudiated. This was not at first understood as a wider loss of function. But decline accelerated in the sixties, masked by the rising service economy, higher education, welfare and health services, entertainment and fashion industries. In the early 1980s, de-industrialisation gathered pace under the Thatcher administration; the hard substances of industrialism, coal and steel, iron and ceramic, fabric and wood, cloth and wool, dematerialised, and sought out the productive power of others in places we had scarcely heard of. The defeat of the miners' strike of 1984 was symbolic, a requiem for heavy industrial work: less a collapse of organised labour than the removal of the reason for its very existence.

The dissolution of industrial life occurred within the twinkling of an eye—far more rapidly than the extinction of agricultural labour, which declined over more than a century to its vestigial role in the workforce. With the disappearance of industrial labour, the main influence upon the lives of the people for six generations, vanished; and with it, the dignity, the potential power of the workers, their organisation and institutions, upon which an alternative to capitalism was, in some versions of a cancelled future, to have been constructed.

So it was that the vindication of the rich, and the reawakening of their slumbering occult powers, took place in step with the eclipse of labourism. It is significant that the prime ministers of Britain in this period were 'ordinary people', lower middle class or working class: Harold Wilson, Edward Heath, James Callaghan, Margaret Thatcher, John Major. The restitution of wealth took place behind the political scenes; and with it, poverty ceased to be a residual problem, but became, once more, structural: the poor no longer laggards of plenty, but its scorned and excluded. The gap between rich and poor widened, and they saw each other again with an estrangement similar to that with which the landed gentry regarded the labouring poor in the late eighteenth century.

During the period of amicable democratisation, in which poverty was apparently reduced, and political struggle muted, there was a simultaneous raising up of certain conspicuous individuals on account of their capacity for heroic consumption. These represented the pinnacle of a way of life, so successful it had become the object of global striving to the new rich of the world; not just to dictators and leaders of military juntas in gold braid and tinkling medals, but glamorous first ladies rigid in metallic couture, hieratic princesses and divinities of mass culture, the figure-heads of extractive international conglomerates, chief executive officers of companies that bestrode the earth, the owners of brands which seared the consciousness of the world, as hot irons stamped the flank of owners' cattle. At the moment when the most savage predations upon the planet were being lauded and raised to universal dream, questions were raised over the long-term viability of wasteful consumption and wanton wealth. It seemed individuals who exhibited an ability to use up the most resources in their brief, overstuffed lifetime had become examples of aspiration to the rest of us. This threatened terrifying impoverishments, not only for the already poor.

The rich occupy once more the exalted position they knew, when this was believed to be evidence of the mysterious workings of Providence, the ordering of their estate by the Almighty, a consequence of blood and breeding. It does not matter if they have attained their present eminence by chance, by marketing some particular talent or skill, by mischief, fraud or even by honest toil: their unassailable status serves as control and social discipline; and that is the main thing, even if planet and people must be sacrificed to maintain this happy and—for the moment—stable condition.

3

WHERE DID THE POOR COME FROM?

Although poverty had troubled authorities, both ecclesiastical and secular, from the Middle Ages, and 'the poor' had seemed at times a threat to stability, at times a test of the Christian conscience, it was not until the eighteenth century that they became a clearly-defined social menace. When their numbers appeared to multiply, even as the general prosperity of the country increased, the time had come for more severe medicine.

Towards the end of this period, poverty—or pauperism, in its darker form—began to be described as plague or contagion, with 'poverty and wretchedness increasing daily, in exact proportion with our efforts to restrain them'.[1] The numbers dependent upon alms or public relief rose. In 1776, administration of the Poor Law cost £1,529,780, but by 1786 it was over £2 million rising to £4,267,000 in 1803 and £8 million in 1818; the cost of maintaining the poor threatened to overwhelm available resources. The pauper was the spectre at the industrialising feast: how could this figure, wolfish and menacing, have become so visible in a country in which 'the universal opulence extends itself to the lowest ranks of the people?' in the words of Adam Smith?[2]

Karl Polanyi in *The Great Transformation*, says, 'The question of where the poor came from was raised by a host of pamphlets and tracts ... in the

[1] Townsend, Joseph, *Dissertation on the Poor Laws*, 1786.
[2] Smith, Adam, *An Inquiry into the Nature and Causes of the Wealth of Nations*, Oxford: Oxford University Press, 1993.

second half of the eighteenth century. The causes of pauperism and the means of combating it could hardly be expected to be kept apart in a literature that was inspired by a conviction that if only the most apparent evils of pauperism could be sufficiently alleviated it would cease to exist altogether.'[3]

Some of these have a striking contemporary ring. No doubt fluctuations in trade, which drew people into the towns and then sent them back to the countryside when trade faltered, were one element. But enclosure and confiscation of common land, upon which cottage industry—and the survival of many country people—depended, also reduced their capacity for self-provision. The Act of Settlement was still on the statute book until 1795, and although it was not enforced with any rigour in prosperous districts and urban areas, where work was available, the idea of 'belonging' to a parish remained. 'Mobility of labour' retained an association with wandering and mendicancy.

Manufacturing was, in any case, believed by many to be an unreliable provider of security, since no country that neglected food production could thrive. Malthus denied that industrial workers added to the wealth of the country: 'He [the industrial labourer] will have added nothing to the gross produce of the land; he has consumed a portion of this gross produce, and has left a bit of lace in return; and although he may sell this bit of lace for three times the quantity of provisions he has consumed whilst he was making it, and thus be a very productive labourer with regard to himself; yet he cannot be considered as having added by his labour to any essential part of the riches of the state....'[4]

Addressing William Pitt in *Thoughts and Details on Scarcity*, apropos of the aid-in-wages method of relieving the poor, Edmund Burke said, 'The labouring people are poor only because they are numerous. Numbers in their nature imply poverty. In a fair distribution among a vast multitude, none can have much. The class of independent pensioners called the rich, is so extremely small, that if all their throats were cut, and a distribution made of all they consume in a year, it would not give a bit of bread and cheese for one night's supper to those who labour, and who in reality feed both the pensioners and themselves.'[5]

[3] Polanyi, Karl, *The Great Transformation*, Boston: Beacon Press, 1944.
[4] Malthus, Thomas Robert, *An Essay on the Principle of Population*, London, 1798.
[5] Burke, Edmund, *Thoughts and Details on Scarcity*, 1795.

WHERE DID THE POOR COME FROM?

Wonder at the spread of pauperism as wealth increased continued into the nineteenth century. In his *Memoir on Pauperism* in 1834, Alexis de Tocqueville said of Europe, 'The countries appearing to be the most impoverished are those which in reality account for the fewest indigents, and among the people most admired for their opulence, one part of the population is obliged to rely on the gifts of the other in order to live.'[6] He describes England as 'the Eden of modern civilisation', but acknowledges with astonishment that 'one-sixth of the inhabitants of this flourishing kingdom live at the expense of public charity'. He also wrote, presciently, of 'the progress of civilisation', which turned more and more 'wants' into 'needs': it was this that produced 'a pauper class in England that is almost rich by the standards of other countries, and at the same time gives rise to a society able and willing to alleviate the condition of that class. Thus it comes about that the richest country has the largest number of paupers.'

Until Marx's account of the relationship between growing wealth and aggravated poverty, observers strove to account for the phenomenon. Some of their explanations are so convincing, they have been reiterated ever since, and continue to be enunciated as words of revelation.

That the Poor Laws exacerbated the ills they were supposed to alleviate was a common criticism, and it anticipates much comment in our time on the welfare state. The principle is sound, the story runs, but the practice defective. There was some truth in this, particularly insofar as setting the unoccupied poor to work was concerned. Denunciation of the Poor Laws led not to complete abolition of them, as advocated by Malthus—after three centuries of Poor Laws, that was too much even for enthusiasts of political economy—but to the stringent reforms of 1834. Sir Frederick Eden, in *The State of the Poor* (1797) said, 'Even to the idle, under certain restrictions, the law of England has assigned a competent provision exacted from the more opulent part of the community. This law has been so modified as sometimes, and in some respects, well nigh to have lost sight of its first aims and intentions, and it may be questioned whether the indigent classes are now proportionately less numerous and less miserable than they were formerly, whether they have benefited by Poor-houses, Houses of Industry, Friendly Societies, and in what degree the present system and administration of our Poor Laws affect either the progress of industry or the blessings of domestic life.'[7]

---

[6] De Tocqueville, Alexis, *Memoir on Pauperism*, London: Civitas, 1997.
[7] Eden, Sir Frederick, *The State of the Poor*, London, 1797.

To some, administrative reform appeared inadequate, since poverty was, under the authority of the Bible, ineradicable. There was no dearth of explanations for the persistence of poverty, despite charity and the institutions set up to dispense it. Despite technological innovation that promised an end to want, the condition was gloomily accepted as a sad but inevitable necessity. For all the dynamism of early industrial society, it was resigned to the persistence of poverty. The words of Christ, 'The poor ye have always with you' became a sorrowing (and much-repeated) axiom; it was even inscribed on the tympanum of many workhouses in Britain after 1834. For this to become a melancholy benediction upon imperishable poverty, it was taken from context. When Christ said this, he did so in response to objections by his disciples that the expensive ointment of spikenard, used by Martha to anoint his feet before the last supper, would have been better sold and its yield given to the poor. His remark, far from the proclamation of lasting poverty, was a prelude to the second—more important—half of the sentence, 'but me ye have not always'. He was referring to his own forthcoming absence from the world, not to the fact that he was leaving the poor in perpetuity behind him, the human hereditament of a departing Saviour.

If these reasons for enduring poverty were insufficient, the most common of all was to treat the poor, those not exempt by an existential incapacity to provide for themselves, as though they were self-generating and existed for perverse moral reasons known only to themselves. This view makes them responsible for their own condition: inherent improvidence, prodigality and idleness. Accessory to their own misery, they breed irresponsibly, have no thought for the future, squander their substance in clement seasons and save nothing for hard times. They are addicted to luxury, drink and 'vice'. In the early industrial period, much as today, it was the irresponsible and dangerous poor who exercised the minds of observers. (Eric Pickles, community secretary, said in an interview given to the *Daily Mail* in June 2012 it was time to blame the '120,000 troubled families at the bottom of society. These folks', he said 'are troubled: they're troubling themselves, they're troubling the neighbourhood. We need to do something about it.')

The distinction between the deserving and undeserving is of great antiquity; and has given rise to a continuous alternation of charitable and punitive impulses. 'He that hath pity on the poor lends unto the Lord' (Proverbs 19:17) confronts 'If any would not work, neither shall he eat'

(II. Thessalonians 3:10). This oscillation between the merciful and the severe has been constant, according to whether the innocent or the immoral poor appear in the ascendant. There is, however, a problem with this distinction. Even when the widows and orphans, the lame, halt and blind, have been separated from the rest, there still remains a division between the compliant and the refractory poor, the acquiescent and the resistant; that is to say, those unable to find work and become independent through their own efforts, and who wait upon their betters to alleviate their poverty, and those who help themselves, sometimes to the goods and belongings of others.

This group rouses strong passions in all who advocate greater stringency against the poor. In the rhetoric, sometimes the submissive poor, unemployed or dispossessed, through no fault of their own, dominate; at other times, the cynically idle prevail, benefit cheats and welfare queens, battening upon the public purse, about whom Something Must Be Done. These people occupy a quantity of energy and emotion disproportionate to their numbers; but their position is crucial—and constant—in the otherwise fluid hierarchies of the poor.

It might be observed that politicians, pamphleteers and divines who fulminated against the addiction of poor labourers to immorality, sexual incontinence and drink, rarely condemned the same characteristics in their social superiors. In an inversion of the morality which judged the poor, these vices became virtues when exhibited by the possessing classes—excess became liberality and open-handedness, drink and idleness were conduct befitting the station of exuberant young men. While the poor pilfered and stole, the rich progressed through the landscapes of imperialism, plundering whatever took their fancy—all extravagances were justified in those who had the means to pursue them. That the rather meagre pleasures of the poor were a tribute to what were esteemed qualities among their betters did little to mitigate the opprobrium to which they were subject.

Wherever the poor came from, it became clear during the nineteenth century that they were no residuum, to be swept away by the riches generated by industrialism. They were a permanent feature of capitalist society. They were not going to be punished into invisibility or drowned in prosperity.

Since the earliest formulation of Poor Laws in England, the poor have been both cared for and excoriated, cherished and held up as a warning and example to the rest; and these conflicting attitudes had co-existed since the consolidation of the Elizabethan Poor Law in 1601. The administration of the poor law was seriously disrupted during the Civil War, although relief of the aged and impotent continued in most parishes untouched by actual conflict. With the Restoration, a more callous attitude appeared: the Act of Settlement dates from 1662; severe game laws in 1671 prevented the poor from supplementing food from the supply of nature; plans for the 'profitable employment of the poor' were proposed; and in 1697 paupers were compelled to wear a badge declaring their status. Yet by the second half of the eighteenth century, the severity had exhausted itself, making way for a more humane view of the poor, in the endowment of schools, prisons and hospitals. This generosity was eclipsed again by the asperities of the 1834 Poor Law Reform Act.

From time to time, the false and dissembling poor have been flushed out of their hiding places among the innocent and deserving. The shelter provided by religious obligation was broken by the destruction of the monasteries. Some who had been fed and housed by them appeared, when cast out into the world, as cheats and knaves, and were to be scourged and beaten. With every such 'cleansing' of the poor, those who have hidden themselves among their guileless peers, must be separated, cunning goats from ingenuous sheep.

Religious establishments served as a kind of material and spiritual welfare state before the 'dissolution' (a term that implies a natural process of solid matter dissolving in liquid, and at the same time, conjures up the alleged licentiousness of the demolished institutions). There have been at least three periods in Britain, when more or less universal provision has been made against the inevitable vicissitudes of life, however imperfect in practice. First was the enduring Christian duty to succour the poor. This had a remarkably tenacious afterlife, and continues to influence duty to the unfortunate in a secular age. It is the staple fare of Archbishops and other ecclesiastical luminaries who claim 'to speak truth to power'; which they do, however quavering and irresolute their tone may have become.

The second attempt to provide a 'right to live' to the working poor came with the system of aid-in-wages from 1795, called Speenhamland, after the parish in Berkshire which initiated it. This came at the end of a reforming interlude in Britain. When the price of bread rose above a certain level, the wages paid by the farmer would be augmented by the parish, according to the number of the labourer's dependants. As a result, wages fell, because farmers knew however little they paid, the deficit up to subsistence level would be made good by the parish; and since the labourer's wages were guaranteed, however scanty his exertions, work was desultory and neglected. The resulting rise in poor rates, and the lassitude of rural life, led directly to the Poor Law Commission and the abrasive Amendment Act of 1834.

The most effective, and truly universal provision, against poverty, unemployment, sickness, disability and old age, came with the welfare state after the Second World War, when the recommendations of the Beveridge Report (1942) were implemented. The preamble to the National Assistance Act of 1948 stated, 'The poor law shall cease to exist'; a promise of deliverance to millions who had lived in the shadow of workhouse, means test, pawn shop and private moneylender. This, the 'post-war settlement', embodied a permanent accommodation between capital and labour. Although contested at the time, and subsequently eroded, a version of it survives; even though now in a state of semi-dissolution (like the monasteries), as pressure on government intensifies to cut benefits to the same legion of cheats, scroungers and other abusers of the generosity of the British who deceived the unworldly occupants of monasteries and took advantage of the Speenhamland arrangement, widely adopted in the South of England. 'Safety nets', a more exiguous provision, are now the preferred metaphor for the protection of the vulnerable; as though being poor had become a dangerous form of aerial acrobatics.

Intermittent exhibitions of tenderness towards the poor, the have-nots, the left-behind of development, are not simply part of a cyclical 're-discovery' of poverty in a very rich country. They have also been inflected by events beyond the borders of Britain. In the 1790s, the rise in wheat prices, fear of agrarian revolt, revolution in France, the Napoleonic wars and fear of invasion, also played a part in the calculations of the governing classes: conciliation of the labouring poor required something more than the access of patriotism which such events prompted. A more generous application of the Poor Laws was part of their response. This led in the 1790s to the aid-in-wages arrangement, which safeguarded the social order of gentry, landlord and farmer.

The welfare state was an even more direct reaction to events outside Britain, the war that left Europe as a site of bones and ashes, the rubble of the Nazi effort to conquer the continent. The war did little for the reputation of a capitalism whose lustre had already been tarnished by the Depression, mass unemployment and poverty. The well-being of the people, which had been the object of the conscience of rulers after the First World War, became as great a concern after 1945 as in the 1790s; the more so since Communism had subdued half of Europe, and socialism was on all the banners of liberation in countries of the disintegrating European empires. Concern for welfare was also part of Cold War rivalry between East and West; a process that was to have far-reaching consequences for the future of poverty.

The very idea of a 'consumer society' was, in part, a strategy to demonstrate to the world, in a time when socialism had enlisted history on its side, that capitalism would prevail. After the war, people fretted at the privations of a joyless peace, which brought few of the rewards anticipated by the triumph of virtue. It was only in the 1950s that rationing ceased completely in Britain, and consumer goods which became part of the domestic landscape of the country, were widely available and affordable. At this time it was not yet clear that the Soviet Union and its satellites in Eastern Europe would not overtake the West, achieve a higher standard of living or a more just society. The first satellite was put into space by Russia in 1957; and at a reception in the Polish Embassy in Moscow, Krushchev made a speech which, though often misquoted as saying to the capitalist West, 'We will bury you', actually had suggested that socialism would be present at the funeral of its capitalist rival. Competition to provide a better life for its peoples nourished the profusion of material goods and although it soon became clear that the Communist countries had been left behind, the dynamic process set in train with the expectation of a constantly rising income in the West, had taken on a life of its own. In the following decades, this evolved into market dependency, an essential aspect of development; and to feed it, excessive resource use, pollution and an assault upon planetary treasures have given growing cause for concern. The global extension of this model, and the apparent impossibility of disengaging from it, lie at the heart of the ecological crisis; irreversibilities, set up for other purposes, have led to new impoverishments, the nature of which are only now becoming visible.

However this may be, and whatever the historical roots of economic practices that appear to elude control, ancient precedent in our treatment of the poor remains. The same sensibility appears with each charitable or punitive pronouncement by our contemporaries. Every analysis, policy, or course of action now advocated, has an echo in our past. Thus David Cameron, Iain Duncan Smith, Nick Clegg, Frank Field, former Archbishop Carey and all the rest appear to receive their recommendations from the long dead. The novelty of these specifics depends upon our readiness to forget the past. They burst forth triumphantly with remedies against poverty, which are paraphrases, less often of the Elizabethan Poor Law than of the Poor Law Amendment Act of 1834. The most resounding rhetoric is reserved for denunciations of the chaotic and unruly poor; contemporary political discourse faithfully repeats (albeit in remarkably inferior style) the observations of Malthus, Joseph Townsend, Jeremy Bentham, David Ricardo, Patrick Colquhoun and Edmund Burke. Perhaps people feel that with the re-iteration of old social and economic prejudices, more troubling problems will go away.

4

CONTINUITIES

HISTORICAL ATTITUDES TOWARDS THE POOR

Poverty and work

Poverty in the modern world is associated with an absence of work. Since the earliest Poor Laws, work has been advocated as the best remedy for the poor. Contemporary politicians repeatedly insist that 'work must pay', and that, like the good woman in the Book of Proverbs, none should 'eat the bread of idleness'. The Christian era has been characterised by the idea of a fair reward for honest labour; but 'work' also evokes an older tradition, namely, that it is the lot of the majority of humankind to labour, whether or not this relieves want.

The etymology of the word for 'work' in most European languages suggests that it is a form of coercion, not for the purpose of mitigating poverty, but as fulfilment of human destiny. Ecclesiastes 22:3 declares, 'There is nothing better than that a man should rejoice in his own works; for that is his portion.' Words for labour have their root in images of compulsion, torment, affliction and persecution. The French word *travail*, like its English counterpart, is derived from vulgar Latin *trepaliare*, to torture, to inflict suffering. *Peíne* in French, meaning penalty or punishment, also indicates strenuous labour. The German *arbeit* suggests effort, hardship and suffering, and is cognate with the Slavonic *rabota* (from which English has taken 'robot'), indicating *corvée*, forced or serf labour. In the Romance languages words derived from Latin *laborare* came to mean ploughing or tilling the earth, although in Italian *lavoro* means work in general; the Latin evoked something accomplished with difficulty or struggle.

The English *work* comes from an Indo-European stem, *werg-* via Greek *ergon*, which is interpreted as deed or action, without punitive connotations, and Latin *urgere*, to press, bear down upon or squeeze, urge or compel. This may be cognate with Gothic *wrikan*, Old English *wrecan*, to persecute. In the simple word 'work' violence is latent, and appears in the form 'wreak', as in havoc or vengeance. 'Toil' also derives from Old French, to argue or dispute, to fight and struggle.

Work was compulsion and punishment, an existential affliction which promised neither well-being nor even an assured sustenance. Traces of this more ancient lineage are present in many Biblical references, from Genesis, 'In the sweat of thy face shalt thou eat bread', to the Book of Proverbs, with its denunciations of idleness and sloth. 'Love not sleep, lest you come to poverty'; 'Through sloth the roof sinks in and through indolence the house leaks'; and 'Whoever is slack in his work is a brother to him who destroys.'

Ancient ideas, especially those buried in the unvisited tombs of words, have a tenacious afterlife. Edmund Burke in the eighteenth century took exception to what he regarded as the canting phrase 'the labouring poor', because it suggested resistance to their fate of those born to work, however pitiful their reward. Work as the destiny of those who have no wealth but their labour, retains its hold on the imagination of political nostalgics of all colours. If work is now offered as a form of secular salvation by contemporary politicians, its redemptive power was acquired slowly and over a long time-span, as the holy poor journeyed on their long descent from closeness to God to a condition of forlorn dispossession.

This ought, perhaps, to give pause to those who recommend the redemptive power of work. Since it is presently estimated that about six million people who work in Britain receive less than a living wage, it is clear that labour continues, despite all the achievements of the modern world, to fulfil its ancient role as the destiny of humanity as much as that of a means of overcoming poverty. Since governments must continue to supplement wages, allot allowances and eke out a grudging dole to the daily labour of people who are employed, suggests that work, far from representing relief from poverty, is a confirmation of the older belief that humanity is destined to 'eat the bread of anxious toil'. Words sometimes tell truths which the increasingly hollow rhetoric of politics conceals.

The beginnings of the Poor Law

After the Black Death, which depopulated England by about one-third between 1348 and 1350, the resulting shortage of labour gave new power to those who survived it. The Statute of Labourers was promulgated under Edward III in 1351, an effort to prohibit any rise in wages over those current in 1346. It recognised the existence of free labourers, who had grown during the long wars with France, since the King had manu-mitted many villeins to replenish exhausted armies. The statute forbade anyone to leave the village to which he belonged; which foreshadowed legislation to come.

It stated, 'Because a great part of the people and especially of the workmen and servants has now died in that pestilence, some, seeing the straights of the masters and the scarcity of servants, are not willing to serve unless they receive excessive wages, and others, rather than labour to gain their living, prefer to beg in idleness: we, considering the grave inconveniences which might come from the lack especially of ploughmen and such labourers, have held deliberation and treaty concerning this with the prelates and nobles and other learned men sitting by us; by whose consentient counsel we have seen fit to ordain that every man and woman in our kingdom of England, of whatever condition, whether bond or free, who is able bodied and below the age of sixty years, not living from trade nor carrying on a fixed craft, nor having of his own the means of living, or land of his own with regard to the cultivation of which he might occupy himself, and not serving another, if he, considering his station, be sought after to serve in a suitable service, he shall be bound to serve him who has seen fit to seek after him; and he shall take only the wages, liveries, meed or salary which, in the places where he sought to serve, were accustomed to be paid in the twentieth year of our reign of England, or the five or six common years next preceding.'

This act could not be enforced: the shortage of manpower gave the labourers physical advantages that could not be legislated away—the sheer scarcity of bodies to perform necessary labour enabled them to command wages higher than those stipulated. Tracts of land left unten-anted offered a chance to those with resources to acquire considerable holdings and to raise themselves out of villeinage. This period saw the emergence of a small, influential class of yeoman farmers, a class later subject to much myth-making: identified as the 'backbone of England', an idea embodied in 'yeoman of the guard', the 'yeomanry', tales of Merrie England; the yeoman as a John Bull figure, sated with English ale and roast beef, of incorruptible obduracy and sense of justice, the progenitor of that part of the middle class which spurned Puritanism, and shimmers over the concept of 'Englishness' to this day.

At the same time, John Wycliffe, Oxford academic and cleric, was preaching that the only true religious authority was the Bible, that the Pope and Catholic Church had deserted the high mission entrusted to them. Wycliffe's teachings gave rise to a sect regarded as highly dangerous, the Lollards, who asserted rights they believed due to them as a result of the unsettling of the natural order by the Black Death. They demanded reform and denounced the wealth of the church. Ideas are rolling stones, which, once set in motion, gather unpredictable kinds of alien moss: John Ball, an itinerant preacher in Kent delivered unsettling sermons, which went beyond anything advocated by Wycliffe. He had been dismissed as a priest in Colchester for his views on rich and poor and in a sermon at Blackheath contested the feudal system: 'From the beginning all men were by nature created alike, and our bondage or servitude came in by the unjust oppression of naughty men. For if God would have had any bondman from the beginning, he would have appointed who should be bond, and who free. And therefore I exhort you to consider that now the time is come, appointed to us by God, in which ye may (if ye will) cast off the yoke of bondage, and recover liberty.'[1] The preachings of Ball were confirmed by the threat of the new child-king Richard II to impose a poll tax of one shilling for every man in the land, which led to the people of Kent and Essex, with Wat Tyler to the fore, marching on the Tower of London in 1381 in the first popular revolt seen in England. Although known as the Peasants' Revolt, it was led by yeomen and lower gentry, many of them liable to pay tax by a decree of 1334. Their grievance, allied to the unenforceable Statute of Labourers, created a strong movement of discontent across social classes.

The army of peasants from Kent and Essex captured the Tower of London. Richard II conceded their demands and urged them to return

[1] Ball, John, Sermon at Blackheath, 1381.

home. Some obeyed, but others returned to the city, killed the Archbishop of Canterbury and the King's Treasurer. A few days later, Richard met the rebels again, outside of the city, but it was a trap and Wat Tyler was killed. John Ball was hanged later in the summer with other leaders from Kent and Essex. However, the poll tax was withdrawn, and the position of peasants strengthened, because harvests still had to be brought in, for which their labour was indispensable.

The Statute of Labourers was the first legislation to link poverty and livelihood, in an effort to moderate wages in the face of a shortage of labour—a situation that was to recur throughout the following centuries. Labour has always been blamed by its employers for improvidence, lack of foresight and a taste for luxury. Living, as labourers did, on the edge of survival, they ought, as the story unfolded in subsequent centuries, to have acquired habits of thrift and restraint. That they have rarely done so has been a continuous irritant to those living under no such constraint.

An Act of 1388 transferred to the district where the poor were obliged to live the responsibility for relieving distress. This began a system of parochial responsibility for assisting the poor, which would have far-reaching consequences. It also reflected unease at the erosion of the feudal system: enclosures, diversion of arable land to pasture for sheep, and the growth of the wool trade removed people from agriculture, but also provided new opportunities in the growing towns. Rootless mendicants became a focus of concern. In the late Middle Ages the word 'vagabond' became current, indicating an aimless itinerant, up to no good, a sinister emblem of unbelonging, who was to be tied down to his (less often, her) parish or returned to his lawful place of abode. In the vagabond appears the later, much reviled figure of the migrant; although of course by the twentieth century, the migrant became emblematic of global displacement, and mobility had long been an indispensable feature of the economic system. Now it is the turn of those who are place-bound, and fail to shift from familiar neighbourhoods in search of work to be stigmatised as feckless; another of the many historic (and ironic) reverses of vice and virtue.

A century later, a law of 1496 deplored the costs to the King's subjects of bringing vagabonds to jails, 'and the long abiding of them therein, whereby, by likelihood, many of them should lose their lives'. This prefigures complaints in our time of the burden of keeping large numbers of people imprisoned. The 1496 Act ordered that vagabonds should no longer be sent to common jails until someone would hire them, but 'vagabonds, idle and suspected persons should be set in the stocks three days and nights, and have no sustenance but bread and water, and afterwards, set at large and obliged to leave the town.' Anyone offering meat and drink to such a person would be fined 12 pence. It was also enacted that every beggar, not able to work, should 'go and rest and abide in the hundred where he was best known, or born, on pain of punishment'.

In 1530 a law granted licences to beg to the old and disabled poor, but excluded the able-bodied, the 'sturdy' and competent (and even an 'impotent' person begging without a licence could be whipped and set in the stocks). 'A vagabond, whole and mighty in body, who should be found begging, was to be whipped until his body was bloody by such whipping, and then sworn to the place where he was born, or last dwelt for three years, and there put himself to labour.'

Five years later, it is stated the preceding act made no provision for 'how poor people and sturdy vagabonds should be ordered at their repair and coming into their countries, nor how the inhabitants of every hundred should be charged for their relief, nor yet for the setting and keeping in work and labour the said valiant beggars, at their repair into every hundred of this realm.' Compulsion to maintain the poor was considered, but no money raised for that purpose. The Act provided that when 'such poor creatures' arrived, the officials and householders of the district should 'charitably receive the same' and should succour and find and keep them by voluntary and charitable alms, so that 'none shall be compelled to go openly a begging, on pain that every parish making default shall pay 20 shillings a month'. This anticipates a contemporary sentimental hankering for a time when the charitable impulse of people sufficed to look after the poor and afflicted, and neither compulsion nor State provision was required; a mythic age and persistent object of the fierce nostalgias of modernity.

Collections were to be made by mayors of towns and churchwardens of smaller communities, 'so that the poor, impotent, lame, feeble, sick and diseased, not able to work, might be relieved, so that none of them be suffered to go openly begging....' Two or three times a week, 'certain of the said poor are to be appointed to collect broken meats and refuse drink of every householder which will be distributed evenly among the poor'.

Any 'ruffler' or valiant beggar sent to his parish from where he had no right to be, was to show a testimonial that he had been whipped; every ten miles he was allowed meat, drink and lodging. If he offended again, he was to be whipped once more and have the upper part of the gristle of his right ear clean cut off. Any further offence, and he risked execution as a common felon.

This began the practice of stigmatising the unmeritorious poor: disfigurement, branding with V for vagabond, amputation, compulsion to wear the P of pauper, the uniform of the workhouse, down to our own time and the 'exposure' of cheats, scroungers and benefit fraudsters in the popular press (a symbolic pillory). The savagery is mitigated with time; the odium remains.

Consolidation of the Poor Law

The destruction of the monasteries by Henry VIII not only abolished hospitals, lazar-houses and educational establishments but also threw out of work many who had depended for livelihood on religious institutions. Sir Frederic Eden, says, 'Some 50,000 monks were commuted to miserable pensioners.'[2] Among the justifications for this act of redistribution was that it cured one baleful effect of monasticism, in that it ceased to offer 'daily relief to a very numerous and very idle Poor'. A number of statutes were passed during the reign of Henry VIII providing for the poor and impotent, who, it was observed, 'had increased strangely of late years'.

In 1547, under the Regency Council—appointed because Edward VI was only nine at the time of accession—the most draconian law against the poor was passed. 'In light of complaints against idleness and vagabondrie it is therefore enacted that if any man or woman able to work should refuse to labour, and live idly for three days, that he, or she, should be branded with a red-hot iron on the breast with the letter V, and should be adjudged the slaves for three years of any person who should inform against the said idler.' The master of such a slave is to feed him bread and water and 'small drink and such refuse meat as he shall think proper; and to cause his slave to work, by beating, chaining or otherwise in such work and labour (how vile so ever it be) as he should put him unto.' If the slave runs away, he is to become a slave for life, branded with an S on the forehead or cheek, and if he absconds a second time, he is to

[2] Eden, *The State of the Poor*, London, 1797.

be put to death. The master can 'sell, bequeath, let out for hire or give the service of these slaves to any person whomsoever on such condition and for such term of years as the said person be adjudged to him for slaves, after the like sort and manner as he may do of any other of his moveable goods and chattels.'

By the same statute, all persons were empowered to take idle children from vagabonds and keep them as apprentices 'till the boys are twenty-four and the girls twenty years of age; and if they run away before the end of their term, the masters might, upon recovering them, punish them, in chains or otherwise and use them as slaves till the time of their apprenticeship shall have expired. A master is likewise authorised to put a ring of iron about the neck, arm or leg of a slave, for more knowledge and surety of keeping him.'

This marked the point of greatest physical cruelty to the poor, at least within Britain. As a model for the treatment of lesser races in subsequent ages, it had a long afterlife. The legislation was repealed three years later. Something of its vindictive temper lingered, and periodically coloured later Poor Laws.

In 1552, collectors of alms for the poor were appointed. These were 'to gently ask and demand of every man and woman what they of their charity would be contented to give weekly toward the relief of the Poor'. The mildness of this admonition undermined its effectiveness.

In the mid-sixteenth century, land cultivated by peasants for food continued to be enclosed, and many were forced from agriculture. It took little more than two decades after the destruction of the monastic houses (1536–1540) for the first Poor Law to be introduced by Parliament in 1563. Further laws followed in 1572, 1576 and 1597. The greatest threat of the hungry and homeless (placards still to be seen around the necks of individuals in public places in the twenty-first century) was to law and order. The first Act was to assess the extent of poverty, and register the poor with each parish. It was suggested that collectors of alms be appointed to administer charitable giving. By 1563, fear of civil disorder led Parliament to make distinctions in classifying the poor—the helpless and the vicious, 'deserving' and 'undeserving'. This seemingly unproblematic distinction in reality created difficulty in administration, since identifying 'the deserving' is more complex than it appears. These were the aged, the sick and children; but there were also 'deserving unemployed', people who would work, but were unable to find it. Almshouses, orphanages and hospitals provided for the 'impotent' poor. The 'undeserving' were criminals, robbers and beggars. These were to be beaten, and anyone repeatedly found begging could be imprisoned or hanged.

The year 1572 saw the first compulsory poor law tax, which compelled each parish to collect and distribute money; an Act of 1576 required each town to find employment for the workless. The first Poorhouses were set up, and Houses of Correction erected for vagrants and beggars. Spoiled harvests in the 1590s led to the 1597 Act, which gave Justices of the Peace more power to raise funds. The Overseer of the Poor was to judge how much was required for the poor of the parish, collect it from owners of property, distribute alms or clothing, and superintend the Poor House.

These laws were consolidated in 1601. They were turned into a national system of poor relief, although based on the parish. Each parish had to levy a poor rate, provide apprenticeships to parish children and to assist the impotent poor in alms-houses, hospitals, poorhouses or in their own homes. The vagrant poor were to be sent to Houses of Correction, and the able-bodied set to work in Houses of Industry, where materials for their labour were to be provided. The Act was known as the 43rd Elizabeth and, however harshly it may have been interpreted in later centuries, its basic provision for the helpless poor indicated a level of humane concern in Britain in advance of that almost anywhere else in Europe.

Throughout the sixteenth century, money taken in fines for offences such as profanity or immorality, was given in poor relief. In 1558, 12 pence was raised from each parishioner who did not go to church on Sundays. The goods of bankrupts could be diverted to charitable ends. The fine for not wearing a woollen cap on Sunday was used for the same purpose.

Labour has always been promoted as the pathway to livelihood, and hence, to self-reliance; poor laws have always sought to set people to work as the surest means of relieving poverty. The Statute of Artificers, 1563, attempted to regulate labour, particularly that of apprentices and young people. Its aim was to create stability at a time of growing population—which increased by almost 40 per cent between the mid-sixteenth and early seventeenth centuries. The statute governed the retention and dismissal of apprentices, servants and labourers, and was intended to keep people in the locality where they were born and to make them follow the calling of their parents. The Act was to 'banish idleness, advance husbandry, and yield unto the hired person both in the time of scarcity and in the time of plenty a convenient proportion of wages'. It was enacted that 'no person which shall retain any servant shall put away his or her said servant, and that no person retained according to this statute shall depart from his master, mistress or dame before the end of his or her term'.

An apprentice, expected to live with his master's family, was to receive moral instruction as well as initiation into a craft; and was forbidden to marry or start a household. Any young person between the ages of twelve and twenty, if not already apprenticed, could not refuse if a householder demanded to employ him. An unmarried girl or woman between the ages of twelve and forty, if unmarried and out of service, could be compelled 'to be retained or serve by the year or by the week or day.' If she refused, she could be made a ward 'until she be bounden to serve as aforesaid.' The Statute was not repealed until 1814, although in 1788 the upper age of twenty-four for men was reduced to twenty-one.

Apprenticeship aimed to prevent poverty. If young people acquired a trade, this would be the surest shield against destitution; a belief which still animates Authority in the twenty-first century, although occupations have often become less material and certainly less durable than they were 400 years ago. The Elizabethan statute also included the children of the poor. In this way, it was thought, poverty would become confined to the sick and aged. The system became degraded in the late seventeenth century, by the effects of the Laws of Settlement (1662), which encouraged parish officers to place pauper children in other parishes, with disastrous results for their security and well-being.

In 1572 provision for the relief of the impotent Poor was ordered in every city, village and hamlet. Any excess would be used for setting rogues and vagabonds to work. The definition of these would last for centuries. It included people falsely claiming to collect the fruits of the benefices of clergymen, practitioners of palmistry, physiognomy or fortune-telling, all persons who could give no reasonable account of themselves (a kind of rudimentary stop-and-search) and who refused to work for reasonable wages, shipmen pretending losses at sea, and counterfeiters of licences to beg. Begging, if the offender was above fourteen years, was to be punished by a grievous whipping and burning through the gristle of the right ear, unless some creditable person would take him into service for a year; if a vagabond above eighteen years offended a second time, he was liable to suffer death as a felon, unless some creditable person would take him into service for two years; a third time, he was to be adjudged a felon and sentenced to death.

By 1576, justices were empowered to hire buildings as houses of correction, and to provide wool, hemp, flax and iron or other materials, so that 'youth might be accustomed and brought up to labour, and then not be likely to grow into idle rogues, and that such as be already grown up in idleness and so rogues of the present, may not have any just excuse in saying that they cannot get service or work'. Finding work for the idle has remained something of an obsession ever since, and has met with a smaller measure of success than any other effort to relieve the poor.

In 1597, a number of Acts referring to vagrancy, mendicancy and other statutes were moulded into a uniform system, anticipating the consolidation of the 43rd Elizabeth in 1601. Penalties were modified—vagabonds, no longer burned through the ears, were to be 'stripped and whipped till their body was bloody' and then sent from parish to parish till they reached the place of their birth. Justices and churchwardens were to build shelters for the impotent Poor. Parents of the blind, lame and other poor persons were bound to relieve them. The family, as the first resource of the afflicted, remains, despite the frayed ties of kinship of the twentieth and twenty-first centuries.

The 1601 Act also insisted that grandparents, parents and children should reciprocally maintain each other. It directed those refusing to work to be sent to jail or the House of Correction. Buildings were to be acquired only for the impotent Poor, with cottages to be built on the waste. Prohibitions upon begging and vagrancy were omitted, and penalties for those who failed in their duty as justices, churchwardens and overseers were imposed.

Objections to laws to protect the poor began with the laws themselves; and with time, although the criticisms became more sophisticated, they did not change in substance. First, it was objected that it was impossible to determine who were 'real paupers', given the ease with which impostors could feign misery and distress. What Thomas Alcock referred to in the eighteenth century as 'the bashful Poor',[3] the most needy, were reluctant to ask for charity, while the bold and impudent showed no such restraint. Secondly, that among the needy, it was impossible to determine who had been brought to want by carelessness and who by misfortune: although the wants of all were the same, their claims on the alms of others were different. Then, the fear of falling into poverty was a salutary

[3] Alcock, Thomas, *Observations on the Defects of the Poor Laws*, London, 1752.

spur to labour and to make provision for those rainy days which seemed, despite Scripture, to occur more frequently in the lives of the poor. Fourthly, when people are compelled to maintain the poor, this destroys the charitable impulse which underlies all giving. Forced donation destroys altruism and creates resentment in those who are taxed for the purpose; and the gratitude of the recipient is diminished by the knowledge that what he or she receives is given involuntarily. One criticism, formerly significant, has lapsed with the secularisation of society. This was that, 'God Almighty, the Helper of the Poor and friendless, seems to have made a human law for relief of them unnecessary, by having implanted a natural Law for the Purpose in every Man's Breast. We have an innate Philanthropy. We carry, I may say, a Poor Law, about with us ... Nature strongly inclines, and even forces us to commiserate and help the Wretched....'[4]

The seventeenth-century poor

In 1604, penalties for the criminal poor were made more severe. 'Rogues adjudged incorrigible and dangerous should be branded on the left shoulder with a hot iron of the breadth of a shilling, having a Roman R upon it, and placed to labour, and if after such punishment, found begging and wandering, they should be adjudged felons and suffer death without benefit of clergy.'

By 1609 it appears many of the proposed Houses of Correction had not been built. The Poor Laws were already being described as operating as a premium on idleness. The Statute of 1609, states, 'many wilful people, finding that they, having children, have some hope of relief from the parish wherein they dwell, being able to labour, thereby to relieve themselves and their families, do nonetheless run away out of the parishes and leave their families upon the parish. If any able to work threatens to run away, they should be sent to the House of Correction and treated as a wandering rogue.'

Pamphlets and publication on the Poor came thick and fast in the seventeenth century, particularly after the end of censorship in 1641. In 1622, *Grievous Grones for the Poor*[5] said that although the statutes were excel-

---

[4] Ibid.
[5] Mackay, Thomas, *Grievous Grones for the Poor*, 1622.

lent, they were not enforced. 'The number of poor daily increases, since there is no collection for them. Not in these seven years in many parishes, especiallie in certain towns, many parishes turn their Poor adrift to beg and steal, so that the country is "pitifully pestered by them".'

In the intellectual ferment of the Civil War, doctrines that vindicated the poor re-emerged, and threatened a social order already under severe strain: Gerard Winstanley, in the *True Levellers' Standard Advanced*, in 1649 wrote, 'In the beginning of Time, the great Creator, Reason, made the Earth to be a common Treasury, to preserve Beasts, Birds, Fishes and Men the Lord that was to govern this Creation; for man had Domination given to him over the Beasts, Birds and Fishes; but not one word was spoken in the beginning, that one branch of mankind should rule over another... And that Earth that is within this Creation made a Common Storehouse for all, is bought and sold and kept in the hands of a few, whereby the great Creator is dishonoured...' Such views were intolerable to the most influential stream of Puritan thought, which was embracing that uncompromising individualism, 'which makes of a man's relationship with God a secret and lonely pact, of which his own conscience was to be sole judge'. This period saw the most dramatic eruption of egalitarian ideas before the industrial era; an assertion of what had always been obvious to the poor (however blasphemous, absurd or unspeakable it might have appeared to established authority) — that labour was an essential part of the production of wealth, and that as such, its share should be greater than the precarious subsistence that had been the fate of most of its producers. This view of labour would swiftly be overtaken by a more austere puritan energy, which saw divine blessing in its own power of accumulation.

A Commonwealth statute of 1656 declared the 'number of wandering, idle, loose, dissolute and disorderly persons is of late much increased by reason of some defects in the laws, and statutes heretofore made and provided for the punishment of rogues, vagabonds and sturdy beggars (they being seldom taken begging), by means whereof divers robberies, burglaries, thefts, insurrections and other misdemeanours have been occasioned, all and every idle, loose and dissolute persons found and taken within the Commonwealth of England, vagrant and wandering from their usual place of living or abode, and [who] shall not have such good and sufficient cause or business for such his or their travelling or wandering' as justices of the peace or mayors or other chief officers approved, were adjudged rogues, vagabonds and sturdy beggars, within the statute of 39 Eliz c. 4, although not found begging; at the same time fiddlers and minstrels were also adjudged rogues, vagabonds and sturdy beggars; and by a statute of the same year, persons having no visible estate, profession or calling answerable to their expenditure were indictable.

The Puritan conscience, sharpened between the opulence and idleness of the court and the slothful indolence of the poor, expressed itself in the view of Cromwell and Ireton in their response to the radicals of the army: freeholders were the foundation of the political body, who were entitled to dispose of their property as they chose, without interference from social superiors, and without regard to the mass of people, who were only tenants at will, and had no fixed interest or share in the land.

In 1656, Joseph Lee, in *A Vindication of Regulated Enclosure*, defending the right of everyone to act according to his own advantage, asserted, 'The advancement of private persons will be the advantage of the public'— foreshadowing by more than a century the authoritative argument of Adam Smith.

In the later seventeenth century, work, and the wealth it created, from being a means of salvation, was becoming the sign of salvation. R. H. Tawney, in *Religion and the Rise of Capitalism*, shows how faith, far from being a steadfast anchor in human societies, is a restless migrant, fixing itself opportunistically upon highly changeable but tenacious orthodoxies; ascribing permanence to its temporary abodes as it moves through time. Tawney's description of the capricious nature of morality appears in the making of the modern world—uncharitable covetousness became economic enterprise, and the medieval character of wealth, which was social, gave way to the inviolability of private property. In sympathy with this, the character of the poor is also constantly changing.

An intensifying individualism characterised the Restoration: the pursuit of private gain identified with the working out in the world of the design of Providence. The obloquy incurred in the Middle Ages by the sins of the rich was diverted to the poor, whose vices became florid, including their alleged love of luxury and intemperance.

The distaste of the rich for the poor always becomes more extreme whenever they have done them some conspicuous injustice. Such was the case at the Restoration, a time of acquisitions of land by speculators and city merchants, as well as enclosures by the Royalist gentry who repossessed their estates after 1660. These were uninterested in common rights, and made a virtue of enclosure, not for the first time, in the name of economic efficiency. They regarded their victims without sympathy, since precarious livelihoods eked out on common lands seemed to them morally injurious to those who practised them, and likely to lead to an unsettling independence of mind. The people would be better under the watchful eye of an employer. Agricultural 'improvements', enclosures and appropriations contributed towards the dispossession of others, and often made the difference between survival and poverty for the labouring classes. Guilt perhaps played a part in the denunciations of the imprudent and idle which resonate down the late seventeenth and early eighteenth centuries, a time when something was clearly being taken away from one part of the population—the poorer part—for the benefit of another. The beneficiaries could scarcely fail to find fault with those whose well-being their enrichment had impaired; a psychological constant in the history of dispossession.

The attitude towards the poor became noticeably harsher in the later seventeenth and early eighteenth centuries; a development that coincided with reactions towards 'natives' in the colonial possessions. This is not surprising, since the people of Britain had been the first to be colonised. Nothing practised elsewhere in the world had not already been tried and tested within the British islands, the destruction of cultures (the clan system in Scotland), famine, evictions of people for more profitable sheep, the alienation of land, transportation for felonies and the bloody penal code.

One clergyman, writing in 1668, thought he could distinguish clearly between the classes of poor. 'Of the Poor there are two sorts, God's poor and the Devil's; impotent poor and impudent poor. The poor on whom we would exercise our beneficence is the honest labourer and the poor householder, who either through the greatness of their charge or badness of their trade; crosses, losses, sickness suretiship or other casualties, being brought behinde hand, and not able in the sweat of their face to earn their bread, or the blinde and maimed, the aged and decrepit, the weak widows or young orphans; which are either past their labour or not yet come into it; these are the principle objects of bounty, and he that is godly and discreet will rather give to them that work and beg not than to them that beg and work not, for according to the Apostles' rule, they that will not labour must not eat. For there are many sturdy beggars and vagrant Rogues, the blemish of our Government and burthen to the Commonwealth; which kind of poor are not to be maintain'd on their wicked courses; to feed these, Rats and Polecats, yea it is to feed vice itself to whom they make themselves servants, and therefore most wisely do our laws punish with a mulct those that do relieve such vagrants; for these are not the poor, but the worst robbers of the poor; we may yet rank them with Usurers, Inclosers, Ingrossers and oppressing land-lords; for this is the reason why the poor indeed do want, and because these counterfeits do snatch it. Men that labour hard often lack bread for their families; while those that refuse all work are full.'[6] It is significant that the rapacious poor should still be categorised with the rapacious rich—the engrosser and usurer; for both work against the blameless poor.

The Law of Settlements

One of the first laws after the Restoration was designed to control more rigorously the movement of people. The Settlement Act of 1662 was to determine the numbers of poor in each parish, and to prevent people from leaving it before they became chargeable, so that the most generous parishes should not attract newcomers and become overburdened with poor. Previously, the industrious poor had been able to seek employment wherever it was to be had—only those unable or unwilling to work had been prevented from moving.

The statute says that: 'by reason of some defects in the law, poor people are not restrained from going from one parish to another, and therefore do endeavour to settle themselves in those parishes where there is the best stock, the largest commons or wastes to build cottages, and the most woods for them to burn and destroy, and, when they have consumed it, then to another parish, and at last become rogues and vagabonds, to the great discouragement of parishes to provide stocks, where it is liable to be devoured by strangers.' This foreshadows efforts in our time to keep out refugees, asylum seekers and economic migrants. It also illustrates parochialism within a Britain, which has for centuries claimed the right of British merchants, adventurers and travellers to go wherever in the world they please. Mobility has been a much disputed issue. Until the industrial era, immobility was the norm; the exhortation to shift to where work is available, to 'get on your bike', is a recent development.

Right to settlement depended upon birth in a parish in which both parents were settled; until 1662, living in a parish for more than three

[6] Young, R., *The Poor's Advocate*, London, 1688.

years gave settlement. After that date, a person could be removed within forty days of arrival. From 1691, an individual had to give forty days' notice before moving into a parish; be employed continuously by a settled resident for more than 365 days (this was avoided by contracts of up to 364 days); hold an official parish appointment; rent property worth more than £10 per annum; have married into the parish; have previously received relief in the parish; or have served an apprenticeship of seven years in the parish.

After 1662, anyone moving out of his parish had to carry a Settlement certificate, by which his home parish would pay for his removal from the parish to which he would go, should he become chargeable on the poor rates. Few parishes freely issued such certificates, and people were discouraged from moving.

The Act of 1662 also addressed the question of fraud practised by some parochial officers. Many inconveniences arose 'by reason of the unlimited power of the churchwardens and overseers of the poor, who do frequently upon frivolous pretences (but chiefly for their own private ends) give relief to what persons and number they think fit; and such persons being entered into the collection bill, do become after that a great charge to the parish, notwithstanding the occasion or pretence of their receiving collection oftentimes ceases, by which means the rates for the poor are daily increased.' To remedy this, a register was to be made with names and dates, to be examined by the vestry, and those to be relieved had to be approved by a justice, except in urgent cases.

The most compelling reason for the necessity of Settlement was argued, almost a century later, by Thomas Alcock.[7] He says, 'The desire of living in Credit and Reputation among their Neighbours, or the fear of the Odium of a contrary Character, is a great Restraint upon the Mass of the People against Immorality and Vice. But Wanderers and Vagabonds, having no settled Residence or Neighbourhood, are Strangers to every Body and consequently are free from this Restraint. Most Pickpockets, House-Breakers, Street-Robbers and Footpads have once been Vagrants.' If the idea of people 'knowing their place' had topographical, as well as social origins, the legitimacy of their whereabouts at any given time could be the more easily ascertained.

Removals of people from parishes where they were likely to become chargeable were selective. Dorothy Marshall says that as time went by,

[7] Ibid.

the overseers 'concentrated their efforts on securing the removal of those classes of persons whom experience had shown to be least capable of maintaining themselves without relief.[8] Those most likely to be removed were married labourers with a large number of children, and unmarried women who were not in service, and whose livelihood depended upon spinning and day-labour for local farmers. Unmarried men, mobile and able to maintain themselves easily, were least likely to be removed.

By the Act of 1662, a settlement was granted to anyone who had served an apprenticeship in the parish. This prompted the overseers to place pauper children in another parish. Forty days after being bound, the child's original parish no longer had any responsibility for him or her. There was no supervision of the fate of such poor children. Many were apprenticed to overcrowded and ill-paid work, 'pauperised' trades like weaving and stocking framework knitting; masters often abused or mistreated them. They lived in dirty lodgings and were badly fed. Most girls were apprenticed to be housewives, which in effect turned them into household drudges. Parish officers could compel masters to take parish apprentices. If they failed to do so, they were liable to a fine. Since workhouse children had a bad reputation, better-off masters preferred to pay the fine to be free of the compulsion; and certain parishes used this as a source of revenue. Some masters took apprentices simply for the sake of the premium, and made no effort to teach them a trade: the runaway apprentice became a characteristic figure in the eighteenth century. Jonas Hanway's Act of 1767 regulated the payment of premiums, so the master received the full amount only after two years.

Dorothy Marshall writes, of the degradation of apprenticeships, 'In no sphere were the original intentions of the [Elizabethan] Act so subverted to the need of keeping the rates down, or the reaction to the Law of Settlements more disastrous.'[9]

Setting the poor on work

Identifying and caring for the aged and impotent has always been relatively easy. The most challenging function of the poor law, to compel the poor to labour, has remained, with greater or lesser coercion, a principal objective ever since.

[8] Marshall, Dorothy, *The English Poor in the Eighteenth Century*, London, 1926.
[9] Ibid.

This desire to make all the able-bodied work is partly dictated by a sense of fairness. But it has also been a matter of privilege, forcing the least able to fulfil burdens no one else will undertake. It is one thing to glorify the dignity of labour and the sturdy sense of independence which eighteenth-century landowners thought they saw in the British labourer, but quite another to expect people of modest competence to devote their entire lives to work that is repetitive, dirty and dangerous. The words of clergymen, landowners and farmers are as unkind as they are hypocritical, when they speak of the reluctance of the poor to labour and the necessity of the goad of hunger to compel them to do so.

Such melancholy reflections are inevitable in the light of the vindictiveness towards this group of people, the criticism of their incompetence and unwillingness to labour. In the 1660s, after the Restoration, emphasis shifted from charitable relief for the helpless to the question of the wilfully idle. Matthew Hale, former Chief Justice, in a posthumous publication of 1683, advocated closer attention to that part of the Poor Law which compelled the idle poor to work.[10] 'Our Populousness, which is the greatest blessing a Kingdom can have, becomes the burden of the Kingdom, and eats out the heart of it' and recommends that 'accustoming the poor sort to a civil and industrial course of life, whereby they would become, not only burdensome, but profitable to the Kingdom and Places where they live'. While men were 'tumultuous and unquiet' and there are many poor, 'the Rich cannot long or safely continue such; Necessity renders men of Phlegmatick and dull natures stupid and indisciplinable; and men of more fiery and active constitutions rapacious and desperate.' Such a course would 'alter the whole state of this Disorder, and bring People and their Children after them into a regular, Orderly and Industrious course of life, which will be as natural to them as now idleness and Begging and Thieving is'.

The language is modified with changing social and economic circumstances, but the sentiments are constant. This should not tempt us to regard the subtleties of thought of the people of the past as inferior to our own. In *The Poor's Advocate*, subtitled *A Sovereign Antidote to Drive Out Discontent*, the cleric R. Young, wrote presciently. 'Daily experience teacheth that as we grow rich in temporals, we grow poor in spirituals ... As fat men are more subject to diseases of the body, so are Rich men to

---

[10] Hale, Matthew, *A Discourse Touching Provision for the Poor*, London, 1683.

those of the minde....'[11] He anticipates decidedly modern observers like Erich Fromm, when he advises: 'Prize not thyself by what thou hast, but by what thou art. For he that makes a bridge of his own shadow cannot but fall into the water.'

The author of a 1673 pamphlet, estimating the Poor Rate at £840,000 a year, says this sum 'is employed only to maintain idle persons and doth great hurt rather than good, makes a world of poor rather than otherwise there would be, prevents industry and laboriousness; men and women growing so idle and proud that they will not work, but lie upon the parish wherein they dwell, for maintenance, applying themselves to nothing but begging and pilfering and breeding up their children accordingly.'

Thomas Firmin, philanthropist and merchant, disagreed with the principle of the workhouse. He set up in the City of London an establishment where poor people could collect hemp flax for spinning, which, he believed, they were likely to do more effectively at home, in the time between their daily duties. 'The only way to provide for our poor,' he wrote, ostensibly in a letter to a friend, 'and to bring them to labour, is to provide such work for them as they may do in their own homes, which though never so mean and homely, is more desired than any other place; and the way which several persons have proposed, of bringing them to a public work-house, will never effect the end intended, for suppose a woman hath a sick husband or child, or some infirmity upon herself, in all such cases she may do something at home, but cannot leave her own house. And supposing that none of these should happen which yet is very frequent, not one person in twenty will endure the thought of working at a public work-house.'[12] His depository in Aldersgate never made a profit, but he said, 'we had much better lose something by the labour of the poor than lose all by letting them live in sloth and idleness'. He continued to make a loss, but subsidised the undertaking rather than discontinuing it. 'And had you seen, as I have done many a time, with what joy and satisfaction many poor people have brought home their work and received their money for it, you would think no charity in the world like unto it.'

Sir William Petty, in his *Essays on Mankind and Political Arithmetic* in the 1670s, advocated setting up a Corporation to create work for the estimated 1,330,000 'cottagers and paupers, including those in poor-houses in cities, towns and villages, and 30,000 vagrants'; 350,000 of these were

[11] Young, *The Poor's Advocate*, op. cit.
[12] Firmin, Thomas, *Some Proposals for the Employment of the Poor*, 1678.

children too young to work, but in the rest he saw a source of potential profit.[13] 'The bodies of men,' wrote Petty, 'are, without doubt, the most valuable treasury of a country, and in their sphere the ordinary people are as serviceable to the commonwealth as the rich if they are employed in honest labour and useful arts, and such being more in number do more contribute to increase the nation's wealth than the highest rank.'

Late seventeenth-century legislation curbed many of the modest liberties of the poor—the Game Laws of 1671 were strengthened, so that hares, partridges and moor fowl could not be hunted by anyone without a freehold of £100 a year; this re-asserted medieval statutes that hunting by the rich should take precedence over poor people's access to food. In 1697, those in receipt of parochial relief were compelled to wear the badge of pauperism.

Sir Josiah Child found the parish itself the problem, since the law assigned to each parish the duty to deal with its own poor. 'The riches of a city as of a nation, consisting in the multitude of its inhabitants, you must allow more inmates or have a city of cottages. And if a right course be taken for the sustention of the Poor, setting them on work, you need no stratagem to keep them out, but rather to bring them in. For the resort of Poor to a city or nation well managed is in effect the conflux of riches to that city or nation, and therefore the subtile Dutch receive and relieve or employ all that come to them, not enquiring which nation, much less what parish they belong to.'[14]

In 1685 Richard Dunning blamed the Poor Laws, which 'making multitudes idle and careless, and allowing them a refuge for relief from their parishes, hath caused them the less to provide for themselves. Indeed, by that law, the parish is (as they commonly say) bound to find us, but in a far other and larger sense than they mean, viz. Work for those that will labour, punishment for those that will not and bread for those that cannot.'[15] The remedy is the strict enforcement of the first two parts of the law, the punitive gaining on the merciful.

John Locke, in his 1699 *Essay on the Poor Law*, ascribed the 'multiplying members of the Poor', not to scarcity of provisions or want of employ-

[13] Petty, Sir William, *Essays on Mankind and Political Arithmetic*, Princeton: Cassells, 1888.
[14] Child, Sir Josiah, *Discourse on Trade*, London, 1751.
[15] Dunning, Richard, *Pamphlet on the Poor Laws*, 1685.

ment, 'since God has blessed these times with plenty'.[16] The growth of the Poor is a result of 'the relaxation of discipline and the corruption of manners'. He estimated that half those receiving relief from the parish are able to gain a livelihood, and recommended enforcing the laws on vagabondage. A majority of poor people were neither unable nor unwilling to work, but through want of employment or unskillfulness, 'do little that turns to any public account'. The same argument is heard three hundred years later: complaints that young people come out of school minimally equipped for the modern economy, unable to adapt to economic demands which even the most far-sighted and sagacious fail to foresee.

Locke's less than original remedy lay in a re-invigoration of the Elizabethan Poor Law, particularly the obligation to work. He recommended 'a restraint of their debauchery by a strict execution of the laws provided against it, more particularly by the suppressing of superfluous brandy-shops and unnecessary alehouses'. His answer was the punishment of vagrants and the setting up of working schools in each parish for children between the ages of three and fourteen. 'We do not suppose that children of three years old will be able, at that age, to get their livelihoods at the working-school; but we are sure that what is necessary for their relief will more effectually have that use if it be distributed to them in bread at that school, than if given to their fathers in money. What they have at home from their parents is seldom more than bread and water, and that many of them very scantily too: if, therefore, care can be taken that they have each of them their bellyful of bread daily at school, they will be in no danger of famishing; but on the contrary they will be healthier and stronger than those who are bred otherwise. Nor will this practice cost the overseers any trouble, for a baker may be agreed with to furnish and bring into the school-house every day, the allowance of bread necessary for all the scholars that are there. And to this may also be added, without any trouble in cold weather, if it be thought needful, a little warm water gruel, for the same fire that warms the room may be used to boil a pot of it.'

If Locke's remedy is grudging, this is because people of quality, however illustrious, were scarcely conscious of the patronising, almost contemptuous, tone in which they spoke of the poor—a 'bellyful of bread' was as much as they could expect; and if a little warm water gruel were really an exceptional luxury, one can only wonder at the monotony of their customary—and unnourishing—diet. To be kept from 'famishing'

---

[16] Locke, John, *Essay on the Poor Law*, 1699.

was enough. The confident assertions by the rich about the poor rarely derive from close contact with them; they express ideas plucked out of the somewhat rarefied air they breathe; the force of prejudice and received opinion as to the material and moral state of the poor was too strong to require mere observation.

According to many writers and pamphleteers, the cost of keeping the poor came from their 'profusion of diet': the poor drink the strongest ale and eat only the finest wheaten bread. One writer, Richard Dunning, estimated relief to be three times the income of an independent labourer with a wife and three children. He also deplored separate accommodation for the poor. 'Several of them have ordinarily one house apiece entirely to themselves, which would conveniently serve three or four of them; and the same fire, candlelight and attendance that now serves one, might serve three or four; in many particulars they might assist, help and comfort one another, only their unwillingness to have their idleness, filching, profuseness in diet, makes them extremely adverse to such cohabiting.'[17] The same writer advocated what would later come to be seen as economies of scale, by having the poor live close together, so that they might conveniently come at one place to eat. 'Whereas the poor are in some places paid once in a fortnight, and some once a month; seldom one of them hath one penny left next day after receiving it, so are forced to live on credit till next pay-day, and to buy dear and lose much in the filching.' He recognised the difficulty of bringing those 'too old to be removed, and too old to be reformed by this method, for old age is incurable; yet the person not likely to be durable'. Beggars, he insisted, must not be choosers.

Ingenious remedies were suggested for the insolent poor, whom no one would employ, for fear lest they spoil the work assigned them. 'A crooked knife', Dunning went on, 'must have a crooked sheath, and such an ill-humoured workman should have as untoward work assigned to him by the overseers; which may be to carry water in buckets from the lower end of some country village, two or three hundred paces or more, and therewith to fill a vessel in the highway; which done, to overturn it in the way so often as filled, and so to continue till he show a willingness to get himself some work, and in the mean time to have only some slender allowance in diet.'[18] Such contrived Sisyphean tasks were to become com-

---

[17] Dunning, Richard, *Bread for the Poor*, pamphlet, Exeter, 1698.
[18] Ibid.

mon in the workhouse system, from picking oakum to breaking stones: work to small purpose, as long as the labour was hard.

It seemed that concentrations of the poor in a single locality would make their maintenance not just economical, but actually profitable. In the workhouse, they might work for their own keep and provide a surplus to comfort the blameless poor. This was to be a pioneering venture at the end of the seventeenth and a panacea for the first half of the eighteenth century.

The best known example was in Bristol, in 1696, an initiative by John Cary, under an Act for Erecting Hospitals and Work-houses at the City of Bristoll, for better Employing and Maintaining the Poor thereof. Eighteen parishes were combined in a single corporation. In 1698, 100 pauper girls assembled in the New Workhouse, engaged upon spinning for ten and half hours a day in summer, a little less in winter. They were taught to read; and when a similar establishment for boys opened a year later, they were taught to write as well. They spun cotton and fustian; and it seemed, briefly, that the scheme might turn a profit. Following this example, in the first half of the eighteenth century several hundred were established in England and Wales, by renting existing properties or the construction of new ones. Pauperism was to be conducted in a business-like way; and houses of industry might transform the pauper into a productive member of society; an objective which, although doomed at the time, has by no means ceased attracting adherents.

John Cary wrote in glowing terms his own account of the Bristol enterprise in 1717,[19] which he addressed To the Most Illustrious and High Born Prince, His Royal Highness, the Prince of Wales; as though he had unlocked the mystery of the marriage of industry with virtue, prescription with practice. After criticising the laws designed to set the Poor at Work as 'short and defective, tending rather to Maintain them so, than to raise them to a better way of living,' he claimed nothing but good Laws may provide Work for those who are willing and force them to Work that are able. 'And for this use I think Work-houses very expedient, but they must be founded on such Principles as may employ the Poor, for which they must be fitted, and the Poor for them, wherein Employments must be provided for all sorts of people, who must also be

[19] Cary, John, *Essay Towards Regulating the Trade and Employing the Poor of the Kingdom*, London, 1717.

compelled to go thither when sent, and the Work-houses to receive them.' His ambition he described as, 'Making multitudes of People serviceable, who are now useless to the Nation; there being scarce any one, who is not capable of doing something towards his Maintenance.'

He reports, 'Before we took the Girls, we at first considered of proper Officers to govern them; and these consisted of a Master, whose Business was to receive work, deliver it out again and keep Accounts of the House &c; a Mistress, whose Business is to look after the Kitchin and Lodgings, to provide their meals at set times, and other things which relate to the Government of the House; Tutresses to teach them to Spin, under each of which we put five and twenty Girls; a School-mistress to teach them to Read; servants in the Kitchin for washing &c., but these were soon discharged and caused our biggest Girls to take their turn every Week. We also appointed an old Man to keep the Door, and to carry forth and to fetch in Work and such kind of Services.' They were set to work at spinning worsted yarn, having been washed and new clothes from head to foot; this, together with 'wholesome Dyet at set hours and good Beds to lye on, so incouraged the Children that they willingly betook themselves to Work.

'We likewise provided for them Apparel for Sunday; they went to Church every Lord's Day; were taught their catechism at home and had Prayers twice a Day; we appointed them set hours for working, eating and playing; and gave them leave to walk on the hills with their Tutresses, when the work was over and the Weather was fair; by which means we won them into Civility and Love of their Labour. But we had a good deal of Trouble with their Parents; those who formerly kept them and who, having lost the sweetness of their Pay, did all they could to set the Children and others against us; but that was soon over.

'The ventures for girls and boys were so successful, that ancient People were then taken in, and here we had principally a regard to such as were impotent, and had no Friends to help them, and to such as we could not keep from the lazy Trade of Begging....Then we called in all the Children that were on the Poor's Books, and put them under Nurses. The Boys are kept at a distance from the ancient People who also lodge in distinct apartments, the men in several Chambers on one Floor, and the Women in another; all do something, though perhaps some of their Labour comes to little, yet it keeps them from Idleness.'

Many similar schemes from this time betray the optimism that the poor could maintain themselves. The intent may have been charitable and humane, but the cost of keeping up the institutions—the Mint workhouse, in which the boys were lodged, absorbed half the annual poor rate of the whole city—and their failure to become self-sustaining, caused the institutions to degenerate. Many survived during the lifetime of their founders thanks to charitable donations. By the time Sir Frederic Eden came to write on the poor in the 1790s, the only work, in what had been the Mint Workhouse, was picking oakum. The quality of provisions had also deteriorated—gruel, bullock's head soup, pease soup, bread and cheese—a far cry from the early days, when Cary prided himself that beef, pease, potatoes, broth, pease-porridge, milk porridge, bread and cheese, good beer, cabbage, carrots and turnips were provided 'on the Advice of our Physician'. By the time of the Poor Law Commission in 1830, it was reported that, 'Prostitutes wore a yellow dress and single pregnant women a red dress; kept separate from the rest and not allowed to associate with the children. The children are taught to read, to knit and to sew, and when of sufficient age, are sent to service.'[20]

The poor in the eighteenth century

Daniel Defoe's essay of 1704, *Giving Alms No Charity and Employing the Poor a Grievance to the Nation*,[21] while acknowledging that 'we are as rich a nation as any in the world', lamented that England was 'burthen'd with a crowd of clamouring, unemployed, unprovided for poor people, who make the nation uneasie, burthen the rich, clog our parishes, and make themselves worthy of laws, and peculiar management to dispose of and direct them.' Many believed poverty was itself a sign of progress, since it was produced by the decline of serfdom and feudalism. Poverty gave evidence of growing freedoms, since the subsistence of the enslaved had depended upon their masters and owners, while the poor of a later age were responsible for their own fate. The freedom to be as poor as one chooses lives on in contemporary libertarian creeds; but the argument has its origins in greater antiquity. Sir Frederic Eden said, 'It is one of the natural consequences of freedom that those who are left to shift for themselves must sometimes be reduced to want. The decrease of villeinage seems to have been the era of the origin of the Poor.'[22]

[20] Eden, *The State of the Poor*, op. cit.
[21] Defoe, Daniel, *Giving Alms No Charity and Employing the Poor a Grievance to the Nation*, London, 1704.
[22] Eden, *The State of the Poor*, op. cit.

Defoe scorns the idea that the Legislature should find work for the Poor, rather than oblige them to find work for themselves. The workhouse is ruinous to manufactures, since work given to paupers removes it from those who undertake it of their own free will; 'begging is, in the able, a scandal upon their industry, and in the impotent, a scandal upon their country'.

Defoe's essay was a vigorous polemic, defending textile workers who had fled the Netherlands, and vehemently denouncing the workless poor. Much of Defoe's rhetoric has proved enduring. 'There is in England more labour than hands to perform it, and consequently a want of people, not of employment.' He believes, 'Truly the scandal lies on our charity: and the people have such a notion in England of being pitiful and charitable, that they encourage vagrants, and by a mistaken zeal do more harm than good.' He also inveighs against setting the poor to labour in poorhouses and houses of correction, since all such work removes it from self-reliant workmen. Defoe re-states the difference between the meritorious and worthless poor. 'The poverty and exigence of the poor in England, is plainly deriv'd from one of these two particular causes, Casualty or Crime. By Casualty, I mean sickness of families, loss of limbs or sight, and any, either natural or accidental, impotence as to labour. These as infirmities merely providential are not at all concern'd in this debate; ever were, will and ought to be the charge and care of the respective parishes where such unhappy people chance to live, nor is there any want of new laws to make provision for them, our ancestors having been always careful to do it.'

Defoe says, 'The English labouring people eat and drink, but especially the latter three times as much in value as any sort of foreigners of the same dimensions in the world... There is a general taint of sloathfulness upon our poor, there's nothing more frequent, than for an Englishman to work till he has got his pocket full of money, and then go and be idle, or perhaps drunk, until 'tis all gone and perhaps himself in debt...' Tis the men that wont work, not the men that can get no work, which makes the numbers of our poor... If such Acts of Parliament may be made as may effectually cure the sloath and luxury of our poor, that shall make drunkards take care of wife and children, spendthrifts lay up for a wet day; idle, lazy fellows diligent and thoughtless sottish men, careful and provident... they will soon find work enough, and there will soon be less poverty among us.'[23]

[23] Defoe, *Giving Alms No Charity*, op. cit.

Severity and leniency

The notion that it is the obligation of the individual to find work for himself or herself was not new, but it became more insistent with the advance of industrial society. The development of a modern economy was perceived by the enthusiasts of political economy as an emanation of nature, a providential arrangement, in which people must find a place for themselves, by compulsion if necessary. Mandeville's 1714 satire, *The Fable of the Bees*, said the poor 'have nothing to stir them up to be serviceable but their wants, which it is prudence to relieve, but folly to cure'.[24]

This view was elaborated later in the century by a clergyman, who wrote, 'The poor know little of the motives which stimulate the higher ranks to action—pride, honour and ambition. In general, it is only hunger which can spur and goad them on to labour; yet our laws have said, they shall never hunger. The laws, it must be confessed, have likewise said that they shall be compelled to work. But then legal constraint is attended with too much trouble, violence and noise; it creates ill will, and can never be productive of good and acceptable service: whereas hunger is not only a peaceable, silent, unremitted pressure, but, as the most natural motive to industry and labour, it calls forth the most powerful exertions; and when satisfied by the free bounty of another, lays a lasting and sure foundation for good will and gratitude.' The 'peaceful' goad of hunger was to be one of the most effective weapons in the armoury of industrial discipline: its merit, impersonality, was that no individual was seen to impose it. The impoverished had no one to blame; the fault must be their own.

Those advocating severity towards the poor drowned out milder voices. John Bellers, whose Quaker workhouse in Clerkenwell received poor children throughout the eighteenth century, re-published in 1714 a tract, in which he said that, 'the poor without employment are like rough diamonds: their worth is unknown'.[25] Taking further the humane initiative of Thomas Firmin, he continued, 'Whereas regularly labouring people are the Kingdom's greatest treasure and strength, for without labourers there can be no lords, and if the poor labourers did not raise much more food and manufactures than what did subsist themselves, every gentleman must be a labourer, and every idle man must starve.' Bellers' remedy was for the poor to reclaim the waste and neglected land.

[24] Mandeville, *Fable of the Bees*, London: Penguin, 1970 [1714].
[25] Bellers, John, *Proposals for Employing the Poor in a College of Industry*, London, 1714.

Rather than enter factories, they should turn wasteland into 'fruitful fields, orchards and gardens'.

But the idea of the workhouse dominated. Whether hired or constructed, it initially made savings, mainly because of the deterrent effect—prefiguring the 'less eligibility' criterion of 1834. The Poor Relief Act of 1723, called Knatchbull's Act after its sponsor in Parliament, sanctioned the construction of workhouses for poor relief, which for the able-bodied was conditional on entering the workhouse. Local justices of the peace were also allowed to contract the administration of relief to those who would feed, clothe and house the poor—an extensive privatisation in effect, which prefigures practice in our time. Relief was given according to a prescribed amount of work, and was calculated to put an end to the 'false and frivolous pretences' under which many persons had found relief.

The eighteenth century was the age of contracting out; an expedient resuscitated today as the most effective means of overseeing the lives of poor people. In the eighteenth century, the poor were to be managed by the contractor at so much per head, or maintained for a lump sum agreed at the outset. In the first case, it was in the contractor's interest to cram as many people as possible into the workhouse; in the second, his interest was to keep them out. This he did by payment of pensions, which cost less than upkeep inside the house. The standard inside was so low that people willingly accepted miserable payments as out-relief. The poor-rates duly declined. Everything that could be was contracted out—physicians for medical services, carpenters for making coffins; the conveyance of vagrants to their place of settlement, pauper shifts and shrouds, shoes and stockings.

Conditions in the workhouses presented 'scenes of filthiness and confusion'. They were 'receptacles of misery', 'mansions of putridity'. Men and women, young and old, sick and healthy shared a miserable existence, some sleeping on straw on brick floors, others three or four in a bed. The parish officers—who performed their duties reluctantly, since they were unpaid, were often in conspiracy with victuallers and suppliers of goods to the workhouse. Overseers were often ignorant men who could not even sign their name.[26]

In keeping with the continuing struggle to separate the poor into innocent and culpable, an Act of 1744 defined three classes of the refrac-

---

[26] See Marshall, *The English Poor in the Eighteenth Century*, op. cit.

tory and predatory poor: 1) idle and disorderly persons; 2) rogues and vagabonds; and 3) incorrigible rogues. The first group included those who threaten to run away and leave their families on the parish; who tipple in ale-houses; who return unlawfully to parishes from which they have been removed; who lie idly and without employment and refuse to work for usual wages; who beg on the streets and highways. The second group was more comprehensive, and touched 'those who go about as patent-gatherers or gatherers of alms under pretence of loss by fire or other calamity'; it also included strolling players, performers, minstrels, people 'who pretend to be, or wander in the habit of gypsies', fortune tellers, gamblers, pedlars. People who 'wandered abroad' were particularly suspect, particularly in ale-houses, or claiming to be soldiers or sailors, or 'pretending to work in the harvest-fields, without a certificate from the parish'. The 'incorrigible' comprised 'persons styled end gatherers', 'buying, collecting or receiving ends of yarn in the woollen branch', escaped rogues and vagabonds, persons escaping the House of Correction and those apprehended a second time as rogues and vagabonds.

Throughout the eighteenth century, work for the poor reflected the growing importance of the discipline required for industrial labour; but was also a consequence of the secularisation of the Puritan belief that work was prayer. If this was so, idleness was a form of blasphemy; a sin on the verge of becoming a crime. As Britain became richer, the number of poor grew; it seemed only natural to blame them for being self-propagating. How, otherwise, to account for such a phenomenon when splendour and opulence were so conspicuous? This also looks forward to our time: in a world of plenty, few concede that those who fail to avail themselves of such easy abundance might do so for reasons other than wilfulness.

The complaint is constant that the poor squander their substance on luxuries. This is usually coupled with protests that they are rising above their station, seeking to mimic their betters. Daniel Defoe singled out female servants in his essay *Everybody's Business is Nobody's Business* in 1725, in which he deplores 'the insolence and intrigues of our servant-maids' and their insistence upon wages that keep them in finery which rivals that of their mistresses. 'It is a hard matter to know the mistress from the maid by their dress, nay, very often the maid shall be much the finer of the two. Our woollen manufacturers suffer much from this, for nothing but silks and satins will go down with our kitchen-wenches; to support which intolerable pride they have insensibly raised their wages to such heights as was never known in any age and any nation.'[27] He regrets that 'plain country Joan is now turned into a fine London madam, can drink tea, take snuff and carry herself as high as the best'. He is in favour of regulating the dress of servants, since he was 'put to the blush' at a friend's house, where, 'by him required to salute the ladies, I kissed the chamber-jade into the bargain, for she was as well-dressed as the best. But I was soon undeceived by the general titter, which gave me the utmost confusion.' Defoe, writing when the population of London had reached about 630,000, reflects the anxieties of the metropolitan elite the in the presence of a growing urban, largely non-industrial, working class, from among whom armies of servants, some of them doubtless unreliable and dishonest, had to be procured. But the sweeping prejudice against them in Defoe's polemic reads oddly now, as does his intense sexualising of them: 'the streets swarm with strumpets', 'trulls', 'wenches', 'prinked-up baggages'. He writes, 'If she be tolerably handsome, and has any share of cunning, the apprentice or his master's son is enticed away and ruined by her. Thus many good families are impoverished and disgraced by these pert sluts who, taking advantage of a young man's simplicity and unruly desires, draws many heedless youths, nay, some of good estates, into their snares; and of this we have but too many instances.' He accuses the women servants of roving 'from bawdy-house to service and from service to bawdy-house again'. He reserves his most sonorous denunciation for those who seduce 'the father or master of the family', who, 'preferring the flirting airs of a young prinked-up strumpet to the artless sincerity of a plain, grave and good wife, gives his desires a loose and destroys soul, body, family and estate'.

Defoe also takes issue with the 'ten thousand wicked, idle, pilfering vagrants permitted to patrol our city streets and suburbs. These are called the black-guard, who black your honour's shoes, and incorporate henchmen under the title of the Worshipful Company of Japanners'. He blames gentlemen's servants for sub-contracting the cleaning of shoes to these 'japanners'. 'I have often observed these rascals sneaking from gentlemen's door with wallets or hats full of good victuals which they either carry to their trulls or sell for a trifle...How many frequent robberies are committed by these japanners? Silver spoons, spurs and other small articles of plate are every day missing, and very often found on

[27] Defoe, Daniel, *Everybody's Business is Nobody's Business*, London, 1725.

these sort of gentlemen... In any riot or other disturbance, these sparks are always the foremost; for most of them can turn their hands to picking of pockets, to run away with goods from a fire or other public confusion, to snatch anything from a woman or child, to strip a house when the door is open, or any other branch of the thief's profession.' Defoe favours placing servants in uniform, and regulating them by means of certificates showing they can fulfil their duties satisfactorily. He would set japanners to labour—the industrious and docile to the wool-combing trade, the refractory to the tanneries and mines and coalworks. As shoeblacks he would use ancient persons, poor widows and others who have not enough from their parishes to maintain them... 'By this means, industry will be encouraged, idleness punished and we shall be famed, as well as happy, for our tranquillity and decorum.'

A generation later, Thomas Alcock elaborated on some of the evils outlined by Defoe.[28] He deplored practices common among the poor, including snuff-taking and tobacco, tea-drinking and 'the wearing of ribands, ruffles, silk and other flight foreign Things that come dear but do little service'; to these, he added dram-drinking, 'which perhaps is worse than all the rest together'. Snuff-taking was 'for some Time practised chiefly among the better Sort; but as Inferiors are always apt to imitate the Ways of their Superiors, tis now become general among the lowest Class'. In the consumption of tea, he distinguishes between rich (to whom it does good) and poor (to whom it can only bring harm). 'Tho' a moderate use of it as a Diluent of the Food and Blood may agree well enough with persons that have good Constitutions, live well, yet in concurrence with a low, coarse, vegetable diet, the chief food of Poor People, its Effects are very mischievous, as it relaxes and weakens the solids, impoverishes the Blood, enervates the Strength and Vigour of the Body. There is also a considerable loss of Time attends this silly habit, in preparing and sipping the Tea, a Circumstance of no small Moment to those who are to live by their Labour.' But he reserves for dram-drinking his most resounding denunciation, as critics of sots, drunkards, soaks, tipplers, boozers and alkies have ever done; one of the most dependable, if destructive, consolations of poverty has remained constant, as has the condemnation of it; only the brewers and distillers who have vigorously defended the right of the working man to his jar of ale have shown them-

---

[28] Alcock, *Observations on Defects of the Poor Law*, op. cit.

selves true friends of the people. Alcock declares, 'If we look abroad into the World and view the Havock and Destruction which Dram-drinking makes among the common People, amongst whom it chiefly prevails, and consider the Miseries and calamities which it brings by that means, upon the Nation in general, every thinking Well-wisher to his Country must be greatly shocked by the sight of such a Scene. This monstrous abuse of Spirituous Liquors has most pernicious Effects; it consumes the Gain and Substance of the People, and reduces them to Poverty and Want; destroys their Health and Strength; and makes hem both unable and unwilling to Work and cuts off the Thread of Life before they have lived out Half their days; it intoxicates the Mind, inflames the Passions and puts them off their Guard and exposes them to all manner of Vice and Corruption.' This is by way of preamble to the denunciation of a law to relieve people brought to want by such extravagances, which is unreasonable and impolitic and in time, 'must prove fatal to the Nation. The number of receivers will become greater than that of the Contributors and these must fall with all the rest, and all come to Poverty, Misery and Confusion'.

Henry Fielding, author of *Tom Jones*, published in 1753 a *Proposal for Making an Effectual Provision for the Poor*.[29] He believed those incapable of work were few, and their welfare best left to private charity. The Act which directed the able poor to be set on work was so general and vague that, given the quality of the overseers, had, unsurprisingly, never been properly carried out. 'So very useless is the heavy tax and so wretched its disposition that it is a question whether the Poor or Rich are more dissatisfied, or have indeed greater reason to be dissatisfied, since the plunder of the one serves so little to the advantage of the other; for while a million yearly is raised among the former, many of the latter are starved; many more languish in want and misery; of the rest, many are found begging or pilfering in the streets today, tomorrow are locked up in jails and bridewells. ... They starve and freeze among themselves; but they beg, steal and rob among their betters.'

In a *Reflection on the Poors' Rates*, prompted by the Abstracts of the Returns of the Overseers of the Poor to the House of Commons in 1776, the anonymous writer deplored, in words that have been uttered by every generation since the first Poor Laws, that the increase in numbers of the poor arises from the Poor Laws themselves, in the sense that they relieve

[29] Fielding, Henry, *Proposal for Making an Effectual Provision for the Poor*, London, 1753.

people, not only suffering poverty, but relieve them also from the necessity of finding work for themselves.[30] The present age is too indulgent and too liberal, which has made the poor idle and insolent to their superiors. 'The labouring people, having lost the desire of laying up any frugal provision for themselves, as they know that the public is bound to provide for them, and that knowledge has made them no longer reckon it a duty to assist even their nearest connections or relations, for they consider all to be lawful gain that they can squeeze from the parish.' The same document quotes from 'a Kentish Man' on the present state of the poor, which suggests growing dissatisfaction with the work-house, 'For they [the inmates of the workhouse] see no want, nor the solicitous care there is in poor industrious families to provide their scanty allowance from day to day; their provisions are all set down before them ready dressed; they hear of no difficulties to procure it; The work they do is by way of stint; for they have either a task or a work of so many hours; when that is done, they think no further of it, nor how they are to contribute to earning the next meal: They are as totally ignorant of every domestic business, whereas in the poorest houses, from their earliest infancy, they set their hands to everything they can possibly do, and never know an end to their work till night calls them to their necessary rest; for the boys rise and go out with their fathers as soon as they can do the least thing; and by that means become handy at country work, and inured to all weathers; which is the constant ruin of every workhouse boy, by being confined in the house, and not so much exposed to the inclemencies of the air, is hardly, if ever, brought to bear it well... And as to the girls, they are also taken in to be doing something with their mother; and though the lowest sort do not make the best of servants they are still good drudges in farmhouses, and always preferable to workhouse girls in the country, whatever they may be in manufacturing town.'

Hopes vested in the workhouse were disappointed: there was no profit to be had from pauper labour, and the cost of maintaining it had other consequences than that of any savings, for children brought up within its walls—if they survived—were good for nothing.

Following a scandal of the excessive number of deaths of babies and young children in the workhouses—more than half failed to reach their sixth birthday—an Act of 1767 obliged all parishes in London and West-

[30] *Reflections on the Poors' Rates*, House of Commons, 1776.

minster to send parish children under six, within a fortnight after birth or after being received into the workhouse, to be nursed outside until they were six years of age, and maintained afterwards until they should be bound apprentices or returned to the workhouse.

A change of heart

The later eighteenth century saw a change in attitude, not only towards the poor. In the 1770s, prices rose and real wages fell; and although the correlation between the economy and social responses is not mechanistic, the idea dawned once more that poverty might be traced to circumstances other than moral failings of the poor. The poor benefited from a new mildness—Hanway's Act against the conditions in which climbing boys worked, John Howard's *State of the Prisons* in 1777[31] and Wilberforce's movement against the slave trade, were part of this movement. Characteristic of the change of heart was a pamphlet of R. Potter, who, inspired by new Houses of Industry erected in Norfolk and Suffolk, described the existing habitations of the poor in his *Observations on the Poor Laws* in 1775, 'These miserable tenantries are, many of them, open to the roof like barns, with ten thousand fluttering cobwebs pendent from the thatch; if they have chambers, they are in this condition, few of them have any floor, besides the naked earth; their site and precinct is generally damp and unwholesome; the door serves to let in the light and let out the smoke, for the windows are generally so small and so patch'd, that they serve to little purpose but to admit the bleak and howling winds and driving snow; their beds are filthy masses of unsheltering rags that beggar description, many of them elevated from the bare earth only by a little rotten straw; in one room you shall find an aged couple, whose shivering limbs ache for want of better covering; contiguous to them a younger pair with three of their children in the same bed, and in a corner of the same room, a son and daughter, each arrived at the age of puberty, couching together. In the same room lodges a decent man of 80, hourly insulted by two wanton wenches each holding to the breast the fruits of unlawfull love.'[32]

The altered sensibility found expression in Gilbert's Act of 1783, which reversed the provisions of the Knatchbull Act. Sub-contracting the

[31] Howard, John, *State of the Prisons*, London, 1777.
[32] Potter, R., *Observations on the Poor Laws*, pamphlet, London, 1775.

maintenance of the poor had led to many abuses: the overseers had, in the words of one observer, 'contrived to contract with obnoxious persons of a savage disposition for the maintenance of the poor, not with a view of making their situation more comfortable, but to hold out a Workhouse as a terrible alternative to those who would not acquiesce in the pittances which the parish officers thought fit to allow them (as out-relief).' Gilbert's Act revoked the power of parish officers to contract with any persons for employing the poor, and directed the appointment of Guardians with the authority to inspect and visit workhouses. Unions of parishes could combine to build workhouses for the old, sick and infirm. The able-bodied were to receive out-relief and employment close to the places where they lived.

Gilbert's Act anticipated the Speenhamland system, adopted by the Berkshire magistrates in 1795; a system of relief, never legislated for, but which became widespread in the southern counties, and even in some of the Northern manufacturing areas (see below).

The punitive tradition

Although Adam Smith is credited with inaugurating the art or science of modern economics, many elements on which he drew were already part of accepted discourse in Britain. More than a hundred years before Smith, Joseph Lee had argued, 'It is an undeniable maxim that everyone by the light of nature and reason will do that which makes for his greatest advantage...The advancement of private persons will be the advantage of the public.'[33] Even Smith's 'invisible hand' had a precedent in Daniel Defoe's *Giving Alms no Charity*.[34] Defoe had spoken, referring to the fate of nations, of 'the secret overruling Hand' (of the Divine Providence). In any case, the idea that the pursuit of individual interests results in the well-being of society is only a more secular reformulation of the medieval view that the harmony of society depends upon the performance by high and low of the duties assigned to them by the authority of God.

Definitions of poverty are always crafted by the rich. The self-preservation of those who have an interest in maintaining the existing order colours their moral evaluation of the poor, who are seen through the

[33] Lee, Joseph, *Vindication of a Regulated Enclosure*, London, 1656.
[34] Defoe, *Giving Alms no Charity*, op. cit.

prism of their own privilege. They assume the poor wish for nothing so much as to rise above their station—to become like them in fact; to spend a life travelling, entertaining, hunting, intermittently overseeing their estates and occasionally, governing the country. The projection onto the poor of 'idleness' and 'luxury' suggests a desire to monopolise these qualities for themselves, and to resist any encroachment upon them, since without the labour of the poor, their own position would be jeopardised.

There is, throughout centuries of instruction to the poor about their own vices, failings and defects, a complex, uniquely British sense of caste. The poor were said to 'breed', while the rich possessed 'breeding'. The poor were born of lowly parentage, where the rich philanthropically, 'gave birth'. The poor were prone to idleness and sloth, for which the pangs of hunger were the best medicine; the rich enjoyed 'leisure'. The poor 'pilfered and stole', while the wealthy ransacked the world of its treasures to ornament their country houses. It is not difficult to perceive in the strictures of the rich on the poor a caricature of their own attributes; these became de-moralised in transference to people who mimicked them, a tendency undiminished in our time, especially when the rich require incentives to encourage them to bestow their talents on society, while the poor must have benefits or subsistence withheld, in order to produce the same effect.

As people in Britain have become better off, they know, by instinct and experience, the appropriate response to those beneath them. The attitudes of privilege are heritable. The ideology of a sometime aristocratic minority was bequeathed, first to the entrepreneurial middle class, and later, to a majority of the people who, no longer poor, knew, by long exposure, how to turn their anger against a poor, reduced now to minority status; a view strengthened by knowledge that the newly enriched remain a minority in the wider world; so that resentment formerly harboured against them can now be turned upon the impoverished of globalism.

In Britain, greater leniency towards the poor at the end of the eighteenth century was accompanied by the elaboration—and hardening—of the ideology of political economy. The rapidity with which the pragmatic humanism of Adam Smith had been transformed by the 1830s, into the rigid creed of the self-regulating market, is astonishing: the need for an ideology was—like some versions of the poor—self-generating. The process began soon after the publication of *The Wealth of Nations*, even though

Smith only once mentions 'the invisible hand', which was to play a fateful part in the beliefs of his successors. Within ten years of the appearance of Smith's book, the Reverend Joseph Townsend was one of many writers of the 1790s who were to become the defining voice of political economy.[35] Townsend anticipates Malthus in his conviction that the resources available to feed the poor lagged far behind the increase in population. The theme is familiar, 'The laws indeed have made provision for their relief, and the contributions collected for their support are more than liberal, but then the laws being inadequate to the purposes for which they were made for industry in distress, does little more than give encouragement to idleness and vice.'

Townsend is in the punitive tradition. 'At the dissolution of the monasteries, the lazy and the indigent, who were deprived of their accustomed food, became clamorous, and having long since forgot to work, were not only ready to join in every scheme for the disturbance of the state, but, as vagrants, by their numbers, by their impostures, and by their thefts, they rendered themselves a public and most intolerable nuisance.'

This is the prelude to a lament that, 'the prodigal must first be fed; the children of the prostitute must first be cloathed'. He asks, 'What cause have they (the poor) to fear, when they are assured, that if by their indolence and extravagance, by their drunkenness and vices, they should be reduced to want, they shall be abundantly supplied, not only with food and raiment, but with their accustomed luxuries, at the expence of others?'

Townsend, vicar of Pewsey in Wiltshire, the physician who originated the treatment of syphilis with mercury and potassium iodide, also had his remedies for shameful social ills. This insight into the impersonal nature of economic pressure subsequently proved to be of great utility.

Townsend speaks of 'the distinctions which exist in nature' and the 'natural obligations which arise from these relations. Among the first of these relations stands the relation of a servant to his master: and the first duty required from a servant is prompt, cheerful and hearty obedience.' Hunger is the remedy for disobedient servants. 'Hunger will tame the fiercest animals, it will teach decency and civility, obedience and subjection, to the most brutish, the most obstinate and the most perverse.'[36]

---

[35] Townsend, Joseph, *Dissertation on the Poor Laws*, London, 1786.
[36] Ibid.

Echoing Defoe and many other casual but authoritative, 'observers' of the poor, Townsend says, 'Drunkenness is the common vice of poverty; not perhaps of poverty as such, but of the uncultivated mind. ... When therefore, by the advance in wages, they (the common people) obtain more than is sufficient for their bare subsistence, they spend the surplus at the alehouse, and neglect their business. Is a man drunk one day? He will have little inclination to work the next. Thus for every drunken fit, two days are lost.'

'It seems to be a law of nature, that the poor should be to a certain degree improvident, that there may always be some to fulfil the most servile, the most sordid, and the most ignoble offices in the community. The stock of human happiness is thereby much increased, whilst the more delicate are not only relieved from drudgery, and freed from those occasional employments which would make them miserable, but are left at liberty, without interruption, to pursue those callings which are suited to their various dispositions, and most useful to the state.'[37]

Providing for the poor undermines their 'cheerful compliance with the tasks society makes on its most indigent members'. The divine harmony of the world is disturbed by their demands. The Poor Laws claim to achieve that which 'in the very nature and constitution of the world, is impracticable'. This leads into his famous parable of the South Seas island, into which goats were introduced by the English for food. The goats multiplied until they placed great pressure on their own food supply. The weakest died and stability was restored. The Spaniards, discovering the English used the island for provisions, introduced dogs to eliminate the goats. These increased and diminished the number of goats. But some goats retired to the rocky heights of the island, and only the weak perished as food for the dogs. The weakest dogs died, and a new balance was established. Prefiguring Malthus, Townsend draws his conclusions for society, 'It is the quantity of food which regulates the numbers of the human species.'[38]

The application of this fable to human affairs placed the economic system securely under the law of the jungle;[39] where, reinforced by the later doctrine of social Darwinism, it has flourished ever since; as popular wisdom about the (largely mistaken) nature of the jungle, dog eat dog

[37] Ibid.
[38] Ibid.
[39] See Polanyi, *The Great Transformation*, Boston: Beacon Press, 1944.

and the rat-race, attests. Thus the common sense of our time has its origin in the distemper of a remote eighteenth-century clergyman. Townsend deplored attempts to relieve poverty by taxing the rich. 'It is not to be imagined that men, who by close application and watchful attention to their business, by rigid frugality and hard labour, have made a decent provision for their families, should freely part with a considerable proportion of their property, or suffer it to be taken from them without strong efforts to retain it.

'It is with the human species as with all other articles of trade without a premium; the demand will regulate the market.'

Amenities taken for granted by the rich become unwarrantable extravagance when the labourer longs for them. 'No man will be an economist of water, if he can go to the well or to the brook as often as he please.' Joseph Townsend commends the inhabitants of Lerwick in the Shetland Islands, who make stockings in their leisure hours, and depend on no other resource than their own industry and frugality. 'They consume neither tea, nor sugar, nor spices, because they cannot afford to purchase these useless articles; neither do they wear stockings or shoes, till by their diligence they have acquired such affluence as to bear this expence. How different is theirs from the dress and diet of our common people, who have lost all ideas of economy....'

In a premonitory gesture to the 'Big Society', Townsend declares, 'To relieve the poor by voluntary donations is not only most wise, politic and just; is not only most agreeable both to reason and to revelation; but it is most effectual in preventing misery, and most excellent in itself, as cherishing, instead of rancour, malice and contention, the opposite and most amiable affections of the human breast, pity, compassion, and benevolence in the rich, love, reverence and gratitude in the poor. Nothing in nature can be more disgusting than a parish pay-table, attendant upon which, in the same objects of misery, are too often found combined, snuff, gin, rags, vermin, insolence and abusive language; nor in nature can any thing be more beautiful than the mild complacency of benevolence, hastening to the humble cottage to relieve the wants of industry and virtue, to feed the hungry, to cloath the naked and to sooth the sorrows of the widow with her tender orphans... When the poor are obliged to cultivate the friendship of the rich, the rich will never want inclination to relieve the distresses of the poor.'[40]

[40] Townsend, *Dissertation on the Poor Laws*, op. cit.

This symmetry of the deferential poor raising their eyes to the benevolent rich has a medieval quality, high and low in their appointed place. This idea reappears in modified guise throughout our history, even when the deity withdraws discreetly from the scene and is replaced by that curious proxy, the market. Only a few years after Townsend, Edmund Burke said, 'We, the people, ought to be made sensible that it is not in breaking the laws of commerce, which are the laws of nature, and consequently the laws of God, that we are to place our hope of softening the Divine displeasure to remove any calamity under which we suffer or which hangs over us.'[41]

Burke makes explicit his abhorrence of the State's involvement in relief of poverty, and objects to any intervention that would raise wages. He asks, '… in calamitous seasons, under accidental illness, in declining life, and with the pressure of numerous offspring, the future nourishers of the community, but the present drains and blood-suckers of those who produce them, what is to be done? When a man cannot live and maintain his family by the natural hire of his labour, ought it not to be raised by authority?'

His answer is a clear negative. 'I premise that labour is, as I have already intimated, a commodity, and as such an article of trade. If I am right in this notion, then labour must be subject to all the laws and principles of trade, and not to regulations foreign to them, and that may be totally inconsistent with those principles and those laws. When any commodity is carried to market, it is not the necessity of the vender, but the necessity of the purchaser that raises the price. The extreme want of the seller has rather (by the nature of things with which we shall in vain contend) the direct contrary operation. If the goods at market are beyond the demand, they fall in value; if below it, they rise. The impossibility of the substance of a man, who carries his labour to market, is totally beside the question in this way of viewing it. The only question is, what is it worth to the buyer?'

The transformation of the labouring part of humanity into commodity must have come easily to people who saw labourers as a class of beings existing principally to serve those above them. Townsend expresses the relationship with unusual clarity. 'He who stately employs the poor in useful labour is their only friend; he who only feeds them is their greatest

---

[41] Burke, *Thoughts and Details on Scarcity*, op. cit.

enemy.' This evaluation of the toilers in farm, field and manufactory was echoed by the rising middle class, the new entrepreneurs and mill-owners, who could not do enough to raise their progeny into the landed classes.

Townsend and Burke were not insensible of the miseries attending the labouring class. But the State has no part to play in alleviating them. 'To provide for us in our necessities is not in the power of Government. ... Whenever it happens that a man can claim nothing according to the rules of commerce, and the principles of justice, he passes out of that depart-ment, and comes within the jurisdiction of mercy. In that province the magistrate has nothing at all to do: his interference is a violation of the property which it is his office to protect. Without all doubt, charity to the poor is a direct and obligatory duty upon all Christians, next in order after the payment of debts, full as strong, and by nature made infinitely more delightful to us.'[42] Burke speaks of the labourer passing from one department to another, a bureaucratic image, as though political econ-omy were one branch of the Divine Providence and mercy another, accommodated, no doubt, in different wings of the flawless neo-classical edifice constructed for the purpose.

Just as it is in the farmer's interest that his men should thrive, so, says Burke, it is 'the first and fundamental interest of the labourer, that the farmer should have a full in-coming profit on the product of his labour. The proposition is self-evident, and nothing but the malignity, perverse-ness and ill-governed passions of mankind, and particularly the envy they have to each other's prosperity, could prevent their seeing and acknowl-edging it, with thankfulness to the benign and wise dispenser of all things, who obliges men, whether they will or not, in pursuing their own selfish interests, to connect the general good with their own individual success. But who are to judge what that profit and advantage ought to be? Cer-tainly no authority on earth...'

Speenhamland

As it turned out, Burke's animadversions on the Speenhamland system were vindicated. While the 'right to life' is a noble principle (echoed in our time by the Green and socialist movements), in practice, it meant that farmers were not required to pay a living wage, since the parish

[42] Ibid.

would make up the difference. At the same time, it gave such security to labourers that it scarcely mattered whether they worked at all, since they were assured an income. The system, which became widespread in the South of England, but not in the North, lasted almost forty years, in defiance of the hardening tenets of political economy. It was in response to its ill effects that the Commission on the Poor Law was set up in 1832.

Karl Polanyi describes Speenhamland as a catastrophe, since the protection it afforded the rural labourer delayed the creation of a capitalist labour market by more than a generation.[43] This was the last effort by representatives of the landed interest to retain power in a country in which the movement towards commerce was well established and in which industry was rapidly gaining ground. The system of aid-in-wages was instituted in the year when the Act of Settlement was repealed, 1795.

Speenhamland affronted the ideology of the free market, and the conviction that the best government was that which forbore to interfere with its workings; despite the fact that facilitating a free market required government activity on a vast scale. It gave rise to an outpouring of angry polemic, diatribes against the omnivorous poor, which continued until the Poor Law Amendment Act of 1834 abolished it.

Speenhamland was, of course, popular; it certainly lessened the harshness of the Anti-Combination laws of 1799, which prevented workers from forming trade unions to raise wages. But this early experiment in the right to livelihood was calamitous. It became difficult for people with large families, not to live 'on the rates'. Similar arguments are heard in contemporary Britain by those who deplore 'the benefit trap' and the unwillingness to work of those who find it easier to live on welfare.

If Speenhamland was an obstacle to the growth of industrial civilisation, the market-system appeared as a deliverance. Polanyi says the degradation inflicted by the free market in labour would not have been enforced with such exuberance, had the devitalising effect of Speenhamland not been carried to a conclusion, whereby the system designed to help the working poor actually finished up by ruining them: warnings issued by generations of opponents of the Poor Law were fulfilled.

This allowance system was a paternalistic rearguard action by the country gentry and squirearchy, although the generous interpretation of the Poor Law did not occur by accident. It was implemented in the after-

---

[43] Polanyi, *The Great Transformation*, op. cit.

math of the French Revolution, and after the disastrous harvests of 1794 and 1795; not for the last time, prudence dictated to the ruling classes greater open-heartedness to the labouring poor, who, the far-sighted feared, might be susceptible to contamination by the French example, let alone spontaneous domestic inspiration, since food riots had occurred throughout the eighteenth century.

The outcome had its effect upon labourers themselves, employers and the payers of the poor rate, many of them employers. Labouring people were pauperised. Enclosure proceeded with increasing speed, and more and more people were forced upon the rates. Wealth in the countryside grew, and with it, the numbers of poor. The whole process ran counter to the spirit of the age, with its rhetoric of the 'free contract' between producer and employee, and prepared the way for that most brutal and utilitarian reaction, the Poor Law Amendment Act of 1834. The humanitarianism of the late eighteenth century was quenched by a mixture of fear produced in the rulers of Britain by the French Revolution and the generosity of Speenhamland, which blurred the distinction between the independent poor and the pauper; a confusion which the Poor Law Commissioners would be at pains to reverse.

The map of Pauperland

Long before the 1832 Reforming government, the reaction had been fierce. One of the most influential writers was Jeremy Bentham, who in 1798 elaborated his earlier ideas for the stricter control of the criminal classes.[44] His detailed proposals were for a National Company (modelled, significantly, on the East India Company), which would set up houses of industry all over the country, within ten miles of each other, each containing up to 2,000 paupers, arranged in such a way that their every action would be visible to those governing the establishment. It would, despite a century of evidence that there was nothing to be got out of paupers but their company and a lot of trouble, provide a profit, part of which would be returned to the rate-payers. Bentham is often described as a major begetter of the Amendment Act of 1834. He elaborated his scheme with great precision, and although he was aggrieved that it was never implemented, many of its principles would haunt the lives of the poor for a century.

[44] Bentham, Jeremy, *Pauper Management Improved*, London, 1798.

He produced what he called a 'Map of Pauperland', the topography, as it were of indigence, with the intention of 'forming a valuation of that part of the natural livestock which has no feathers to it and walks upon two legs'. The description of people as 'stock' is a measure of the distance between masters and people, since the latter are perceived as closer to the beasts of the field than to the vault of heaven.

The spirit of Bentham informed many of the rigid policies of the 1834 Act. One of the principles in his Houses of Industry was sexual segregation, which was indeed incorporated into the workhouse system. Among reasons for separation of paupers was 'the prevention of unsatisfiable desires'. The vigilance with which the appetites of the poor were to be curbed runs through the literature; if it now reads oddly, this is because prohibition of desires considered dangerous has long been lifted, since these are now a source of profitable economic activity.

'There would be separation of the indigenous and quasi-indigenous stock of the non-adult class, from the coming-and-going stock, who might excite hankering after emancipation by flattering pictures of the world at large.' In a more enlightened age, such discrimination has proved unnecessary, since rich and poor are self-segregating, each contained within their own spatial sphere, which permits them to lead lives apart, and to follow trajectories which rarely intersect.

Bentham starkly enunciates the value-system of the self-regulating market, to which he ascribes miraculous powers, since through its workings, human nature, with all its vicious propensities, would emerge, cleansed and capable of social good. Capitalism was to become redemptive: in its baptism of the people by total immersion, it scooped up and absorbed some of the beliefs of Christianity. Similar patterns of feeling would later nourish Marx, whose transforming doctrines also focussed on a form of redemption, albeit secular. 'Every system of management,' wrote Bentham, 'which has disinterestedness, pretended or real, for its foundation, is rotten at the root, susceptible of a momentary prosperity at the outset, but sure to perish in the long run. That principle of action most to be depended upon, whose influence is most powerful, most constant, most uniform, is the most lasting and most general among mankind. Personal interest is that principle; a system of economy built on any other foundation is built upon a quicksand.'[45] The only constant is that

[45] Ibid.

83

the poor remain recipients of the savage wisdom of their betters—
oppressive then, but later, when rich pickings were to be had from the
relaxation of industrial discipline, more permissive. It is this loosening of
discipline that has led, in our time, to complaints about spoonfeeding and
nannying, loss of independence, the hour of the sponger, the cheat and
the fraud; and with it, a clamour for 'crackdowns', stampings out, clamp-
downs and a return to the salutary severities of the Poor Law.

It was Bentham's belief that no element of labour, however feeble
should be wasted. 'Not one in a hundred is incapable of all employment.
Not the motion of a finger—not a step—not a wink—not a whisper—but
ought to be turned to account in the way of profit in a system of such
magnitude... Employment may be afforded to every fragment of ability,
however minute.' This sentiment lingers. Britain's Coalition government, having contracted out to private entities a labour test on those
previously on disability benefit, has discovered that there are people suffering from terminal illness and in extreme pain, who are nevertheless 'fit
for work.'

Bentham was as keen to break 'the paupership habit' as any twenty-
first century politician is to destroy 'welfare dependency'. Not even the
smallest detail escaped his eye, vigilant as he was for potential waste; in
the cheeseparing minutiae the ancestry of Thatcher is clearly detectable.
He would cut away any useless material from the clothing of the poor:
even hats should be brimless, in the same parsimonious endeavour. Bed-
sheets should be fastened on hooks, pins or buttons, 'to save the quantity
usually added for tucking in'.

In a surreal section he describes 'hands', a collage of the instruments
of labour of the poor—'unripe hands', 'feeble hands', sick hands', 'insane
hands', 'imperfect hands', tender hands', 'past-prosperity hands', 'hands
of the dangerous and disreputable classes', 'unwilling hands', 'extra-ability
hands', 'inadequate-ability hands'; the only omission the helping or
tending.

Bentham's strictures on begging also resonate in the popular press of
the twenty-first century. 'Begging is a species of extortion to which the
tender-hearted, and they only, are exposed. Every penny spent is the
reward of industry; every penny given is a bounty on idleness. The luxuries seen in many instances to be enjoyed by beggars are a sort of insult to
the hard-working child of industry: by holding him out as a dupe, who
toils and torments himself to earn a maintenance inferior to that which
is earned by canting and grimace.'

In another anticipation of familiar debates, Bentham advocates loans rather than gifts to the poor. 'Loans preserve unimpaired the spirit of frugality and industry, by leading them to transfer their dependence from their own exertions to those of others.' He deprecates savings, since they present, 'the difficulty of opposing a never-ending temptation afforded by the instruments of sensual enjoyment, where the means of purchasing them are constantly at hand.' The lack of willpower of the poor troubled observers, until it was discovered that the absence of such power would drive, in the twentieth century, the new cult of consumerism.

Bentham deplored the Act of Settlement. He proposed 'frugality inns' as staging posts for conveying the poor (the 'transferable classes') to places wherever food or labour is cheapest, a primitive version of urging the unemployed to move to the nearest site of labour. He also insists 'how little comfort depends on money, and how much on the attention and felicity with which it is disposed'.[46]

The inadequacy of 43 Elizabeth: Malthus[47]

The Elizabethan Poor Law remained the standard by which subsequent changes were measured; and in the seventeenth and eighteenth centuries, the gap between its intention and its implementation was a continuous irritant. The Elizabethan law was part of a wider scheme, of which prevention of depopulation and enclosures, control of food prices and stability of employment, were also part. By the eighteenth century, the Poor Laws could not cope with what was later to be perceived as 'economic distress'. Parts of the law had also been ignored: and although labour was still advocated as the most effective remedy for poverty, deficiency in 'setting the poor on work' remained. There was little provision of the materials with which to work; houses of industry were criticised for degenerating into castles of indolence.

In the early nineteenth century, growing industrial towns had drawn large-scale migrations, and a radical disturbance of population; and now the Settlement laws were called into question by industry and commerce, which saw them as an obstacle to the mobility of labour; a concern which prefigures contemporary anguish over how to stem the flow

---

[46] Ibid.

[47] Malthus, *An Essay on the Principle of Population*, London, 1798.

of migrant labour. The landed interests wished to maintain a demographic stability which would never again be known. Disputes arose as to whether manufacturing was a fleeting and impermanent activity, the production of food being the real function of the labouring classes. The first census of 1801 made clear the extent of the increase in population. Far-reaching change, not yet fully understood, was everywhere apparent, susceptible to a range of interpretations. The last gasps of feudalism raged against the industrial future, but at the time, few had any idea of the nature of the society coming into existence. What everyone could agree upon was the growth in 'pauperism', the 'surplus population', large numbers of whom would require subsistence from the parish, and for whom either sexual abstinence or forced emigration were recommended as the principal palliatives.

In the circumstances, it is unsurprising if the preachers of apocalypse were in the ascendant. It was a day of (secular) judgement, although many saw the time as a divine reckoning, apparent in the millennial cults, the emergence of prophets and seers, and the intense religious emotion of Non-conformists in their sooty chapels.

The supreme representative of lurid pessimism—ironically, at the very moment when Britain was about to enter its most dynamic period of industrial wealth-creation—was Thomas Malthus, whose diagnosis of the maladies of the time profoundly influenced following generations. His *Essay on the Principle of Population* was a response to the rhapsodic predictions of William Godwin who saw a future humanity capable of such improvement that it would eventually transcend its own sexual nature and even its own mortality.

It is never difficult to refute doctrines of the perfectibility of man; and by contrast with the absurdity of Godwin's beliefs, Malthus' own extreme views appeared plausible. His contention, that 'population, when unchecked increases in a geometrical ratio, while subsistence increases only in an arithmetical ratio', took on a life of its own in the convulsed society of the 1790s. Malthus wanted to show that population growth would exhaust the capabilities of the earth to provide food. A similar argument has resurfaced in our time in the Green movement, although most see the issue as an abuse of the resources of the earth, rather than the effect of population on the food supply. The contemporary argument takes a stand against consumption by a minority, of a disproportionate share of what the earth provides. But the premise is similar, and demands 'restraint' of a different kind from the 'moral restraint' (sexual abstinence) which Malthus held out as a possible source of population control in a later, less gloomy, version of his work.

Discoveries in science and natural history in the eighteenth century were influential in the interpretation of changes in society. Observers of the early industrial period concentrated on the human consequences of industrialism, rather than on the technology, engineering and productive power of the age, which would eventually allay anxieties about population, resources and social upheaval. Attitudes were, for the most part, anchored in traditional views of a human nature defined by the story of the Fall, redemption and salvation; a spiritual heritage which in the material world of early industrialism, became poverty, labour and affluence.

What Malthus could not have known was that, as people became more secure, they would limit the size of their families. When survival was more or less assured, population would take care of itself. High levels of infant mortality appeared a permanent feature of social life; and although child deaths were in fact declining, his projections took no account, either of the undermining of his own argument through the number of infants who perished, or of any future change. As for birth control, to Malthus, this was part of the portmanteau of 'vice', which, as a clergyman, he could not bring himself to name—prostitution, homosexuality, onanism or any other sexual practice that inhibited conception. Delay in marriage was productive of 'vice', whereas the pursuit of natural instincts led to misery. The lesson of Malthus was that severity equalled benevolence, since anything else only increased the numbers of the poor.

Perhaps more instructive in those who predict the future than their formal prognostications are all the things they fail to foresee. No less powerful than the theory of the press of population upon the food supply was the necessary proportion of poor (large) to rich (small). Malthus states, 'No possible form of society could prevent the almost constant action of misery upon a great part of mankind, if in a state of inequality, and upon all, if all were equal.' It is unthinkable that 'station' or 'estate' or 'rank' should be called into question, and for a very good reason. The rich were a very small section of the population; and if all their wealth were redistributed, as Burke observed, 'it would scarcely provide bread and cheese for a day's supper for the legions of labouring poor'. Malthus emphasised the inevitability of social stratification, 'Man cannot live in the midst of plenty. All cannot share alike the bounties of nature. Were there no established administration of property, every man would be obliged to guard with force his little store. Selfishness would be triumphant. The subjects of contention would be perpetual. Every individual mind would be under a constant anxiety about corporal support; and not a single intellect would be left free to expatiate in the field of thought.' The inexorable laws of nature decree that 'some human beings must suffer from want. These are the unhappy persons who, in the great lottery of life, have drawn a blank.' This unfortunate metaphor sits ill with the efforts of Malthus to demonstrate that this is part of the plan of Providence for our moral, if not material, improvement. He refers elsewhere to 'those roughnesses and inequalities of life, which querulous man too frequently makes the subject of his complaint against the God of nature... The savage would slumber for ever under his tree, unless he were roused from his torpor by the cravings of hunger or the pinchings of cold. ...The necessity for food for the support of life, gives rise, probably, to a greater quantity of exertion, than any other art, bodily or mental. To furnish the most unremitted excitements of this kind, and urge a man to further the gracious designs of Providence, by the full cultivation of the earth, it has ordained that population should increase much faster than food.' It is only a step from regarding these salubrious necessities as an argument in favour of the abolition of the Poor Laws, since these only interfere with the workings of Providence.

The assimilation of 'the savage' to the 'labouring poor' is not accidental; for both were regarded by those who oversaw their plight, from the same distance. The powerful spoke within their own secure sense of place in society; theirs was an imperial mindset, which regarded the inhabitants of remote territories with the same gaze they turned upon the occupants of Pauperland. They had little imaginative understanding of the lives of the labouring poor. Since their own position in society was divinely appointed, it was not difficult to see those in lowlier stations placed there by the same wisdom.

'To remedy the distresses of the common people, the poor-laws of England have been instituted; but it is to be feared, that though they may have alleviated a little the intensity of individual misfortune, they have spread the general evil over a much larger surface... I feel no doubt whatever that the parish laws of England have contributed to raise the price of provisions and to lower the real price of labour. They have therefore contributed to impoverish that class of people whose only possession is their labour...The labouring poor, to use a vulgar expression, seem always to live from hand to mouth. Their present wants employ their whole attention, and they seldom think of the future. Even when they have an opportunity of saving they seldom exercise it; but all that is beyond their present necessities goes, generally speaking, to the ale-house. The poor laws of England may therefore be said to diminish both the power and the will to save, among the common people, and thus to weaken one of the strongest incentives to sobriety and industry, and consequently to happiness.'[48]

Although the Poor Law Commission of 1834 did not follow the teaching of Malthus and do away with the Poor Laws, his spirit, like that of Bentham, informed its deliberations; coercive management of the poor the dominant tone.

Later, Malthus, in an 1803 edition of his *Essay*, added the famous fable of Nature's banquet, which suggests his ideas had found a receptive environment, even though he was widely criticised as heartless. His revision did little to diminish this reputation. In the next edition he wrote:

'A man who is born into a world already possessed, if he cannot get subsistence from his parents on whom he has a just demand, and if the society do not want his labour, he has no claim of *right* to the smallest portion of foods, and in fact, has no business to be where he is. At nature's mighty feast there is no cover for him. She tells him to be gone, and will quickly execute her own orders, if he does not work upon the compassion of some of her guests. If these guests get up and make room for him, other intruders immediately appear demanding the same favour. The report of a provision for all that come fills the hall with numerous claimants. The order and harmony of the feast is disturbed, the plenty that before reigned is changed into scarcity ... the guests learn too late their error, in counteracting those strict orders to all intruders, issued by the great mistress of the feast, who, wishing that all her guests should have plenty, and knowing that she could not provide for unlimited numbers, humanely refused to admit fresh comers when her table was already full.'[49]

Poets and writers detested his doctrines, but he gained influence among politicians and economists, his melancholy view so powerful that it rendered foregone the conclusion of the work of the Commission on

[48] Ibid.
[49] Ibid.

the Poor Law in 1834. Although Nassau Senior—with Edwin Chadwick, the principal author of the report—repudiated Malthus, the sheer numbers of clamorous, incontinent, improvident poor crowd the report from beginning to end; and the 'evidence' is presented in such a way that there is little doubt that the recommendations will be incorporated into the Act of Parliament. This, like much legislation described as 'reform', is designed to make sharper the already pointed goad of pauperism.

The Poor Law Amendment Act, 1834

The Commission, set up following the agrarian riots of 1830, began taking evidence before the election of the Reform government of 1832. In *The Problem of Poverty 1660–1834*, Geoffrey Taylor observed that the Old Poor Law, 'essentially had ceased to be a system long before 1834, but as a device for dealing with surplus labour in an expanding economy, it was not ineffective'.[50] After thirty-five years of Speenhamland, change was urgently needed; and the shape of that change had been outlined in the consensus of commentators on the poor at the close of the eighteenth and early nineteenth centuries; a view saturated with the ideology of political economy, tempered by vestiges of patrician charity. Patrick Colquhoun's *Treatise on Indigence* explained the distinction between poverty and indigence.[51]

'Poverty is that state or condition in society where the individual has no surplus labour in store, and consequently no property but what is derived from the constant exercise of industry in the occupations of life; or in other words, it is the state of everyone who must labour for subsistence.' Poverty, he argued, is indispensable, since it is the spur to labour, 'and without labour there would be no riches, no refinement, no comfort and no benefit to those who may be possessed of wealth'. Against this necessary spur to exertion, Colquhoun places 'indigence', 'that condition of society that implies want, misery and distress. It is the state of anyone destitute of the means of subsistence and unable to labour to procure it as nature requires.' Indigence is of two kinds—innocent and culpable. He estimates three-quarters of recipients of parish relief in 1803—well over a million—culpably indigent. Resources for employment of both males and females are greater than exist in any country in the world; no

---

[50] Taylor, G., *The Problem of Poverty: 1660–1834*, London: Longman, 1969.
[51] Colquhoun, Patrick, *Treatise on Indigence*, London, 1806.

individual, having labour to dispose of and with a good character, ought to find any difficulty in finding a purchaser; a view which finds widespread support today.

Colquhoun's definition of poverty corresponds to Burke's idea of the natural condition of the labourer, which Burke, however, would not acknowledge as poverty. Burke would allow no lamentation of their condition, since there was no point in complaint against nature. Colquhoun wanted to restore the indigent to a state of dignified poverty; the difference was semantic.

Neither Burke nor Colquhoun was indifferent to the suffering of those who fell on evil days. Burke would not violate the laws which he held to be sacred, but for Colquhoun, the laws of political economy were a little less stringent, although he felt it necessary to reaffirm them. 'It is an axiom in politics, that the legislature should do nothing to disturb the exertions of individuals, aided by capitals, in every fair pursuit to improve their condition, since such improvements tend to the general good. Agriculture and manufactures and commerce, upon this principle, ought to experience no legislative obstruction. To the effect of this principle we owe much of the success, which, in these great branches of industry, has elevated this country above all the nations of the world.'[52] There was, however, an exception to this wisdom, which would be clearly reflected in the Commissioners' Report. 'In the operation, however, of such a principle, a power of individual exertion is implied, susceptible of that species of impulse which leads to a successful issue. It differs widely from the principle which applies to the labouring classes; who require to be assisted and guided into the way of helping themselves, and of maintaining their independence; first, by a religious and moral education; secondly, by a proper introduction into life, by acquiring a knowledge of some useful employment; thirdly, by provident habits and forethought; and fourthly, by such information as shall enable them to make the most of their earnings for the benefit of their families.'

Governing elites had to confront the churning of the labouring poor, and the metamorphosis that was changing them into an industrial working class. This disturbing development exempted it from the rules of laissez-faire; and the Report recommended an extensive programme of government involvement in the administration of the poor, a procedure dramatically out of keeping with the prevailing ideology.

[52] Ibid.

From the start, the conclusions of the Report are plain. 'It is now our painful duty,' say Edwin Chadwick and Nassau Senior, its principal authors, not without relish, 'to report that the greater part of the districts which we have been able to examine (about one-third of the 15,000 parishes in England and Wales), the fund, which the 43rd Elizabeth directed to be employed in setting to work children and persons able to labour, but using no daily trade, and in the necessary relief of the impotent, is applied to purposes opposed to the letter, and still more to the spirit of that Law, and destructive to the morals of the most numerous class, and to the welfare of all.'[53]

The degree of regulation of the poor was to be unparalleled. And although the recommendations were mitigated before being enshrined in law—and even that law was never fully and comprehensively implemented—the tone and intention of the Poor Law Amendment Act quickly became a source of fear and anxiety to the industrial poor. In theory, the government was undoing the mischief caused by the laxity with which relief had been provided under the Speenhamland system; so they regarded their activity as returning to its 'natural' state, the condition of the poor. The first part of the report assembles the evidence that fitted their preconception, and the second defines the remedies for evils already well known, and widely aired by influential opinion.

The other characteristic of this long, prolix document is the visceral loathing for the dependent poor by the individuals who gave evidence to the Commission. The poor who would not work, the indolent, improvident and vicious, were the main objects of attention; and for reasons which may or may not have coincided with the base qualities supposed to animate them; for the uncompliant poor interfered with the ideology of the self-correcting market, that natural phenomenon of supernaturally inspired symmetry and beauty. If the pursuit of individual self-interest really was to the benefit of all society, those who did not act in conformity with the ideology were guilty of wilful obstruction; what other explanation could there be for those who did not observe the rules of the game? This echoes in our time: in 2011, Iain Duncan Smith referred with explicit approval to people 'who play by the rules'. These rules were formulated by privilege for a game, in the creation of which the poor had no part and over the purpose of which they were never consulted.

[53] *Report of the Poor Law Commissioners*, 1834.

A central purpose of the Report was, in its words, to clarify 'the mischievous ambiguity of the word poor', and to underline, both in theory and in practice, the distinction between 'the poor' and 'the pauper'. The law of 'less eligibility' was to demonstrate this, since although the faultless poor would be accommodated, conditions for the able-bodied poor would be made so disagreeable in the workhouse, that only those who genuinely could find no employment outside would avail themselves of its forbidding hospitality.

The Commission did uncover much corruption in the administration of the 'old' poor law; and the poor of the period should not be elevated into martyrs. But neither were they wily and cunning predators on the public purse, as their betters of the early nineteenth century alleged. It is important, then as now, to distinguish between those living off the parish and those prevented from working, not only because of physical infirmity and age, but also because of other, less visible, injuries to the psyche and spirit, the weak, those of unsound mind, of limited intelligence, the wounded and humiliated of industrialising society, the able and intelligent denied the chance for self-improvement. Lazy and rapacious some certainly were; but the understanding of posterity tempered some of the harsher judgements of those who helped lead Britain to its position of supremacy in the world.

If the failings of the poor are on display in the Report, so, too are the prejudices of the dominant. Significantly, there is a meeting of minds between the ideological partisans of severity towards the poor and the immediate administrators of the Poor Law—overseers, parish officials and modest poor-rate payers. Their antagonists are liberal-minded magistrates and landowners, whose sense of responsibility towards the poor and (in the judgement of the Commissioners) their unfamiliarity with their scheming ways, led them to grant relief where it would be withheld by the overseers. There is a clear class distinction here, which pre-dates the class antagonisms of industrial society; an animosity which, despite the outbreaks of violence in 1830 against enclosures and threshing machines that displaced labour, was no less virulent in the minds of those who had agreed with the rancorous ideas on the labouring poor of Bentham, Townsend, Malthus and many others in preceding decades, and indeed, centuries.

The principal target of the Report was the relief given in aid of wages, tied to the scale according to the price of bread and the size of the labourer's family. Of the extent of this allowance, Cambridge was offered as one of many examples:

A single woman was entitled to the equivalent of three quartern loaves a week.

A single man: four quartern loaves (The quartern loaf was made of 3.5 pounds of flour and weighed 4.33 pounds.)

Man and wife: seven quartern loaves.

Man, wife and one child: eight quartern loaves.

Man, wife and two children: nine quartern loaves.

Man, wife and three children ten quartern loaves.

Man, wife and four children and upwards, two quartern loaves per head per week.

The value of the quartern loaf varied; but at ten pence, a man, wife and four children would be entitled to the equivalent of 5 shillings a week.[54]

Abuses of the system were widespread. People failed to declare their full wages. Farmers had an interest in lowering the income of labourers, since the rate-payers would make up the difference. The Commissioner reported that the vestry clerk of Old Swinford (Worcestershire) told him that, 'Men with families were in the habit of being relieved, who were known to earn 16s or 18s a week, and unless it were shown that the earnings of the family amounted to 25s a week, allowance was not refused. This I was hardly able to credit at first, but he stated that when trade was good, people were able to earn these wages, and it had been considered since that time a standard for allowance. The character of a large portion of these people was described as being reckless and dissolute beyond any others.'

In Berkshire and Wiltshire, 'the parish gives the labourer, out of the poor rates, what they sometimes call their "make-up pay" and sometimes their "bread-money". The bread-money is calculated weekly, at the price of two gallon loaves (the equivalent of four quartern loaves) for the husband, one for the wife, and one for each of the children, be the number what it may; ... No attention is paid either to the character of the applicant or to the causes of his distress.'

'Bread-money' came to be regarded as a right, quite distinct from 'going on the parish'. In many parishes, an agreement was made between parish officers and farmers to sell the labour of paupers at a certain price.

54 Ibid.

This was often done by auction. In Sulgrave, Northamptonshire, 'the old and infirm are sold at a monthly meeting to the best bidder, at prices varying, according to the time of year, from 1s.6d a week to 3s. At Yardley Hastings, all the unemployed men were put up for sale weekly, and the clergyman of the parish told the Commissioners he had seen ten men knocked down to one farmer for 5 shillings.'

The complaint was universal, that magistrates, when appealed to by the paupers, overruled the overseers and ordered relief to be given. Magistrates followed the desire of the landowners in the area, who wanted peace and order on their estates, farms and villages.

Nor were the able poor set to work, despite parish employment: in 1832, only £354,000 out of more than £7 million collected through the poor-rate was paid out for work on roads and in workhouses. 'In the parish of Mancetter in Warwickshire, the overseer stated that young able men received 2s 6d a week, and the magistrates would not allow the parish to employ them more than 3 days a week, that they might get work for themselves. Upon inquiry, it appeared that their characters soon became so infamous, that no person would employ them, having devoted their spare time to thieving and poaching.'

In places where parish labour was trifling, the paupers received more than the independent labourers. In Eastbourne, where the average wage of individuals was 12s a week, the parish paid for nominal labour as much as 16s. It was reported that the wives of the few independent labourers regretted that their husbands were not paupers.

'At Burnash in Sussex, in 1822, the surplus labourers were put up to auction and hired as low as 2d or 3d a day; the rest of their maintenance being made up by the parish. The consequence was that the farmers turned off their regular hands in order to hire them by auction when they wanted them.'

Out-relief was the particular bugbear of the Commissioners, since this was the most extensively given form of relief, and because 'it appears to contain in itself the elements of an almost indefinite extension'. This was occasioned by 'the diminishing reluctance to claim an apparent benefit, which imposes no sacrifice, except a sensation of shame quickly obliterated by habit'. Overseers from London parishes attested to the dangers arising out of this most mischievous portion of the Poor Law. The 'utmost vigilance' cannot eradicate fraud. 'Even respectable mechanics and classes of person now claim relief, apart from the "worthless people".'

'We have a pauper father, pauper wife, pauper son and pauper grandchildren, frequently applying on the same relief-day.' Pauperism is described as a 'contagion', 'an inherited condition'. 'The only protection for the parish is to make the parish the hardest taskmaster and the worst paymaster that can be applied to.'

It was particularly difficult to distinguish paupers by character. If extra were allowed to the deserving, the Poor Laws would 'constitute the distributors of relief into a tribunal for the reward of merit, out of the property of others'.

'It appears from our returns that in every district the discontent of the labouring classes is proportioned to the money dispensed in poor's-rates or in voluntary charities. The able-bodied unmarried labourers are discontented from being put to a disadvantage as compared with the married. The paupers are discontented, from their expectations being raised by the ordinary administration of the system, beyond any means of satisfying them.'

'They, as well as the independent labourers, to whom the term poor is equally employed, are instructed,' says Mr Chadwick, 'that they have a right to a reasonable subsistence, or a fair subsistence, or an adequate subsistence. When I have asked of the rate distributors what fair or reasonable or adequate mean, I have in every instance been answered differently; some stating they thought it meant such as would give a good allowance of "meat every day" which no poor man (meaning a pauper) should be without; although a large proportion of the ratepayers do go without it. It is abundantly shown in the course of this inquiry, that where the terms used by the public authorities are vague, they are always filled up by the desires of the claimant, and the desires always wait on the imagination, which is the worst regulated and the most vivid in the most ignorant of the people.' This concern of Chadwick recurs in the constantly expanding universe of capitalism, which defies all attempts to define sufficiency. 'How many loaves? how much meat? constitute enough. Ale-houses are frequented by those on relief as much as by the independent labourer. Is beer or gin a necessary of life to the paupers?' The Commissioners did not measure the comforts and convenience of their own lives by the standards they brought to those of the poor. If it was impossible to define an upper limit to the requirements of paupers, it most assuredly would be within their powers to prescribe a minimum for survival. No leisure, no space for play, for tenderness or affection, was a necessary consolation for lives of drudgery; recourse to the ale-house was simply weakness, not the sole means of escape from exposure to wind, rain and cold throughout the year, with only hay-time, harvest as relief—and that also required redoubled labour before the brief time of festival. Sir Frederic Eden, not excessively indulgent towards the poor, observed, 'With respect to that unremitting labour which almost every political writer insists on as necessary for the promotion of individual happiness and national prosperity, it may be questioned whether it is not very discouraging to the efforts of men in social life, to say that whatever improvements may take place in civilization, it must be the lot of many to spend their lives, except for meal times and rest in unceasing bodily labour.'[55]

But the ideology illuminates the text from within. 'It appears to the pauper that the Government has undertaken to repeal, in his favour, the ordinary laws of nature, to enact that the children shall not suffer for the misconduct of their parents—the wife for that of the husband, or the husband for that of the wife; that no one shall lose the means of comfortable subsistence, whatever be his indolence, prodigality or vice: in short, that the penalty which, after all, must be paid by someone for idleness and improvidence, is to fall, not on the guilty person or on his family, but on the proprietors of the lands and houses encumbered by his settlement.'[56]

The laws of nature are constantly invoked; at a time when nature itself was being vanquished by human mastery. In any case, nature, like the people of Britain, was also in the process of migration, taking up residence in the laws of political economy; once enthroned there, it exercised a tyranny the more powerful for appearing as part of the divine plan.

The judgements anticipate the recommendations: the allowance system should be discontinued, and relief afforded to the able-bodied only on the harshest terms inside the workhouse: 'Where the allowance system does not operate, workmen are diligent and their labour good; in areas where it operates, they are idle, fraudulent and worthless. ... Allowance has destroyed the industry and morals of labourers who were bred under a happier system, and has educated a new generation in idleness, ignorance and dishonesty.' 'Bred under a happier system'; the past takes

[55] Eden, *The State of the Poor*, op. cit.
[56] *Report of the Poor Law Commissioners*, 1834.

on the contours of the lost paradise, and ensures nourishment for inexhaustible nostalgias.

The report was less concerned with workers in large manufactories, since 'the object of machinery is to diminish the want, not only of physical, but of moral and intellectual qualities on the part of the workman. In many cases it enables the master to confine him to narrow routine of similar operations, in which the least error or delay is capable of immediate detection. Judgement or intelligence are not required for processes which can be performed only in one mode, and which constant repetition has made mechanical.' Given the dishonesty, indolence and profligacy the Commissioners found among the agricultural labourers, it is surprising that they did not reflect a little more on the diminished 'moral and intellectual qualities' required by manufacturing. Preoccupied with recent riots, they had small understanding of the vast changes sweeping the country, whose poor would assume an even more menacing aspect, once they were concentrated in the slums of the Midlands and North, of Scotland and Wales.

Among the labourers from whom the Commissioners took evidence was Thomas Pearce, in Sussex.

'At first the witness appeared to be a stout hard-working young man... [He] was examined as to the diet and usual mode of living of the labourers of that district. His evidence was confirmatory of that which is elsewhere stated, as to the modest living of the labouring classes, and as to the superiority of the condition of the paupers.

'In your parish, are there many able-bodied men upon the parish?'— 'There are a great many men in our parish who like it better than being at work.'

'Why do they like it better?'—'They get the same money and don't do so much work. They don't work like me. They be'an't at it so many hours, and when they be at it, they're doing no good, and are only waiting for dinner time and night; they be'an't working, it's only waiting.'

'How have you managed to live without parish relief?'—'By working hard.'

'What do the paupers say to you?'—'They blame me for what I do. They say to me "What are you working for?" I say "For myself." They say "You are only doing it to save the parish, and if you didn't do it, you would get the same as another man has, and would get money for smoking your pipe and doing nothing."'

'The constant war which the pauper has to wage with all who employ or pay him, is destruction to his honesty and temper; as his subsistence does not depend upon his exertions, he loses all that sweetens labour, its association with reward, and gets through his work, such as it is, with the reluctance of a slave. His pay, earned by importunity or fraud, or even violence, is not husbanded with the carefulness which would be given to the results of industry, but wasted in the intemperance to which his ample leisure invites him.'

'It is a striking fact that in Colesbury (a parish in Buckinghamshire, where the cost of the poor-rate exceeded the value of the land) "where out of 139 individuals, only 35 persons of all ages, including the clergyman and his family, are supported by their own exertions", there are two public houses. The character and habits of the labourer have, by this scale system (the allowance made according to size of the family and price of bread), been completely changed. Industry fails, moral character is annihilated, and the poor man of twenty years ago, who tried to earn his money and was thankful for it, is now converted into an insolent, discontented, surly, thoughtless pauper, who talks of "right and income", and who will soon fight for these supposed rights and income unless some step is taken to arrest his progress to open violence.'

The assistant overseer of the poor at Windsor, in reply to a question about the characteristics of the wives and families of paupers, said, 'The wives of the paupers are dirty and nasty and indolent; and the children generally neglected and dirty, and vagrants and immoral.'

The deep roots of class are everywhere visible; distinctions of caste calculated to prolong the supremacy of elites and the ancient destiny of the rest to labour. Indeed, the only characteristic of the labourer is his fulfilment of a function for which he is uniquely fitted, and in which there is no place for intelligence, imagination or creativity. A rare concession is that a small allotment of land may help a labourer become more self-reliant; 'a man who works for a farmer for twelve hours, from six till six, with the help of his wife and family, can manage half an acre, for a pig and potatoes'.

But generally, 'Hodge', the familiar name given to the peasant, clod-hopping, earthy, was the embodiment of what Marx—in his dramatic over-evaluation of the intelligence of urbanism—was to call the 'idiocy of rural life'. The Commissioners thought they saw in the workings of the poor law an effect later assigned to capitalist individualism: 'Natural affections are weakened: pauperism seems to be an engine for the purpose of disconnecting each member of the family from all the others; of reducing all to the state of domestic animals, fed, lodged and provided for by the parish, without mutual dependence or mutual interest.'

'Unhappily,' say the Commissioners, in the credo that was to become known as laissez-faire, 'no knowledge is so rare as the knowledge when to do nothing.' This piece of wisdom is astonishing, since what they recommended was a vast, centralising activity on the part of government, deemed essential to restore the natural state of affairs in which nothing more would ever again be required to be done.

A great deal of the material resonates with the contemporary reader: why migrant Irish labour is employed in Spitalfields rather than its English equivalent, for instance; the salutary effects of stringent labour upon those who have not worked for years because of alleged infirmity; but especially, the effects of the Poor Laws on unmarried mothers and illegitimate children: the support of illegitimate children, the relief afforded to their mothers and the attempts made to obtain the repayment of the expenses from their supposed fathers. From Berkshire came the view that: 'The certainty of women obtaining care and provision for themselves during pregnancy and birth of children born in bastardy, as well as parish allowance for the maintenance of children so born, tends to remove those checks to irregular intercourse which might otherwise operate were they in such cases left more dependent upon the honour and ability of the men to support them in such difficulties. No restraint is now imposed by necessity of circumstances to influence women to observe caution or forbearance, or even decent scruples, in their choice.'

On the question of illegitimacy, women were always the object of censure. 'The sum allowed to the mother of a bastard is generally greater than that given to the mother of a legitimate child; indeed the whole treatment of the former is a direct encouragement to vice.' From Holbeach, Lincolnshire: 'An unmarried girl upon leaving the workhouse after her fourth confinement, said to the master, "Well, if I have the good luck to have another child, I shall draw a good sum from the parish, and with what I can earn myself, I shall be better off than any married woman in the parish."'

At the heart of the report is an issue which had previously exercised Edmund Burke—'the distinction between pauperism and independence'. Burke had taken issue with the very words 'the labouring poor'.[57]

[57] Burke, *Thoughts and Details on Scarcity*, op. cit.

'Nothing can be so base and so wicked as the political canting language "The Labouring Poor". Let compassion be shewn in action, the more the better, according to every man's ability, but let there be no lamentation of their condition. It is no relief to their miserable circumstances; it is only an insult to their miserable understandings. It arises from a total want of charity, or a total want of thought. Want of one kind was never relieved by want of any other kind. Patience, labour, sobriety, frugality, religion should be recommended to them: all the rest is downright fraud. It is horrible to call them the once happy labourer.... Labour is a commodity like any other, and rises and falls according to the demand. This is the nature of things; however, the nature of things has provided for their necessities.'

It can be seen how Adam Smith's 'invisible hand' had become explicitly the 'benign and wise dispenser of all things', and how the self-interest of the butcher and baker had been erected into a system which equated the pursuit of individual gain with the general good of society. Within twenty years it had ossified into ideology; assisted by the experience of Speenhamland, its supporters had raised doctrine to dogma.

The Poor Law Commissioners had assimilated all this; and they set themselves to treat all expenditure for the relief of the poor as so much taken from the labouring classes, 'as if those classes were naturally pensioners on the charity of their superiors, and relief, not wages, were the proper fund for their support: as if the independent labourers themselves were not, directly or indirectly, losers by all expenditures on paupers; as if those who would be raised from pauperism to independence would not be the greatest gainers by the change; as if, to use the expression of one of the witnesses we have quoted,' the meat of industry were worse than the bread of idleness.'

There was only one way to isolate the independent labourer from the pauper, particularly the vicious, rapacious pauper. 'In no part of Europe except England,' the report goes on, 'has it been thought fit that the provision [for the poor] whether compulsory or voluntary, should be applied to more than the relief of indigence, the state of a person unable to labour, or unable to obtain, in return for his labour, the means of subsistence. It has never been deemed expedient that the provision should extend to the relief of poverty, that is the state of one who, in order to obtain a mere subsistence, is forced to have recourse to labour.'[58]

[58] *Report of the Poor Law Commissioners*, 1834.

Thus are the labouring poor—in the phrase repudiated by Burke—distinguished from the indigent, who are elevated only by impotence and incapacity from the idler and the vagrant; the latter to be set to work, if not by accepting the wages of poverty, then by subsistence as defined by the workhouse.

In this way, those incapable of acquiring livelihood through their labour may be distinguished from those who refuse to do so. What the report did not explain was what to do with those who can, and do labour, but attain an income insufficient for subsistence. The distinction could not be sustained; and many people, in the 1830s, and for the next four or five generations, unable to find work on which they could survive, were also compelled into the workhouse. This was a source of bitterness in industrial communities; for although out-relief never ceased in the industrial towns and cities, and was formally re-introduced through means-tested benefits in the twentieth century, the stigma of the pauper lingered. In contemporary life it re-appears as the woman who becomes pregnant to get priority housing, the benefit cheat and welfare queen, the shirker and the 'problem family', all who mock the 'decent hard-working majority of those who play by the rules'.

For the Poor Law Amendment Act to work, 'the first and most essential of all conditions' was required, 'a principle which we find universally admitted, even by those whose practice is at variance with it, is, that his (i.e. the pauper's) situation on the whole shall not be made really or apparently so eligible as the situation of the independent labourer of the lowest class.'

The Commissioners believed wages adequate for survival were assured by the 'natural' balance of forces. 'We can state, as the result of the extensive inquiries made into the circumstances of the labouring classes, that the agricultural labourers when in employment, in common with the other classes of labourer throughout the country, have greatly advanced in their condition; that their wages will now produce them more of the necessaries and comforts of life than at any other period.' This proved untrue.

Failure of the system was determined by the ideological basis of its conception. Workhouses had to be well regulated. They weren't. The Andover workhouse scandal occurred in 1847, when the inmates were discovered to have been eating rotten meat from the bones they were supposed to be rendering for glue. The wages of the lowest class of labourer could not be regulated, so for some, greater security was to be found in the workhouse or the jail than was available outside. But the people continued to be blamed for their own moral defects. Enthusiasts of the self-regulating market believed that this was because the market had not been totally freed from government control, and the remedy was more deregulation. At the same time, the realities of industrial life demanded Factory Acts, limits on the hours of labour of children and women, public health legislation, extension of the franchise, and greater protection against the abrasive freedoms of the market. Society had to be protected from the effects of the free market which, fettered as it may have remained according to its supporters, nevertheless ravaged the lives of those caught up in its grim mechanism.

The ideology, formulated in the late eighteenth and early nineteenth centuries continued its hold over governing classes, and lingered, even when officially forsworn in the presence of organisation by the poor themselves and the later socialist threat; pervasive as an odourless but deadly gas, it lay inert during the time of State intervention and welfarism following the breakdown of capitalism in Europe in the first half of the twentieth century. But it lived on, revived by the eclipse of Communism and the retreat of the welfare state; and has dominated the era of globalisation, when it was re-animated, clad in the shining armour of neo-liberalism in the 1970s and 1980s. It became the guiding principle of the world economy, triumphant, cleansed of association with the miseries of the nineteenth century, promising an era of unparalleled increase, in which the poor would be reduced, even in China and India, to a minority, a dwindling remnant, waiting for their moment to be brought by a mixture of its magic and miracles, into the embrace of universal prosperity.

5

VOICES OF THE POOR

Historians have regularly regretted the absence of the voices of the poor, which have generally been drowned out by their more assertive social superiors. But the experience of the poor has not been lost. It may be gathered from scattered testimonies and the occasional memoir. I have in my hands, for instance, a compilation of early memories of people who grew up in rural Britain before the repeal of the Corn Laws; a volume drawn up by Jane Cobden Unwin.[1] These stories were submitted to the editor in writing, and, although many individuals were self-taught, which appears from the spelling and grammatical errors in their testimonies, they are often bitterly articulate, and offer an authentic account of the life of farm labourers in the first half of the nineteenth century.

Joseph Boddington, born 1827, Northamptonshire. 'Our family consisted of seven brothers, two sisters, father and mother. I was the youngest but one. Father was hedge-cutter and thatcher, and all hard work of any kind. I had to go to work with him from the age of six years, weather hot or cold. My little hands would suffer very much with the frost and the cold. We used to live on barley-bread, but we could not do without mixing it with wheat-flour. I worked with my father till I was twelve years old ...We was not allowed free speech, so I would just pull a face at my mother at meals, and then she would say, "Boy, I cannot eat this crust", and oh, the joy it would bring into my little heart. At night, we would

[1] Unwin, Jane Cobden, *The Hungry Forties*, London: T. Fisher Unwin, 1904.

have a three-leg iron pot and a good dose of small potatoes and a little bit of fat to keep them from burning; and oh, the eyes and ears that watched and listened to them as they were being roasted!

'At twelve I went to a farm where I lodged, out of the village, to work from six in the morning till six in the evening. My wages up to sixteen years old was five pence a day—2/6 a week. I worked for one farmer who gave me the sack because I asked the servant girl to go to chapel with me. I have seen fourteen young strong men stand in the village with nothing to do.'

William Prestidge, born 1828, Warwickshire. 'My father's wages were but nine shillings a week, with the twopence I got for frightening the crows off a farmer's wheat, making another eleven pence a week to keep seven of us. Father had to pay six pounds a year out of that for the house to live in, so you may guess how we lived with the four-pound loaf at eleven and a half pence, tea from five to eight shillings a pound, and vile sugar at ninepence a pound. Then meat—mutton, beef and poultry—we could only see those things. One ounce of tea a week and a pound of bacon a week, with a dish or two of Swedes thrown in if we could get them, as the potatoes were a great failure after the disease set in, which has continued more or less ever since, and was the cause of thousands of deaths in Ireland. And from frightening the crows off the farmer's wheat, when I got a bit older, I used to help my father thrash the corn, with two heavy sticks swinging over my head all day, on barley-and-wheat bread and small beer in the farmer's barn; and we used to have "tea-kettle broth" for breakfast (i.e. water). I never had a day's schooling in my life, but was always brought up to behave myself lowly and reverently to my betters.'

Richard Rigg, Hertfordshire. 'I was born in Maresworth in 1804 and worked early. I worked as a ploughboy, with my mother's boots tied onto my feet with string. My first engagement was with a farmer who, in return for my labour, gave me free food and no wages. When I was too ragged to be decent, my master applied to the parish for clothes for me. We used to wear sheepskin breeches, and when we got them wet through, we lay on them all night to get them dry for morning. At sixteen years of age, I worked for £5 a year and received board free.

'Sunday was a high day of course. We might get a penny black pudding for breakfast, suet pudding and a pig's foot for five of us to feast on. Beef? Yes, we might get a small piece at our feast, and a bullock's heart at Christmas. We did occasionally get a pennyworth of bullock's liver, if we happened to be going to town—about three miles—for the doctor during the week. Beverage? Well. Yes, we used to have as much as four ounces of tea and two of coffee for three weeks and one pound of sugar a week. To illuminate our cottage in winter we would get half a pound of candles (ten pence) and a rush light for father to retire and rise with, as it did not consume so rapidly. As an additional drink, we had mint-tea for summer, and we might eat toast and water, especially when ailing, in winter.

'Many families would have to go into debt, trusting to extra pay in harvest, and the gleanings of the family to enable them to pay the shoe-maker and so on. Some would purchase tailing corn (i.e. that had sprouted), and if a sheep or other animal died, would perhaps get a part or the whole of the carcase on the cheap. Within my recollection there was scarcely a trade cart came to the villages to call on labourers. Two vehicles we did see. The relieving officer used to come once a week—bread was then served out—and a hearse to bring from the infirmary or workhouse the remains of a former resident.

'My earliest recollection is of four cottages in a row, five overhead bedrooms and representative of eight families. Then how were they furnished? Many would have a few rush-bottomed chairs, a few stools and round deal table, some trenchers and wooden spoons to match, with the sun to tell the time of day and "Old Moore" for those who could make out the time of year.'

John Hawker, Leicestershire. 'I was born in 1836. I was sent into the fields to scare crows, and when I had done a full week, seven days, I had one shilling. My first week's money bought one loaf. In 1844 men was brought to justice for sheep-stealing, sent to Van Demon's Land for fourteen years. If you took a pheasant by night, fourteen years. Two men in this village had fourteen, Jack Burrell and Bill Devenport. In 1844, it was not safe to go out after dark if you had any money on you. Burglary, highway robbery, fowl-stealing, because men were starving. Men would steal to be sent away. They had freedom when they got there. When we have to be sent away as convicts to get liberty, we quietly sit at home as slaves. I was the oldest of seven; and when I was old enough, I crept into the wood by the light of the moon, and once brought out five pheasants to keep my father, mother, brothers and sisters from starving.'

Edwin Cook, Suffolk, born 1844. 'My farther was an agricultural labourer in the parish of Ickingham in the county of Suffolk. My grand-father was a widouer, lived with us. I was the third child born of a family of seven. My grandfather was born in 1780; he commenced work when seven years of age. And ceased working for wages in 1854, and his wages never exceeded eight shillings a week. I have heard him relate the terrible condition of himself and others in the village befor I was born. Barley bread was the staple articul of food. My father was born in 1814, and commenced work with his father at eight years of age. Who was a Shepard for the esquire of the village. When in his teens he commenced general farm work, and his wages never rose higher than seven shillings a week till 1840, when he wooed and won my mother, then he obtained the extra shilling a week allowed to married men. I was the third child and my first vivid recollection of hunger was in February 1849. My sister, who had evidently done the same thing before, took me to the cabbage bed and pulled up some of the cabbage stalks and peeled off the outer rind and the centre we ate for our dinner, and many times after we did the same thing.

'How to exist and keep honest—this was the mistery that confronted my parents; final result, it could not be done. My father, therefore, like others in the same predicament, brought home from the farm potatoes, turnips, carrots, in fact, anything that was eatable.

'But our condition up to this time was louxerous compared to what we suffered in the winter of 1854–1855, when bread rose to famine prices. I remember my father had 20 roods of allotment ground, for which he paid the Esquire ten shillings per annum, but through insufficiency of manure and constantly being cropped with potatoes, they often proved a failir. So to give the land a chance he decided to plant it with parsnips, intending to sell parsnips and buy potatoes with the money. Poor man! He never seemed to have asked himself the question "Who could buy them?" The result was they could be neither sold nor exchanged for potatoes; we had therefore to eat them; and to add to our misery, owing to bad weather my father lost a great deal of work, so with scarcely any bread, we practicly lived on parsnips—in fact, like Daniel's prayers, they came three times a day.

'After the harvest of 1855, my father obtained work in the gravel pits, riddeling stones for the roads. The working of this gravel was let by the Esquire to a contractor, who employed the men; as this was piece work, the men sometimes made eleven or twelve shillings a week. With this prospect in view, we entered the winter of 1856 with bright prospects, till one Saturday night, just into the new year, when my father handed my mother his week's wages he told her there was no more work at the gravel pits, as the Esquire had stoped the work. This news brought consternation into our litel camp, for this arbitrary conduct on the part of the Esquire, we afterwards learned, was because of something the gravel workers had been boasting at the village pub, that they were independent of the Esquire and his farms. When this got to his ears, he at once gave orders that no more gravel was to be won. Of cours, my father had to suffer with the reste. He now tramped from farm to farm, but no work could be obtained. Maddend by his non-success, he arrived home one evening and declared he would take us all to the workhouse. This declaration raised my mother's temper, and she said "Never!" we would all die rather than go their. In vain he pleaded with her, and young as I was, I put in a word, and said "Mother, Bill Capp said he got plenty of bread when he was in; let us go!" This brought tears all round. My grandfather, who through old age and infirmity was receiving four shillings a week from a friendly society, said "No", we should not go to the workhouse; we should share with him. My father, dispareing of perswading my mother to take us to the workhouse, declared he would run away and leave us, as he could not stop and hear us crying for bread; and poor fellow he did go, we knew not whither. In a fortnight's time he returned, all smiles; he had succeeded in obtaining work in the neighbourhood of Ely, and by ruffing it in both lodging and food he was able to bring home a few shillings to mother.'

Between 1770 and 1830 more than six million acres of common land was enclosed in Britain. Landlords petitioned Parliament: most were uncontested and received royal assent. The best of this land had already fallen into the possession of local proprietors, but local people could continue to graze cattle, grow vegetables, gather brushwood and turf for fuel, and to collect the gleaning after harvest. Most worked as labourers for farmers or small gentry, but the fraction of shared land provided about one quarter of their subsistence, which could mean the difference between subsistence and hunger.

These testimonies were from a self-selecting group. Coloured by an intense feeling of injustice, they are not less tendentious than the evidence given by informants to the Commission on the Poor Law. When regrets are expressed that the voices of the poor were rarely heard, this is not always because they never spoke, or were struck dumb in the presence of their betters, but is more often because what they said was suppressed or dismissed as unworthy of record or unreliable.

6

THE INDUSTRIAL POOR

Rich and poor: the widening division

By 1834, the ideology governing attitudes towards the poor was settled; and everything that occurred subsequently was a working out of the conflict between doctrines of the free market and the need to temper its most baleful effects by legislation. The context in which this took place was determined, first of all, by a recognition that the best protection for the working (and non-working) poor lay in collective action and organisation. Confronted by growing assertiveness of the labour movement, governments responded with increasing solicitude, passing laws which prohibited the most exploitative practices, as well as providing public amenities which would not be furnished by the market; sanitation and water, education, and later, housing, welfare, and in the reforming Liberal government of 1906, old-age pensions.

The condition of the poor in industrial society is well known, although as with the agricultural labourers, their experience is represented chiefly by observations of articulate outsiders, at least until the twentieth century. Engels' lurid vision of the fate of the working class, impoverished and doomed to become even poorer, was taken up by Marx; although by the time *Das Kapital* was translated into English, the scenes of dereliction (already passing as Engels wrote) had already become archaic. But the impression of absolute destitution survived, a mirror-image of the fabulous wealth-creating capacities of the early days of capitalism. Rich and

PAUPERLAND

poor remained apart, through Disraeli's *Two Nations*, Mrs Gaskell's *North and South*, Dickens' *Hard Times* and George Eliot's *Felix Holt*. Most Victorian writers, following traditional distinctions, were anxious to clarify the difference between the respectable and the disgruntled poor. Into the latter group fell not only wild political radicals, but also what Marx referred to as 'lumpen' elements, the 'dangerous class or social scum, that passively rotting mass thrown off by the lowest layers of old society', in the expressive phrase of the *Communist Manifesto*. Radicals and outcasts presented problems of a different kind, to the progress of capitalist society: the first suggested its possible overthrow by force, the second its contamination by vice, squalor and disaffection.

The poor took on a more threatening aspect with industrialism: added to the idleness and improvidence of the rural labourer, the urban labouring class was increasingly identified as wild, intractable, a race of 'savages', like the inhabitants of the imperial possessions; of which the great towns and cities of Britain were also potent examples. Some faint sense of the estrangement of their inhabitants remains to this day a tendency to misbehave, to congregate in threatening gangs, and when policing is relaxed, to riot or loot.

The places which industrial labourers called home were described by Labour historians J. L. and Barbara Hammond as 'barracks'.[1] They represented what Lewis Mumford, in his denunciation of the 'palaeotechnic town', referred to as 'Abbau', or unbuilding, the reduction of the complexity of the city to a single productive activity.[2] Dickens' Coketown is the model, 'a town of red brick, or of brick that would have been red if the smoke and ashes had allowed it, but as matters stood, it was a town of unnatural red and black like the painted face of a savage. It was a town of machinery and tall chimneys, out of which interminable serpents of smoke trailed themselves for ever and ever, and never got uncoiled. It had a black canal in it and a river that ran purple with ill-smelling dye, and vast piles of building full of windows where there was a rattling and trembling all day long...'[3]

De Tocqueville, writing of Manchester, says in that city, 'humanity attains its most complete development and its most brutish; here civiliza-

---

[1] Hammond, John Lawrence and Hammond, Barbara, *The Rise of Modern Industry*, London: Methuen, 1925.
[2] Mumford, Lewis, *The City in History*, London: Pelican Books, 1866.
[3] Dickens, Charles, *Hard Times*, London: Household Words, 1854.

tion works its miracles, and civilized man is turned back almost into a savage'.[4] We know only too well the fate of 'savages'. The connection between the poor of Britain and the peoples of empire pre-dates the nineteenth century. Before the Baptist missionary William Carey went to Bengal in 1792, he wrote, 'It has been objected that there are multitudes of our own nation, and within our immediate sphere of action, who are as ignorant as the South Sea savages, and that, therefore, we have work enough at home, without going to other countries.'[5]

Even in 1831, Matthew Crabtree, a respondent to the *Sadler Report*—evidence given to the committee set up to support the bill regulating the hours of labour in textile mills—speaking of child labour in a mill in Dewsbury said, 'I have seen at that mill, and I have experienced and mentioned it with grief, that the English children were enslaved worse than the Africans. Once when Mr Wood was saying to the carrier who brought his work in and out; "How long has that horse of mine been at work?" and the carrier told him the time, and he said, "Loose him directly, he has been in too long." I made this reply to him, "You have more mercy and pity for your horse than you have for your men."'

Later in the century, William Booth, founder of the Salvation Army, wrote of his expeditions into 'Darkest London', taking the image directly from explorer Henry Stanley's account of his journeyings in Africa.[6] Booth said, 'While brooding over the awful presentation of life as it exists in the vast African forest, it seemed to me only too vivid a picture of many parts of our own land. As there is darkest Africa is there not also a darkest England? Civilisation, which can breed its own barbarians, does it not also breed its own pygmies? May we not find a parallel at our own doors, and discover within a stone's throw of our cathedrals and palaces similar horrors to those which Stanley has found existing in the great equatorial forest?...' He refers to 'the two tribes of savages—the vicious lazy lout and the toiling slave'. As late as 1902, Jack London, in his *People of the Abyss*, (London's East End) wrote of people as 'a new species, a breed of city savages'.[7] 'The streets and houses, alleys and courts, are their hunt-

[4] De Tocqueville, *Memoir on Pauperism*, London: Civitas, 1997.
[5] Carey, William, *Enquiry into the Obligations of Christians to Use Means for the Conversion of the Heathen*, London, 1792.
[6] Booth, William, *In Darkest London and the Way Out*, London: Salvation Army, 1890.
[7] London, Jack, *People of the Abyss*, London: Macmillan, 1902.

ing grounds. As valley and mountain are to the natural savage, street and building are valley and mountain to them. The slum is their jungle, and they live and prey in the jungle.'

The labouring classes of Britain were regarded in much the same way as the peoples of Asia and Africa. The comparison is significant, since it implies the poor of Britain had been reduced to the status of the weavers of Bengal, the coolies, ryots and peasants of empire, a condition only to be expected in those sombre lands, but shameful at home.

The metaphor is persistent. If the squalor of industrial Britain finds its equal only in the imperial territories, this is because these are the natural sites of the primitive and uninstructed. J. L. and Barbara Hammond, observed, 'In South Wales ... the conditions were more like those of a newly discovered goldfield, or a plantation in tropical Africa; the restraints of tradition, of a common history, of experience and government, were all wanting.'[8] They quote an unnamed writer of 1848, who gave this account of Merthyr Tydfil, then the largest town in Wales: 'The footways are seldom flagged, the streets are ill-paved, and with bad materials, and are not lighted. The drainage is very imperfect; there are few underground sewers, no house drains, and the open gutters are not regularly cleaned. Dust bins and similar receptacles are unknown; the refuse is thrown onto the streets. Bombay itself, reputed to be the filthiest town under British sway, is scarcely worse! The houses are badly built, and planned without any regard to the comfort of the tenants, whole families being frequently lodged—sometimes sixteen in number—in one chamber, sleeping there indiscriminately.' The offensive circumstances of life in Africa, or Bombay were referred to principally to point up the mistreatment of people at home. 'Natives', as 'savages', were not worthy of the zeal of reformers, although they might have been of interest to missionaries.

The restlessness of poverty

Despite the distinction between the worthy and worthless, the industrial poor were considered, especially by those who sought their emancipation, a more or less solid and enduring mass of people. But poverty is anything but static. It is as mobile and flexible as capital itself, protean and arbitrary, an unwelcome companion in homes believed to be secure against

---

[8] Hammond and Hammond, *The Rise of Modern Industry*, op. cit.

it, a grim attendant on the careful and parsimonious, a sudden visitor in places of plenty.

The causes of poverty are complex: an interaction of changing social circumstances and fluctuating personal fortunes. These are also inflected by cycles of boom and slump, and to an even greater degree by wider change, epochal shifts in livelihood: in the late eighteenth and early nineteenth centuries, in the movement from agriculture to manufacturing, in the late twentieth century, in the shift from manufacturing to services. What is spoken of as 'social change' or 'economic re-structuring', have profound effects upon the psyche and imagination of the people. Who can now imagine the view of the world of the agricultural labourer, who read in the fields and skies, in flowers and clouds, signs of life and death, whose children picked stones in the cornfields and scared away the rooks, to whom news came by carrier's cart and for whom there was no world beyond walking distance? It has become almost as difficult now to enter into the psyche of the industrial worker, whose labour chafed at bone and flesh, the woman with a baby always at the breast and another in the belly, their penitential work of keeping the grime and dirt that provided livelihood out of their homes and lungs, the eager draught of oblivion in the dark corner pub, pigeons released into the sky as emblems of a freedom they could never attain, the power of a foreman to deprive a man of work if he disliked the look on his face? And how is either of these kinds of human being comprehensible to a generation raised on desire and hope, on the longings that attach themselves to ubiquitous goods which lay siege to and overwhelm the spirit, chased by the rising income and the fevers of wanting, to which jobs, not work, are the elusive key? If the people of Britain are conservative, this is because so much radical change has been demanded of them at their core, estranging one generation from another, and always primarily in the interests of others. Who has measured the poverties which attend these changes of personality, of mental and psychological structures?

Migration from agriculture to industrial society favoured certain groups and disadvantaged others, just as the change from manufacturing to service industries discarded some cohorts of people, de-skilled and ejected them from the labour force, while elevating others. Within each period, technological innovation, the displacement of abilities and the requirements of an altered division of labour, thrust people out of familiar occupations and compelled them—or their children—to new competences and skills. In early industrialism, workers abandoned ancient crafts and resigned themselves to simple repetitive actions, which replaced their capacity to create a shoe, a length of lace, a stocking or a horseshoe, a silk cloth or a basket, out of materials at hand; or they would develop muscles required for lifting, shovelling, pounding or winnowing, until these were taken out of their fingers and vested in machines, which they were called upon to mind and to watch. This may have relieved labour, but was often felt as degradation. Adam Smith was an early observer of this: 'The understandings of the greater part of men are necessarily formed by their ordinary employments. The man whose whole life is spent performing a few simple operations, of which the effects too are, perhaps, always the same, or very nearly the same, has no occasion to exert his understanding, or to exercise his invention in finding out expedients for removing difficulties which never occur. He naturally loses, therefore, the habit of such exertion, and generally becomes as stupid and ignorant as it is possible for a human creature to become. The torpor of his mind renders him, not only incapable of relishing or bearing a part in any rational conversation, but of conceiving any generous, noble, or tender sentiment, and consequently of forming any just judgment concerning many even of the ordinary duties of private life.'[9]

The chasm between rulers and ruled was carried from rural into industrial life. Although much was made of 'one nation', and the common interests of employer and worker, the experience of each remained largely inaccessible to the other. Characteristically, the rich lived on the salubrious western slopes of the city, in stone villas with crystal conservatories screened by evergreens, while the smoke and grit of the factory chimneys scribbled its enigmatic messages on a darker sky, borne eastwards on the prevailing wind, and settled on washing on clothes lines in the yards and tenements where the factory labourers lived.

Handloom weavers, who flourished during the Napoleonic Wars, worked on in their unrepaired cottages, where mice nested in the thatch and wind blew through the broken windows, until their income was reduced to starvation level; then they went, or sent their children, into airless mills, where they choked on lint and dust, resenting the confiscation of time they had called their own. Later, many of the ingenious

[9] Smith, Adam, *An Inquiry into the Nature and Causes of the Wealth of Nations*, Oxford: Oxford University Press, 1993.

occupations of Mayhew's[10] street-people, from rat-catchers to collectors of 'dog-pure', dredgermen, mudlarks and bone-graters, serving on the margins of metropolitan life, were rendered obsolete by more efficient management of waste; while collectors of chickweed and groundsel, cress-sellers, nettle-gatherers and turf-cutters for the food and roost of captive skylarks, sellers of squirrels and songbirds prolonged a memory of rural life. Street-performers, presenters of giants, pygmies, sapient pigs and equilibrists, eventually lost their fragile livelihoods to more showy entertainers in music hall, freak show and menagerie. Workers with horses were dispossessed by the internal combustion engine; farriers, stablers, curriers, ostlers, blacksmiths, harness- and carriage-makers were compelled into new crafts, in which some succeeded and some, wounded by loss, pined, became bitter, and failed to adapt to changes for which they were not prepared or forewarned. The daughters of agricultural labourers, summoned into service in towns and cities, lodged in garrets and basements, in hierarchies of servitude, dressed in the appropriate uniform of kitchen, in-between and parlour-maids, as nurses, nannies and attendants; for those of higher station, as companions, or as governesses, often to imperious children, who soon learned their calls would be obeyed. Many such women were rewarded in retirement, and sat, knitting in old age by a meagre fire in a distant room of the house; others were left to fend for themselves in grudging boarding-houses when their years of usefulness were past.

New technologies, fresh ways of doing old things, the decay of trades, changes in fashion, social customs that fell into disuse—people were summoned in and out of employment by the gravitational pull of unpredictable markets. 'Demand', or loss of it, sometimes operated severely upon people who thought they were provided with a skill for life, but found themselves by-passed or incapable of adapting to altered circumstances. At the same time, their inventiveness is striking, their capacity to improvise and create for themselves some income: the street-people of Mayhew who worked as illusionists, tricksters and dealers in unlikely commodities, prefigure the ingenuity of their counterparts today in Mumbai, Dhaka and Lagos, who insert themselves into urban economies and make a living driving cycle-rickshaws, selling broken toys, rusty keys, wornout garments or mouldy oranges. Some people, injured by the rejec-

[10] Mayhew, Henry, *London's Underworld*, London: Spring Books, 1850.

tion of hardwon skills, were also impoverished, since they could only mourn the golden age in which the articles they made, or the services they provided, were much sought-after. Some lost skills are embalmed in English surnames—fletchers and thatchers, pargeters, glovers. The domestic work of families up to the early nineteenth century, making fabrics or shoes at home, while keeping a pig on a piece of common land, cultivating vegetables on the waste, was disrupted by enclosures and the containment of labour in factories and mills. Competition from Germany and the USA demanded a more skilled workforce; and this compelled children into state schooling from the 1870s. Many parents yielded reluctantly to loss of control over their children's earning-power; August was conceded as holiday, so their residual labour was available at harvest-time. My oldest aunt left school at the age of eleven in 1880, when her presence was required, tying knots in a boot factory; her siblings' destiny was to perform the same function, but their education was prolonged by a year; when her youngest sister, my mother, left school in 1918, instruction until fourteen was necessary to work in a brush-factory, operating a machine that pulled bristles through the head.

The rise and fall of products, and the labour that went into their making, called forth workers equipped with the acquirements needed, often instructed by older workers in the task, since this was not on any educational programme. In addition to shifting technologies, times of economic contraction and expansion also benefited, or took their toll on, different groups of workers. As light and airy factories were opened along the Great West Road, producing for a mass market face-powder, rouge and talcum powder, side-cars for motorcycles and domestic appliances, these were overshadowed by the Depression in the 1920s and 1930s, images of men in cloth caps, stub of a cigarette burning their lips, leaning against the factory wall, on which No Hands Wanted expresses their despair, haunting impressions of an unemployment that could no longer be convincingly ascribed to the laziness of employees. Newsreels of crowds leaving work at the same time, filling the streets of Huddersfield or Bolton, men in flat caps, gabardine raincoats and grey flannels, women with hair in headscarves, pinafores and flat shoes, phalanxes of bicycles, men carrying snap-tins, or dazzled by daylight as they emerged from the pit, waiting at the docks for a day's labour as foremen examined muscles and assessed their ability to carry loads that would curve their spine and result in untreated hernias; all of this was set against a uniform background of red-brick terraces, smoking chimneys and street-corners, the frosted glass of pubs, factory hoists or the dank breath of chapels.

Some of the streets still stand, silent now, as steel and glass pyramids of banking, retailing or the health service encroach upon their shrinking localities, absorbing a more varied population of women and men, smartly dressed, differentiated in ways undreamt-of in the early post-war period. The recruitment of labour in the Caribbean and South Asia in the 1950s was a temporary expedient with permanent consequences. They answered labour shortages of a period of full employment, a mythical age now that jobs are scarce again, and the workless drag their canvas shoes and blow on their frozen hands in the cold. Many of the children and grandchildren of former migrants, whose economic utility proved brief, have been drawn into new forms of poverty.

The theoretical equilibrium of 'free markets' has never been achieved. Yet faith in it is persistent; and efforts to bring about the 'natural' balance have come at a high cost to many groups of people through time. The idea of the economy as natural phenomenon dies hard; and it is comforting for those doing very well to believe that people out of work are idlers, the lazybones of industry, rather than victims of vagaries of expansion and contraction. People who accept responsibility for success at times of good fortune, are dismayed and aggrieved when they fail through no fault of their own, and find themselves open to the judgements they were ready to pass on others.

Added to unpredictable movements of permanent economic evolution is the familiar life-cycle, the expectations that come with health and vigour and pass with debility or age. The chances of work and its nature depend upon how these intersect with periods of recession or prosperity: older people and inexperienced workers find an occupation when business flourishes, but are the first to be laid off in hard times. There are peaks and troughs in the lives of those who depend upon their labour for income: perversely, periods of hardship usually occur at the time when money is most needed, while times of greater ease come when urgency has passed.

These cycles of impoverishment and prosperity were first noted by B. Seebohm Rowntree at the beginning of the twentieth century.[11] He

---

[11] Rowntree, B. Seebohm, *Poverty: A Study of Town Life*, Bristol: The Policy Press, 2000.

noted five periods of life, three of which were threatened by poverty. When children are dependent, families are more likely to be poor, their poverty intensified according to the number of young children. When these leave school, they have, historically, contributed to family income—which is why many parents removed them from school and placed them in a factory as soon as the law allowed; although recently, prolonged years of education and high unemployment among the young have brought less relief to family hardship than formerly. When young people left home to set up an independent household, their parents would be relatively well off, especially if they were still in work. Meanwhile, young adults were self-reliant until they started a family, and then they again became poor. (This has changed to some degree with the return of women to work when their children are still young.) Old age was traditionally a time when people once more knew penury, particularly if they depended for their income on weekly wages spoken for in advance, and in retirement, on the state pension. Today's minimum income for the elderly cannot alleviate the pain of ageing, but it removes anxieties over some of the consequences of longevity. It has been one of the most humane contributions of the welfare state, that it remedies anomalies caused by entirely predictable circumstances of existence, by its allowances for children, old age pensions, unemployment pay, compensatory incomes according to the vulnerability of people at times of loss or need; although these are always under threat in the interests of 'efficiency', sparing the taxpayer or the alleged raiding of the public purse by fraudsters and cheats.

Rowntree differentiated primary from secondary poverty: the latter occurs when the actual income would be enough to maintain physical efficiency, were it not for 'wasteful' spending, especially on alcohol. Many of these 'extravagances' may be interpreted as attempts to make bearable lives that would otherwise have been insupportable; and in this light, were perhaps closer to necessities than they appeared to outsiders.

This schematic overview of the incidence of poverty is modified by other circumstances, including chronic sickness, accidents, psychological injury—victims of depression, psychiatric illness or simply despair. The demoralised and hopeless are also part of the workforce, even though largely non-functioning. Their ability to labour may be impaired by conditions which receive scant sympathy. Nor should poor mental attainment be underestimated as a source of poverty. For many years I worked with the families of people euphemistically styled educationally handi-

capped. Research shows that such people are disproportionately represented in prisons and psychiatric hospitals. Young people who have been
in care and people with disability are also at a disadvantage, and appear
in numbers in all measures of poverty. Ex-offenders are rarely very afflu-
ent, unless they have master-minded bank robberies and decamped to
countries with which Britain has no extradition treaty. Impoverished, too
are the socially isolated, those without family, relatives or close personal
relationships. People who never go out, the 'shut-ins', those suffering
from irrational fears which abstract them from the labour market, are
also condemned to lives of insufficiency. I worked with a family, whose
mother had not been outside the house for twelve years. She was afraid
people were watching her, talking about her. She felt ugly and conspicuous; and concealed her 'shame' from the outside world. Whenever people
boast of their success, I always think of these, their nominal 'competi-
tors', whose handicaps help the assertive and aggressive to shine, and take
for themselves more credit for achievement than may be due.

The complicated interplay between economy, society and personal
experience makes of poverty an arbitrary visitation. This is reflected in
our confused social and political responses. Poor people are often
encumbered with a burden of culpability forced on them by their more
favoured peers or neighbours. It is easy to applaud those who work val-
iantly for low wages, and make sacrifices for the sake of their children; to
sympathise with those for whom only part-time work is available, and for
whom (in an echo of Speenhamland) governments have provided 'tax
credits'. Nor is it hard to feel warmly for those willing to work, but for
whom, because of economic downturn, or their own incapacity, work is
unavailable. But the category of 'labour', does not distinguish defeated
people, victims of broken relationships, child cruelty or abuse, scars that
never heal, any more than it recognises the qualities of disorganisation
and insecurity, rarely regarded as warranting abstention from work;
although many such people find it difficult to get up in the morning, face
another day, come off anti-depressants. Those damaged by drug and
alcohol abuse, not for any moral failing, but to escape their own unhappiness, loneliness or other emotional affliction, seldom find the judgement of the majority suspended in their favour.

Even if shreds of sympathy do attach to these, there remains the most
troubling category, the unwilling and refractory poor, the 'dangerous and
perishing classes', as they were called in the nineteenth century, who see

no reason why others should not maintain them, if not legitimately, then by force, by robbery, stealing or fraud.

This group plays a particular role in the war against the poor, since they are the most defiant of the 'undeserving', cheats and con men, amoral, conscienceless, beggars and survivors, living off the generosity or gullibility of others. They are not as numerous as the popular press makes them out to be, but they are highly symbolic. They are human scarecrows to the respectable, inspire revulsion and indignation in those who conform. These are the people Marx called 'lumpen proletariat', the ready tools of capital to subvert the inexorable advance of the workers. If this was their function in the early nineteenth century, they certainly don't look like lackeys of capitalism now; rather, they are a subversive irritant in the smooth machinery of wealth creation. Having survived the centuries, they appear in their post-manufacturing guise much as they did before the industrial era, seemingly indestructible. They have withstood the strictures of clerics, politicians and moralists, impervious to threats to compel them into whatever passes for righteousness in contemporary life. They continue their irresistible progression, indifferent to damning rhetoric as to coercive legislation, nemesis of liberals and spectre at the universal feast. In a sense, their conservatism, like their durability, is reassuring. Always present in the dance of poverty, like their partners, wealth and privilege, they have come unscathed through all the upheavals of industrial life. But through such people campaigns against the poor are waged, and with some success: they make others, however innocent, vulnerable to the obloquy to which their conduct gives rise.

There are, of course, other developments which impoverish or enrich whole societies. The Gross National Product is acknowledged as an indication of the wealth of countries; yet this is remarkable, less for what it includes, although that is significant enough (accidents, disasters and sickness all add to this curious 'product')—than for what is uncounted. For non-market transactions do not appear; the free gifts of humanity, the daily gestures of kindness, solidarity and compassion, have no existence in the calculus; neither does illegal economic activity, the dealing in drugs, contraband, fake branded goods, smuggled and trafficked objects, let alone people who cross borders for slavery or prostitution. Other exchanges—reciprocal services, goods given or bartered—are also not part of this sombre aggregate. Apart from these shortcomings, when the wealth of a country is unfairly distributed, it may create discontent and a sense of injustice, which disrupt 'ordinary' economic transactions, by political protest or criminal operations. At the same time, the growth of GDP also depletes the resource-base of the earth, which diminishes well-being in ways less familiar and unresponsive to traditional gauges of wealth or poverty. GDP originated as a way of measuring the extent of the Depression in the United States in the 1930s (then called Gross National Product). It became a convenient fiction applied to all national economies, and has remained so. Such indices are treacherous; we depend upon them to ascertain whether we are rich or poor, although these, not rooted in experience, are the stuff of theory, or worse, ideology.

7

THE ENDURING IMAGE OF POVERTY

The industrial town

The iconography of the nineteenth century industrial poor persisted well into the twentieth century; their suffering left deep scars on the consciousness of Britain. Only in our time have the echoes of these, the reproachful or indignant poor, people moved to righteous anger by social injustice, begun to fade and lose their power. The intelligence of generations was stifled by poverty and lack of educational opportunity, despite the rich instruction many garnered from industrial life. Many of these poor devoted themselves to the uplift, material and moral, of the people. They worked for the education and political understanding of neighbours and friends, often with limited success. They were a considerable leaven in a working class which, however perversely it pursued its own way, looked to them for assistance in an adversity which was as familiar as it was persistent. Among these poor were trades unionists, office holders in the Labour party, secretaries of workers' educational associations, collectors for friendly societies and burial clubs. These 'grass roots' have now, like so much of the countryside where they delighted to cycle, discuss and picnic, been covered with concrete. They were affected, if distantly, by the great myth propounded by Marx, but more immediate influences were Robert Blatchford, William Morris, George Bernard Shaw, Keir Hardie and the Independent Labour Party, H. G. Wells, Vera Brittain and Rebecca West, and the novels of Charles Dickens.

They had humanity and humour; they saw the pathos of lives dominated by labour, pub and pawn-shop, the pooling of meagre resources, the spontaneity of mutual help, fear of the workhouse, women who concealed the growth in the stomach or the lump in the breast until it almost killed them, neighbours who took in the children of the woman who put her head in the gas oven, the woman who voluntarily got into bed with the dying so they should be less alone, the organisers of street parties and celebrations; they spoke for the poor, and came as close as anyone to representing the (now eroded) sensibility of industrial poverty. They showed that to be poor was not to be without dignity. It was, of course, a male-dominated culture; but male strength was all that stood between families and destitution; and the work of women, in softening the harshness of want and hunger, was scarcely an ignoble undertaking.

The combined effect of growing popular intolerance of poverty and the prudent actions of government to alleviate the worst of it, created a sense of continuous 'progress'; and people did not compare their lives with those who had so much more, nor even with what might have been possible, but with the even more desperate want of previous generations. This kept alive a hope of sustained improvement.

My own early memories were overlaid by those of the Edwardian childhood of my mother and her sisters: their stories were so vivid I felt I was present in them. I saw the naphtha flares on the market stalls late in the evening, as the children scrambled between the wooden trestles, rescuing mildewed oranges, burst tomatoes and specked brown apples. I could smell the faint vanilla of stale pastries which bakers shovelled into their empty pillow-cases as the shops were closing. I could see the daylight through the hessian sacking at the windows, which my grandmother had pinned against the wood to make believe it was night and banish their hunger. The smell of scraps of leather waste with which they tried to kindle a fire was in my nostrils, and the aroma of years of the Saturday penny bloater lingered on the whipcord horsehair sofa of my grandmother's house, which was still illuminated with gaslight in the 1940s. The wound of intelligence prevented from flowering was still sore; and the dismissal of boys from the factory when they reached eighteen or twenty-one and were due an adult wage still rankled. My Aunt was caught one morning before work practising the Valeta between the rows of machines in the finishing room, and was told she could bloody well Valeta down to the Labour exchange and get herself a new job. I could see the half-mittens of the man in the pawnshop with the Cyclops eye of his examining glass in his forehead, as he took the bundle of Sunday clothing across the worn wooden counter on Monday morning, and I glimpsed the smudged faces of paupers behind the workhouse windows, as the hearse rattled over the courtyard with the corpse unfollowed to a lonely grave. I sometimes looked up to the picture rail, wondering if the stair-rod, with which their father claimed he taught them right from wrong, was still lying there; and I could taste the free cocoa and currant bun given to pious children who sat on the hard benches at the Band of Hope, and their tearful oath that spirituous liquor would never pass their lips. I felt the agitation of children whenever their father was expected home—from work, when he lifted his boots for his wife to untie the laces and pull them from his stinking feet, or from the pub, when he would sometimes fall over the bicycle in the passage, and lie prone and cursing on the stringy linoleum, waiting for someone to help him to his feet. The dust had left its sour traces on the chenille tablecloth, and a papery scent of fear arose when we opened the few books in the house—a grisly version of Jack the Ripper, with a frightened woman of easy virtue gazing at her attacker over her shoulder, and a medical book full of terrifying black and white photographs of melancholy women with tumours and children with rickets. It was a festival when life improved, and they moved to a house on the sunny side of the street for an extra sixpence a week rent. The sheets steeped in Jeyes fluid still seemed to flap at the doors of sick rooms, where scarlet fever and diphtheria held children's lives in the balance for long quiet days, as adults stirred the fire and hoped the sparks flying up the chimney were not really souls going to heaven....

Their childhood coincided with the growing self-consciousness of the Labour movement, and the emergence of new assessors of poverty like B. Seebohm Rowntree, whose study of York in 1900 uncovered unfamiliar gradations of poverty, as well as its known degradations.[1] Low wages were the overwhelming cause of poverty, since 43 per cent of the wage-earning class were poor. The pay for unskilled labour could not provide food, shelter and clothing to keep a family of moderate size in a state of physical sufficiency, that is, at the level of the occupants of the workhouse, with their diet of bread, broth, porridge, gruel, skim milk, cheese and potatoes, and the occasional luxury of treacle. 'And this means physical efficiency.

[1] Ibid.

A family on the workhouse estimate must never spend a penny on the railway or omnibus. They must never go into the country, unless they walk. They must write no letters to absent children. They may not contribute to church or chapel or help a neighbour. They cannot save, join a trade union or sick club. They may spend nothing on toys or sweets for the children. Father must neither smoke nor drink. Mother must never buy pretty clothes for herself. If a child is sick, the parish doctor must be called, if it dies, it must be buried by the parish. The wage earner must never be absent from work for one day.'

Rowntree's work built on the pioneering study of Charles Booth, who began publishing his report on *Life and Labour of the People in London* in 1889 and finished only in 1902.[2] Booth devised the 'poverty line', an income relative to the size of a family, below which it could be said to be in poverty. He found almost one-third of the people of London living in poverty, a proportion similar to that of Rowntree. He divided people into eight classes, from A to H, the poorest being in Class A and so on. He used a variety of informants, from the School Board, missionaries, rent collectors and visitors from the Charity Organisation Society; and although the quality of contact with the people varies, his compilation provides unique insight into how the poor lived. Observation was close and sharp, nowhere more so than in reports from some of the poorest streets. In Shelton Street, close to Drury Lane, two hundred families lived in forty houses, five people in a room eight feet square. They worked casually as market porters, sellers of flowers, fruit, vegetables and fowls. A majority were Irish, and their lives were characterised by debt, drunkenness and dirt. In hot weather, the vermin were so intolerable that people did not go to bed at all, but sat up through the night sleeping in chairs. Doors were open day and night. A closet and a single tap in the yard served six or seven families.[3]

The stories offer poignant vignettes of poor people's lives: a child of five fell sick, and died on its way to hospital. 'The parents had neither money nor goods, but borrowed sufficient for wax candles to burn near the body and light the poor little soul to paradise.' In one house, where the husband had gone to the USA, leaving his wife and four children,

---

[2] Booth, Charles, *Life and Labour of the People in London*, 17 vols., London: Macmillan, 1902–1903.

[3] Ibid.

'their mother had to lock them in the room while she went to sell oranges in the streets'.

Of one couple: 'They were not married; the banns were published, but on the morning when the marriage should have been solemnised, the two fell out and he blackened her eye, so the ceremony had to be postponed; and the man dying suddenly, it never came off.' In a parlour at No. 8, a man one day told the visitor that, 'although a Catholic, he did not believe in anything but beer'. The same visitor tells of a family who had 'seven children, but about eight years ago, two of them, aged nine and eleven, going to school in the morning, have never been heard of since'. 'A quiet and sober, though rather shiftless man, had apparently lost all heart, and only wished to be gone from a world of suffering.' 'On the ground floor lived a widow, paralysed so as to be almost speechless. Still, she pushed a barrow and sold mussels in the street, and would sometimes be out many hours and travel miles to take a few pence.'

'About nine years ago a woman was killed in this house. She had discharged herself from the St Giles' Workhouse, and returning to this house, where she had been before, she chose a certain bed that was vacant, but another woman present wanted the same bed, and in a quarrel that ensued the woman from the workhouse, knocked down, fell against the bedstead and death instantly ensued. The woman who struck the blow was arrested and taken to Bow Street, where the very next day in the cell, she gave birth to a child. She was sentenced to twelve months imprisonment. When the missionary called on the following Sunday, he was told by the "deputy" and others that no one would sleep in the corner where the death had happened, because of the fearful noises which were heard, and he was begged to offer prayers against the infliction. He did so, using the occasion to give solemn warning to those present, and on the Sunday next succeeding heard that since the prayers had been offered in the room, nobody had been disturbed.'

'A woman married an Irishman, and they had no children, but one day a boy was left on the doorstep, and she took him in and kept him for twelve months, when one day, he was taken off and a little girl (his sister) left in his place. A man who came to live at a common lodging-house in Short's Gardens, whose wife had left him, found out that the children were his, and his wife had left them. The father died in hospital, and the girl stayed on, and still lives with her adopted mother, who is now a widow.'

The pages of Booth's work evoke the sombre landscapes of the East End, stone-yards next to the cowsheds, mortuary and music-hall, which had taken over two adjacent houses to provide exits from the theatre, soup sent by neighbouring clergy to consumptive children, families who could afford one penny a meal for each person, vows of temperance and repeated drunkenness, casual work in the hop-fields in September, lungs destroyed by labour in the Lead Works, the same set of garments taken weekly in and out of pawn, a pinch of tea for three-farthings, the repayment of debts for funerals, games of pitch-ha'penny in the streets, clay pipes and jugs of beer, the woman wearing odd boots, 'because she could afford to buy only one at a time', the boatman who committed suicide, leaving his widow with eleven children.

The labour, too, of the poor is akin to that of Mayhew's people: they earn a livelihood shelling peas, throwing out drunkards from the music-hall, rat-catching (the ratcatcher's room is full of ferrets and surly dogs), going out of London to gather groundsel or chickweed for birds, or creeping-Jenny and sprays of ivy which they then sell in the streets; boot box making, matchbox making, dyeing children's hats in a portable boiler, slipper making, making toy whips, bill posting, pew opening, mantle making, dealing in sawdust, working as piano tuner, dog doctor or prostitute's 'bully'. At one German bakery, workers laboured between 110 and 112 hours a week: this was exceptional—seventy or eighty was more usual. 'Greeners' straight from immigrant boats were employed in the sweated trades, small masters who operated workshops in their own home, and who paid them little more than their keep.

'At number 35, on the top floor lived Mr Warner, a "shoe-doctor": he would buy old shoes and make them up with paper, paste and polish, and when necessary, with leather, for sale in Dudley Street market, where they might be bought for less than one shilling a pair. Given fine weather, they would stand a few weeks' wear, but go to pieces on the first wet day.' The work of women included washing, mangling, making kettle- and iron-holders. One woman 'would pick up odds and ends in the street and bring them home, thinking they would be useful one day—old rags, bits of cloth and string, dirty paper, an old boot, an old hat or some bones—or perhaps with the idea of selling them'. Another woman of eighty worked as a crossing sweeper.

'A widow aged 60, gained her living by weaving carriage-lace on an old loom. She was paid a penny-halfpenny a yard and could earn ninepence for a full day's work. Sitting at her loom has so cramped her that she was bowed together and could not lift herself up. She was sometimes without food or tea.'

A missionary reported of a Covent Garden porter: 'The man is a notorious Atheist, one who holds forth on behalf of his creed under railway arches, saying that if there be a God, he must be a monster to permit such misery as exists. The man suffers from heart disease, and the doctor tells him that one day in his excitement he will drop down dead. His room is full of Freethought publications.'

The Rowntree study[4] does not have the humane quality of Booth's work. It is altogether more 'scientific', and contains only laconic biographies of the poorest: No occupation. Married. Age sixty-four. Two rooms. The man 'has not had his boots on' for twelve months. He is suffering from dropsy. His wife cleans schools. The family shares one closet with eight other houses and one water-tap with four others. Rent 2s.6d.

Labourer. Foundry. Married. Four rooms. Four children. Steady; work regular. Man has bad eyesight and poor wages accordingly. Family live in the midst of smoke. Rent 3s.

Out of work. Married. Four rooms. Five children. Drinks. 'Chucked his work over a row'. Very poor. Have to pawn furniture to keep children. Rent 4s.

Widow. Four rooms. Grandson, 1, sleeps here. Parish relief. Woman takes lodgers when she can get them, but that is seldom. Do not know how she manages to live. Rent 4s.6d.

Spinster. Blind. Two rooms. Earns a little by knitting. Parish relief; also two shillings a week from a former employer. Very clean. Spends a lot of time with relatives. This house shares one water-tap with seven other houses and one closet with one other. Rent 2s.6d.

Charwoman. Two rooms. Son twenty. Casual labourer. Husband in workhouse. Dirt and drink in plenty. This house shares one water-tap with six other houses and one closet with two others. Rent 2s.

So many spinsters—evidence of sexual repression and of the expectation that a girl would stay and look after her elderly parents. So many widows, too—suggesting that many men had died young, consequence of neglect of safety at work, industrial accidents and sickness, but also that desertion was an option to men; it was not available to women.

---

[4] Rowntree, B. Seebohm, *Poverty: A Study of Town Life*, Bristol: The Policy Press, 2000.

Even these relatively sympathetic accounts of the poor and their lives are still saturated with the moral judgements of the observers. What are referred to as 'drink, gambling or other extravagances', shortcomings ascribed to lack of 'character', force many who might otherwise have enough to sustain them, into poverty. Relatively secure artisans are described as having 'a narrow intellectual outlook. They do not as children stay long enough at school to acquire intellectual tastes, or even the power of applied reading and study. Their reading is confined to evening papers, more or less sentimental or sensational novels, or to the endless periodicals made up of short stories, scrappy paragraphic comments upon men and events, columns of jokes and riddles and similar items of a merely trivial character.'

The renewed interest in poverty was prompted in part by the poor physique and malnourishment of recruits into the army (more than 47 per cent were unfit), particularly at the time of the Boer war. Charles Booth's work on London and Rowntree's survey of York, led to the setting up of the Poor Law Commission of 1906. Just as compulsory education in 1870 had been an answer to fear of a more educated and competitive labour force in Germany and the USA, so the physical condition of the people was the focus of concern in the early twentieth century, because a fit and competent work-force made economic sense. Rowntree made this explicit: 'Within the last thirty years Germany, Belgium and even Russia have transformed themselves economically. The two former are now highly developed industrial states claiming a large share of the world's markets, while we are also face to face with the unprecedented competition from the US. ... Other nations have been moving up to our standards of efficiency, so that British labour does not enjoy the same incontestable high relative position that it formerly did.'

The Commission of 1906 was far from the exhaustive ideological exposition of 1834. It addressed the problem of overlapping, fragmented provision which had developed in the three-quarters of a century since. The majority report recommended the replacement of the Poor Law Authority by a 'Public Assistance Authority', which would deal with all aspects of pauperism (a curious word with its overtones of poverty as a profession or calling). It was criticised by minority Commissioners Sidney and Beatrice Webb (who had originally worked with Charles Booth, her cousin), founders of the Fabian Society, since it retained the principle of deterrence and waited until destitution had occurred before intervention would take place. The Webbs insisted that prevention be the purpose of any effective policy. This they saw as a 'more humane, as well as a more effective, form of deterrence than that of the 1834 Poor Law. The new preventive authorities deter from falling into destitution, not by fear of what will happen when the fall has taken place, but by timely insistence upon the performance of the social duties that will prevent the fall.'

The inter-war years

After the First World War, which had enclosed revolution in Russia, a war within a war, penitence was in the ever alert minds of the ruling classes; particularly since the slaughter had robbed every street and every village of young men, leaving pallid spinsters with blighted trousseaus to mourn the love they lost and the children they never bore. A generation, disparagingly referred to as 'old maids', had been, at the time, young maidens, bereaved of lovers unreturned from the trenches. War Memorials were erected all over the country, the metal panel of names discoloured now by verdigris, a bunch of cotton poppies left at the site each November, to commemorate their deaths.

Those who returned were to take comfort from unemployment benefit introduced for the first time, a concession supposed to be supplemented by homes fit for heroes, and more ample life-chances for survivors. Many of these I remember, since they lived on into my childhood. They were conspicuous on the streets of our town, selling matches or bootlaces, their stump sewn into the dead-end of a trouser-leg, or the arm of their jacket limp from its missing limb.

The idea gained ground that the world had changed, that the country to which they were returning, would make amends, not only for the shedding of so much blood, but also for conditions in times of apparent peace, which had stunted minds and wasted bodies. Unemployment pay soon came to be called 'the dole', meaning a handout, and from its inception suggested dependency on public charity. The government required local authorities for the first time to provide subsidised housing, to replace the worst slums. All this seemed to indicate a diffuse, if not entirely convincing, repentance for the human tribute of a war, the objectives of which had been as obscure to its casualties as to its instigators.

The immediate boom after the war quickly gave way to slump; and when the coal-owners wanted to reduce pay and lengthen the working day of miners (who had numbered a million in 1914), the Conservative government announced the formation of a Commission of Inquiry into the industry. While the evidence was being collected, preparations were made for the strike foreseen; and the report duly confirmed the need for reorganising the mining industry, and cutting the wages of miners. It seemed, from its swift dissipation, that the tenderness for the 'heroes' of 1918 had been somewhat shallow. A general strike was called in May 1926, but lasted only nine days; however its defeat exacerbated the abrasive enmities of class, and stored up rancour which expressed itself only after the Second World War and the Labour landslide of 1945.

The depression of the 1930s was darkened further by the Means Test: public assistance would be given only to those who could prove their destitution. It involved an intrusive regime of inspection of the incomes and assets of the poor. Stories were told of people compelled to sell a piano, a tea-set, pieces of family jewellery, the 'luxuries' for which the poor had long been supposed to have developed a taste. In any case, most who applied for relief had already deposited anything of value at the pawnshop, in the window of which they could identify their small unredeemed treasures until these were sold.

A system of spying existed: an employee of the Public Assistance Committee would take up position in the balcony of cinemas in Bolton or South Shields, to observe who was idling money and time away, watching *The Garden of Allah* or *Poor Little Rich Girl*, when they ought to have been pounding the streets in search of an outlet for their unwanted labour; informants were reputed to stand all night outside certain houses, to make sure no undeclared lodger or relative was sleeping there. People picking coal fallen from railway wagons were charged with theft, and even those gathering fuel in the woods were considered to be conducting a profitable business. Many who had been active in the General Strike were told they would 'never work again'; a promise, in many cases fulfilled by a combination of vengeful employers.

The victims of punitive employment and niggardly welfare brooded over these multiple injustices. I visited a man in Sunderland in 1980, who fetched down a painted biscuit tin, in which he kept, not family photographs, but pictures of the people of his town taken during the Depression. 'There's not a day goes by but what I feel bitterness and shame at what this country did to millions of its working people,' he said. The photographs, faded with age, fan out across a threadbare chenille tablecloth. He indicates a young woman with braided hair and a graceful plinth of neck: 'She came from a TB family. You knew who the TB families were, you knew you had not to marry into them if you wanted your children to survive. She died at nineteen.' There is a picture of a misty street, with a cluster of men on the corner, hands in pockets, bodies arched against the cold. A man looks unsmilingly into the camera, flat cap, muffler parted to reveal a collarless shirt. 'He was a miner. After the general strike he never found work again. He cut his throat one afternoon in 1931. It was July. I can remember it like yesterday. I came home from school and found him. He'd left a message written with a cake of soap on the looking-glass, saying he was sorry. He was my father...'[5]

George Orwell reported, 'The favourite joke in Wigan was about a man who was refused relief on the grounds that he "had a job carting firewood". He had been seen, it was said, carting firewood at night. He had to explain that he was not carting firewood but doing a moonlight flit. The "firewood" was his furniture.'[6]

A woman in Bolton told me in 1980 that she had seen children lick the grease off paper that chips had been wrapped in. She left school on her thirteenth birthday and two days later started work as a spinner. '19s.10d a week, that was good wages in 1919, just after the War. But those years were soon gone. Our wages went down; they kept knocking a shilling off and a shilling off till they reached 11 shillings...I was married on the dole. My husband came to me just as he was, with no second shirt, no change of clothing, nothing. He was out of work for five years. It was munitions that got him back to work. Then he had to go in the army. After the war, he went working in the pits, but he had a dropped stomach and had to come out. Then he worked in a quarry, then a brick croft; and then he went into an iron foundry and that just about finished him. When I think about him, bless him, I don't know which was worse, having no work at all, or watch his health go down doing the jobs he hated.'

Survivors have become anthropologists investigating their own past lives. 'I grew up knowing nothing about sex. At one time, we had a couple living in our house, and the woman was having a baby. I was lying there half asleep, I heard my sister's baby say, "Mama". I said to my Mam, "Hark, it's talking". I didn't know children couldn't talk when they were

[5] Seabrook, Jeremy, *Unemployment*, London: Quartet, 1982.
[6] Orwell, George, *The Road to Wigan Pier*, London: Victor Gollancz, 1937.

newborn. At nineteen, I still didn't know how babies came. You used to hear snatches from the girls in the mill, but you never put it all together, you didn't half believe it. I was nineteen when my mother died, and I don't know if it was the shock, but my courses stopped for three months. And I used to sweat real heavy. The girls in the mill assumed I was having a baby. They said, "Come on, tell the truth, you've been with a lad haven't you? You only need to go with a boy once to get pregnant." I thought, "Oh ee, I did go out with that boy to the pictures, and he twisted my wrist. It must be that makes you pregnant." I was that ignorant. I said "Yes", and they took me to the doctor. I nearly lost my job over it. I'd never once put my stockings on in front of my father or seen any part of a man. My Mam used to say she'd tell me; and then she died, so she never did.'

A woman in Wigan woke her husband when she went into labour in the middle of the night. She said to him 'The baby's coming.' He turned over and said,'Well put it back till morning.'

The aftermath of poverty

Memories of this tenacious poverty in the industrial towns embittered many who lived through it and survived into the age of affluence: this was another migration, although they went nowhere. They became social refugees, remnants of another age and carried remembered worlds to an altered sensibility, which looked upon their stories with wondering incomprehension. The eclipse of the industrial mentality has been similar to the effacement of its agricultural predecessor, but it occurred in a shorter time: rural experience was slower to fade, and memories of the countryside, use of herbal remedies, gathering of free foodstuffs—mushrooms, chestnuts and hazelnuts, blackberries, wild strawberries—and the recall of old superstitions, eased the transition; whereas the decay of industrial life was accelerated by the onset of the culture of commerce and consumption.

I went to Lancashire in the 1960s, to record some of the last recollections of mill-workers. By this time, the cotton industry had declined to a fraction of what it had been. The trauma of its origins had been succeeded by pride that Lancashire goods were known all over the world: I had seen machinery redundant in Lancashire in various 'Manchesters of the East'—Ahmedabad, Ludhiana, Kanpur and the mill-area of Bombay, where the black metal looms bore the names of foundries in Oldham or Bolton.

Cotton was so much part of people's lives that Manchester was called 'Cottonopolis', as though cotton itself originated there, sprung between the cobbles and the humid tenements where it was transformed into garments. Cotton did become became part of the people's bodies, since the dust entered their lungs, creating illnesses like 'mill fever' and respiratory diseases that took a heavy toll among the operatives. In the 1861 census, 'cotton weaver' was the most common occupation in Lancashire, far ahead of 'servant', 'housekeeper' and 'labourer'.

Blackburn was one of the larger satellite towns of Manchester. The population grew rapidly in the first half of the nineteenth century, although the actual area of the city barely increased. Occupation became denser, as cellar dwellings were excavated beneath existing buildings, and former houses of the middle class were divided into tenements. Spaces between properties, gardens and open ground were filled with housing devoid of amenity, without running water, with shared privies. Roads narrower than twelve feet did not count as highways and remained unpaved. Waste matter collected in the streets and choked the Blakewater river, so the town was pervaded by the smell of rotting vegetable and animal matter, bones, eggshells, peelings and rind, broken crockery, wood, torn garments and discarded fabric. Whole families lived in a single room, rarely changed their clothes, while bedcovers were scarcely removed from one year to another. Frequent outbreaks of cholera and typhoid made people dread the brief humid summer for fear of the fevers it brought. People were wakened by 'knockers-up' in the early morning, men who struck bedroom windows with a long pole, human alarm-clocks. The clatter of looms filled the streets until late at night, when people went to market in search of a meagre supper—offal, stale vegetables, penny bloaters, mildewy fruit, which they examined by the light of naphtha flares; household lighting depended on candles until gaslight was installed in the mid-nineteenth century. Nursing children were taken to the mills to be fed by their mothers in brief breaks from work. Women learned to lip-read because of the noise of the looms, and many became deaf in early adulthood. Sickness remained untreated, bones knitted unevenly after breakages, leaving people with a permanent limp; consumption and lung diseases affected almost every household; while a high level of child mortality made women bear children with passive, compensatory fatalism. Even the cemeteries were neglected, so the dead, consigned to shared paupers' graves, remained imperfectly buried, and the smell of death inhabited the places of the living; while the chapels, on almost every street corner, with their barely detectable doctrinal difference, offered a sooty solace and promises of a better world, which was certainly not this one.

A hundred years' later, traces of this remained: slum housing, much of it condemned, shabby curtains torn by broken windows, moss-grown cobbles which had seen no sunlight for 150 years, collapsed roofs, kitchens with plaster sinks and stone floors, grates still choked with the ashes of long-spent fires, abandoned belongings, photographs in old shoeboxes, deal tables and hard Windsor chairs, rag-rugs made by the elderly from patches of wornout clothing, crumbling masonry, soot-blackened stonework, buddleia growing out of broken chimney pots, acres of fireweed beside rusty railtracks, damp stone where frogs croaked, rusty pails and scrubbing brushes with which six generations of women had performed a penitential labour of cleaning.

Bitterness remained, when to the scars of old injustice was added a new sense of disorientation which came with the decline of the cotton industry. That, too, had been a long process, since it began after the First World War; although dissolution was more rapid after 1945, leaving a void of ruinous mills of crumbling brick, broken windowpanes that reflected fragments of sky and the spread of magenta willow-herb. The last efforts to revive—or prolong by a few years—the textile industry relied on the import of labour from the sub-continent to staff mills to sustain a faltering profitability. People from Pakistan, and its then Eastern Province (later to become Bangladesh), came for a brief interlude, working twelve-hour shifts, before they, too, were thrown out of work, and the mills crashed into dust beneath the bulldozer and the demolitionist's ball and chain. If the imposition of industry had been trauma, its removal was to those who lived through it, no liberation, because with it went a sense that, whatever they had endured, they had at least contributed materially to the necessary work of society.

In the 1960s, the town was full of memories which spoke through people to anyone who would listen; a plaintive claim for recognition by those discarded by a system they had humanised, who had made life more bearable in the industrial exile now over, as people glimpsed the glittering towers which some (mis)took for the new Jerusalem.

By that time, Blackburn had shrunk in importance and grandeur since its mid-Victorian prosperity. People still celebrated the dying music of a vanishing industrial culture, remembering their former selves, the mill-workers they had been, as though these had become strangers, or belonged to some dimly recollected anterior existence, faintly incredulous now about what they had lived through. 'It was a lifetime away,' said the old weavers, wiping away tears of laughter and regret, recalling the children they had been, starting as part-timers in the mill, standing on orange-boxes to reach the loom, working barefoot and in terror of the overseer, and to whom the mill-owner was a being from another world.[7] 'Every time the boss came to the mill, the doors would open, and there would be a carriage and pair outside with a liveried coachman ...The boss's son came to work on horseback. And us kids, watched down by the canal as they came along, one a chestnut and th'other a dappled grey. They rode like cavalrymen with two or three Dalmatians behind.'

I've got a notice here from a mill, working rules and regulations. It dates from about 1900. 'Any person coming late shall be fined as follows: five minutes, 2d; ten minutes 4d; fifteen minutes 6d, and so on. Any person found leaving their work and talking with any other work people will be fined 2d for each offence. For every oath and insolent language, 3d for the first offence, and if repeated, they shall be dismissed. The management would recommend that all their work people wash themselves each morning, but they shall wash themselves at least twice a week, Monday and Thursday morning, and any found not washed shall be fined 3d for each offence. Any person wilfully damaging this notice shall be instantly dismissed.'

'There's a chap one morning, walking along the canal bank from Moorgate to Whiteley's Mill to see if he could get sick-weaving or something like that. And as he's between Moorgate Bridge and Whiteley's Bridge, he sees a chap drowning in the canal. He's shouting, "Save me, save me." He asks, "What's thee name?" He says, "Never mind that, save me." He says again, "What's thee name?" He says, "Billy Ockison, save me." He says, "Where's tha work?" He says, "Whiteley's." So the fellow walks on and Ockison is drowned. He goes to Whiteley's and he says, "You've four looms to let." Manager says, "I haven't." He says, "Yes you have." He says, "Whose are they?" He says, "Billy Ockison's." He says, "Why, he's all right." He says, "Nay, he isn't. Bugger's just drownded in t'canal."'

'I used to go to school with the door keys round me neck. I came home from school and lit the fire. A lad near me used to go and light the fire for

[7] Seabrook, Jeremy, *What Went Wrong*, London: Victor Gollancz, 1979.

the woman next door. Her husband died, and he laid dead in his coffin. This lad said to the kids, "Come on in, he won't hurt you", and he used to pick up his hands and poke him in the belly, and all us kids trooped in to look at him. His wife had to go to work, even though her husband laid dead in the house.'

'We lived in Inkerman Street. The woman next door had two babies, she breast-fed both of them. And I used to go up and run down to the mill with them to feed them at eight o'clock. Then I'd to bring them back and leave them in the house. I don't know who looked after them the rest of the day. I had to go to school.'

'People who had money used to take their children out to be breastfed by poor people. This is what used to happen rather than that the rich man's wife should be put to the inconvenience of breast-feeding her own children.'

'We had a family near us, they used to fill up two pews at church, each row seated eight, and on Monday morning, there was father, mother and about ten children all down one alley at the mill, and they ran about forty looms between them.'

'The Church seated about a thousand people, and sometimes you couldn't get in. In them days, people followed their employer's religion to get a higher position ...Every Christmas our church used to give the Messiah. I've seen that church full, with extra chairs down the aisle. That's the kind of people they were. They were good people.'

'Young people's lives used to revolve around the church. Christmas coffee and buns, and an outing in the summer, these were the highlights of our life.'

'And sitting round the piano on a Sunday night. We used to sing "Yield Not to Temptation".'

'Dare to be a Daniel.'

'Here's one I used to recite.' An elderly man rises to his feet and declaims:

> 'Th'art bonniest brid we han in nest
> Come up closer to me breast
> For I'm thee Dad.
> But tha shouldn't a-come just when tha did
> We're short of pobbies for our Joe.
> But tha didn't know
> Did tha, lad?

THE ENDURING IMAGE OF POVERTY

> I've often heard me feyther tell
> When I coom in the world mesel'
> Trade was slack.
> And now it's hard work getting through
> But I mustn't blame thee;
> If I do,
> Tha'll go back.'

'We had nine children. They often went without, but they grew up to be decent people. Our next-door was complaining one day about people who have too many children. I said, "You mean me. Do you?" "If the cap fits, wear it." I called all my children into the yard, and lined them up. "Now then," I said to him, "you look at them, and *you* tell *me* which ones I should not have had".'

'After the First War, men were reduced to singing in the streets go get the money for a night's lodging.'

'When the men came out of work, there'd be a swarm of children standing round the works' gate, who'd run up to them and say, "Have you any bread left mister?"'

'My mother was in service. Nine o'clock one night, she sat darning a hole in her stocking. The employer came in. "What are you doing?" "Mending my stocking." "You don't do that. I'll find something for you to do. You do that in your spare time." She had one Sunday afternoon off in two.'

'They took lads on at fourteen, then sacked them at sixteen, to take on younger ones. Then the older lads joined the army, because that was the surest way of getting something to eat.'

'There were earth closets, and all the ash and cinders went where the excreta went. The night-soil men used to come and clean it out once a week. You always kept your windows shut that night. They shovelled it out into a barrow in the middle of the road. The men who did it were known as the shit divers.'

'Where we lived, you had to walk a hundred yards to the toilet; and that was shared with all the other houses in the yard. If it was occupied, you had to jump on your bike into town.'

'I rode a pony delivering meat. I had to deliver it to Park Towers, where the MP lived. One day, I was delivering meat, and to my surprise I saw another butcher drive up in a van. I said to him, "How come there's two of us delivering meat to the same house?" He said, "Mine is for the household, yours is for the staff."'

'I was a wire drawer and flattener. The first thing I can remember after the First World War, they were telling us about foreign competition. I led a strike. The employers told me I'd never work again in the town again. And I didn't.'

'In the mill the overseer appointed a woman to time you when you went to the toilet, to make sure you weren't stealing time from the employer. She was known as the shit-house cop.'

'A lot of the unemployed in the twenties had been in the war. We were disciplined. We went for marches, we were strict. Many of the leaders had also been brought up to church and Sunday school. They might have abandoned their religion, but it left something, a feeling for justice, what was right and what wasn't.'

'On the hunger march, one day, I remember, somebody called the cook a bastard. We took it seriously. We had a parade. Now then, who called the cook a bastard? Some chap pipes up, "Who called the bastard a cook?"'

'As young lads, we used to talk together. About war, unemployment, poverty. What we all agreed was we wanted to leave the world better than we found it. And we were only apprentices, sixteen, seventeen.'

'We slept, eleven of us in one room, the boys in one bed, the girls in another, me Grandma and Auntie Nellie in another, and me, Mam and Dad on the landing. It wasn't terrible. We told each other stories and jokes. Affection and warmth, I've never known anything like it since.'

'Our family was poor, but I was educated. People used to ask, "Why are you wasting education on girls—they're only going to get married." He said they may lose their husbands to war or industrial accidents, and then they could get their own livelihood.'

'When my schoolmaster said to me, "You're a good lad," the tears ran down my cheek. They weren't lavish with praise, but when they said owt, you knew they meant it. It was a waste of talent, they just threw everybody into the factory, regardless of what you were capable of.'

'I went down the pits at fourteen, and I went to chapel till I was seventeen. I left the church because we asked the Minister to give a socialist sermon. He said if he did he would lose his job—preachers were virtually colliery officials. We were just workers. The chapels taught us patience and forgiveness, when they should have called for anger and justice.'

Lily is ninety-four. She cannot walk, and says she rarely sleeps. 'I don't go to bed. They'll put me there with a shovel soon enough.' Her mind is sharp, and she watches TV with one eye, commenting on the news as it breaks. She shows me ancient scars on her arms. 'They were from my stepfather's buckle. My father left my Mam when I was four. She lived with another man and had ten kids with him. He hated me. My brother ran away to the Navy when he was fourteen. His ship was sunk in the First War. He was fifteen. I worked from thirteen in the Cherry Blossom polish factory. My playtime was spent stealing cinders from the trucks in the railway sidings. That was my contribution to the household. My stepfather said to me, "I'm gonna show you what discipline means." He wasn't joking. I ran away. When they wrote and told me he was dead, I said, "Let's put the flags out and have a party." They put him away twice. A violent man. My mother was scared of him, she never stood up for me. I pushed a truck loaded with pig-iron from the factory to the sidings. My horse was my best friend. My husband was crippled in the First War, a bullet through his jaw and a smashed pelvis. He died in 1961. He was a golden man. I brought up my five children and fostered five others. I laid out the dead, six in that house opposite, two next door. The only thing that really upset me was having to lay out small babbies. I feel sorry for young people. They have no purpose in life. We worked, we suffered, but be knew what we had to do. Women are stronger than men. We have to be. When they lose their job, they've nothing left but their pride. They race pigeons and hang around the unemployment office. It's not a life.'

These people were articulate and self-taught, animated by a fierce resolve to change the world, and dreaming of the socialism that would come; a day of secular judgement, a vindication of the suffering of those they loved, children whose small mounds filled the graveyard, men uncompensated for industrial sickness, women aged prematurely by childbearing, the war-mutilated begging, the glitter in the eyes of the consumptive youth planning for a future cancelled. They were patient visionaries, aware of the double misfortune of those who, unlike themselves, could not see beyond the end of the week; and if they yearned for justice on their behalf, it didn't occur to them that the future beneficiaries of their sacrifice would repudiate their efforts; any more than they could have imagined that the inheritors of the Labour party would consign their painful struggle to oblivion as a lost cause, in the superior interests of securing for their children a place in the capitalist garden of earthly delights.

They transmitted an industrial wisdom through time only for as long as it was required as a guide for living by those who remained poor. It was a subterranean flow of knowledge, strategies for survival, avoidance of authority, the seizure of a few moments of peace and comfort from a world determined to withhold them. Their values became public—as writing, recorded or broadcast material—only as it was passing into oblivion, and a new generation had no further use for it. We, who recorded what we thought was the culture of an enduring industrial working class in the 1960s, were actually listening to the last sigh of a dying tradition. Nothing is forgotten so quickly as poverty by the no-longer poor; and all the subterfuges and expedients which helped to make it bearable were swept away by the advent (and its appearance was quasi-miraculous in the austere environment of the working poor) of an affluence that transformed the landscapes of poverty.

An inherited role

In spite of the re-modelling of the mills and the burial of the sites of misery, a ghostly reminder lingers of the way of life in the industrial graveyards. It is found among more recent migrants to Lancashire. It should not be thought that the griefs and joys witnessed by the nineteenth-century streets in the northern towns disappeared when the people who had lived there departed for the suburbs. The sorrows and pleasures, cares and loves of the old inhabitants linger in dusty cupboards and cellars, in attics and dark corners, ready to reclaim the next generation of occupants, wherever they may come from.

It is a cliché to dwell on the sameness of human emotions independent of ethnicity, religion or culture. But the exactitude with which communities from Pakistan and Bangladesh recreate the situation of a white working class which, only yesterday lived in the crowded terraces behind the city centre, is astonishing. Echoes and correspondences of a way of life that, superficially, could not be more different, create a powerful sense of history revisited in the dwindling streets of the inner city.

It is not the differences between people that cause friction and a sense of displacement, but the samenesses: it is continuities which tug at the heart and memory, and set up strange pathologies that make people view incomers and migrants as usurpers; when they are fulfilling roles and functions which were, until recently, those of a white working class.

People are always poor in the same way. Insufficiency, and insecurity do not distinguish between forms of worship (or the absence of them), the using up of flesh and blood has no regard for skin colour. Inadequate income, the pooling of resources (including human resources), contriving to make ends meet—all this was not long ago second nature to working communities in Britain. The phenomenon of the 'labouring poor' never went away; some people, however hard they work, can barely provide for their family.

The economic position of migrants and their descendants, whatever the impulse was not the only reason for their arrival in the memory-saturated streets of Blackburn, Keighley, Bolton or Leeds: the social arrangements by which they get by also reflect forms of survival common in these streets ever since they were first built.

The people of the industrial era were also migrants. With what trepidation they left enclosed commons and impoverished villages in the early nineteenth century for the raw red-brick towns smothering the fields and meadows of Lancashire. Who knows of the injuries sustained by the sensibility of old countrypeople, as they adapted to the changed rhythm and tempo of industry? What was, two centuries ago, disturbance and insecurity, experienced afresh by anxious arrivals from rural Punjab or Sylhet in the 1960s into the soft drizzle and swollen skies of Lancashire and Yorkshire. That the first arrived on foot with their thin belongings on a handcart was no less an upheaval than that of people who came by air, battered suitcases tied up with string, and ancient trunks and jute sacks from an East Pakistan soon to become Bangladesh.

If the economic and social conditions which impelled people to move, both in the early nineteenth and mid-twentieth centuries, were similar, patterns of family life, roles and relationships also recreate the obligations that animated people who lived in the now wasting streets, when these were first constructed to accommodate migrants from the countryside.

Women have the same protective role, using up their energies to keep body and soul—and the family—together. The same mothers look anxiously at their sons, wondering at the company they keep, and how to preserve them from a life of petty, or serious crime; they regard with apprehension the young women their boys may meet, a girl from Somalia or Sylhet, or worse, from the English suburbs, who cannot be expected to adapt to customs and practices of home. Similar doubts clouded the eyes of mothers two or three generations ago, when their young formed friendships with boys or girls who were not chapel, or came from the rough, rather than the respectable, parts of town. The men, too, privileged patriarchs, whose word is no longer law, seek in vain to compel their refractory children to habits of obedience, sometime using canes or fists, just as fathers in the same houses taught children right from wrong with the help of the buckle-end of their strap.

In Nadim Aslam's *Maps for Lost Lovers*, Kaukab, the fretful mother, with her declining powers, trying to conciliate her children, including the daughter who has been to university, is not an exotic personage of fiction, but plays out well-known conflicts and remembered struggles.[8] Monica Ali's evocation of London's East End in *Brick Lane*—that re-making of a provincial town in Sylhet, with its secret world of women's solidarity and power—is also, in part, the Bolton in which she grew up, a place haunted by the ghosts of the millworkers who preceded her.

The family remains the centre of social life. Extended families of uncles, aunts and cousins live next door, in the same street, around the corner. The small rivalries of siblings cover deeper commitment, and older children help bring up the younger. Even religious observances of more recent comers are not the outlandish practices they appear to a generation schooled to a society that calls itself secular: they rekindle memories of chapel teas, church festivals, the Messiah, Whitsun walks and an archaic belief in a better hereafter, where all who had died would be waiting in streets of jasper and gold to welcome them to the everlasting feast.

How familiar it is. For the old working class lived, like communities of Bengalis and Pakistanis, a life apart. Of course, migrants and their children are minorities; but the working class (always a majority of the population), rarely figured in the iconography of the nation, except as 'masses', workers, or when wars were fought, as soldiers and dead heroes.

The differences are shades, the similarities starkly conspicuous. It is not to the unrelatedness of experience that the source of smouldering resentments is to be traced, but to what we recognise too well. Migrant communities, with their close, closed networks of kin, neighbourhood and religion, illuminate the elided costs of the improvements proclaimed, the suppressed, uncounted payment for the terms on which the lives of the majority have been bettered. They show how far we have travelled, and into what uncharted lands.

[8] Aslam, Nadim, *Maps for Lost Lovers*, London: Faber and Faber, 2004.

8

AN IMPERMANENT SETTLEMENT

The voices of the industrial poor have also fallen silent now that the sites where they lived and died have been re-shaped, so that grass covers the slag-heaps and parkland occupies places where factories filled the air with soot and smoke; canals, polluted with chemicals and dead domestic animals, have been reclaimed for the tranquil passage of holiday boats; workshops rehabilitated by a sanitised heritage industry for schoolchildren to look upon with astonished disconnectedness from their own past. If conditions were degrading and people perished, poverty also called forth resistance and dignity, mutuality and self-sacrifice, a sensibility reminiscent, if of anything, of the elective holy poverty of the early saints; lived out in the devotion and selflessness of those who worked for the better world they did not doubt would come after the years of the industrial wilderness. How easy it was to read Biblical images into the landscapes of their lives, ideas with which the dim stony interiors of the chapels echoed—exile and wandering, promise and its fulfilment, the righteous and the wicked, justice and reward.

What the labour movement wanted was what Edwin Chadwick had declared in 1834 impossible to define: a fair sufficiency. The labour movement did not come into existence to bring about consumerism or the contrivances of excess; if it was only on its own terms that capitalism offered improvement, this counterfeit went largely unnoticed by those who acted in good faith in the compromise between labour and capital in 1945.

For a moment, it seemed to some that the working poor might evolve an alternative culture to that of capital: a different social organisation from that founded on profit; based upon mutuality, collective protection, shared experience. It was a short-lived dream of sufficiency and equality, an imperfect sketch of an imagined future, since the fate of women, gays, minorities had scarcely been considered in its rudimentary vision. But as long as the labouring poor threatened with its own visions the malignant money-drenched fantasies of power, it was the objective of capital to destroy it. That better world was finally drowned, the golden city submerged in the great flood of consumerism: capitalism's unsustainable cult of prosperity, which ousted the meagre prize of a sober, modest plenty.

As a result of suppression of alternatives, the poor, like the rest of society, have been re-made in the image of wealth. That is to say, the poor are a caricature of the rich. The danger these now present to wealth is no longer a threat to usurp their power by violent expropriation; it lies in the fact that they demonstrate too clearly the values of those who inspire them: greed, selfishness and rapacity betray the origins of the principles they embody with uninhibited exuberance. Just as the rich suppressed the subversive ambitions of the labour movement, now they are at pains to distance themselves from those who impersonate them, and demonstrate a version of wealth they would rather conceal from the world.

The welfare state carried the collective hopes and ambitions of those who had laboured in mill, mine, factory and fields. It was also of great utility to wealth and power, following the breakdown of capitalism in the 1920s and 1930s, when the heart of 'civilisation' was crushed by Nazism and Fascism, the outcrop of a racist ideology which had also pervaded half a millennium of imperial adventures across the globe, repatriated, as it were, to the extermination camps of the 1940s. The provision of security for the people would protect them against what William Beveridge, whose report formed the basis of the welfare state, called the five giants—Idleness, Disease, Ignorance, Squalor and Want; spectres we can now see, seventy years' later, that were never exorcised; but banished for a season by the bright lights of a regenerated capitalism.

Because the collapse of civilised life in Germany had been caused by economic disaster, inflation and unemployment, and the self-regulating market had failed to repair itself without human casualties on an unprecedented scale, it was in the realm of the economy that redemption—not for the first time—had to be sought. Not only did penance have to be made for the failure to protect the Jews of Europe, it was also necessary to restore faith in the capacity of capitalism to provide a decent life—and more—for the people. Repentance was written into the statutes of the welfare state, which was accompanied by a chorus of 'Never Again'. Not since the French Revolution had threatened to contaminate the peaceful, stolid peasantry of Britain with its dangerous example, and aid-in-wages had been devised to preserve stability in the countryside, had such a comprehensive system been erected for the defence of the people against the ravages of free markets; or was it to defend free markets from the ravages of the people?

A national health service, secure income for the elderly, support to the sick and unemployed, represented a security unheard of in the history of industrial capitalism. And for a people liberated from ancient scourges of want and hunger, Britain was ready for a prosperity that promised—and indeed, has delivered (in more ways than one)—the earth.

The 'settlement' appeared a permanent compromise between capital and labour. For three decades, it seemed, old antagonisms had been laid to rest. The amicable, if somewhat tense, agreement held. Governing parties formally recognised their obligation to protect the vulnerable, not only against recession, worklessness and hardship, but also against the certainties of ageing, sickness and death. This merging of a single defence against the vicissitudes of an economic system with those of life itself, was to have fateful consequences.

The sleepy ideology of the self-regulating market was, after all, only resting, hiding its shame until it could emerge, refreshed and rejuvenated after the years of discreet torpor and of forgetting. It still appeared sporadically, even in the early years of the welfare state, in those who resented it, and complained that free health care had pushed the working classes to have their teeth pulled to enjoy the amenity of free dentures, and to ornament themselves with eyeglasses, because these could be had for nothing. A murmur of resentment was heard, words that would have been familiar to early Victorian England—the welfare state cosseted the people, 'sapped their moral fibre', ruined character and destroyed the sturdy independence for which British people were renowned. They were being 'feather-bedded', and the system of assistance provided a refuge for the idle and workshy. The economy was being held back by over-mighty trade unions and excessive payments to people who preferred to sit on their backsides rather than doing an honest day's work, or pleading poverty, instead of rather than rolling up their sleeves and earning a livelihood by their own efforts.

With the rehabilitation of the free market in the early 1980s, complaints of red tape, government interference, high taxes, the stifling of enterprise and the crushing of initiative, the time was ripe for an assault on the welfare state, as invented by do-gooders to make people supine and demanding. And the principal object of wrath was, once more, the poor; not the impotent poor (although even these are now considered by government proper targets for surgical strikes on welfare), but the able-bodied poor, the army of shirkers and losers who take the piss and have a laugh at the taxpayer's expense.

The popular press is the principal conduit for outrage against the rediscovered arrogance of the poor. Stories of benefit cheats echo the catalogue of abuse compiled by the Poor Law Commissioners in 1834: a woman claims benefit for children who do not exist; people on disability benefit are working out at the gym or playing football; teenage girls have babies to get social housing; a man keeps his mother's body in the freezer after she dies, so he can keep on drawing her pension; a man claims for three wives and nine children; a woman arranges with a relative to 'kidnap' her nine-year-old daughter, who is then kept in confinement, while the weeping mother appeals on TV for help in finding her. A demonic folklore hovers around hosts of freeloaders and exploiters of the hard-working majority. This development is made easier in a society where the poor pose no serious electoral threat. Vengefulness is never far from the impulse to be charitable; perhaps a retrospective determination to punish those who, while they formed the larger part of the population, created so much uneasiness in their rulers. So the hunt is on for the cheat and the thief, the raider of public bounty, and the vigilant are invited to call a confidential helpline. Resentment and hatred are staples of the rhetoric; the world is full, not of family, friends and neighbours, but of junkies and alkies, peds and pervs, beasts and monsters, loonies and weirdos, con-artists and crooks, rapists and muggers; a rapacious humanity out to take advantage of the thin charity and grudging compassion of our miserly wealth.

The welfare state is now beginning to appear as fragile and temporary an expedient as the forgotten mercies of Speenhamland. And if the most solid religious establishments were unable to withstand the onslaught of power in the sixteenth century, what chance is there that secular refuges should outlive their usefulness, no matter how great the dedication of their servants? The principal target of assault upon the citadels of what was called, quaintly, the caring society, is, as ever, the rough and recalcitrant; since through them, the case can be more easily made for the demolition of shelter against poverty wages, unemployment and underemployment. Later, this can be extended to the dismantling of protection against the inevitable tragedies of living, sickness, old age and loss, with which it will become necessary, in time, for people to make their own private accommodation.

The attack on the poor—in the form of welfare—has reached a paroxysm. Politicians, journalists, ideologues, polemicists, some members of the clergy, taxpayers' organisations, commerce and business unite in condemnation of those who drain the public purse to no positive effect; a project made easier by mobilising majorities against those who have nothing. Of course, just as Malthus' desire to abolish the Poor Laws completely was doomed, so it is impossible to demolish absolutely the welfare state, since many thriving industries depend upon the security of the people: it is hard to imagine leisure industries, entertainment, music, fashion, travel, mobility, if people were exposed to want and hunger: anorexic models may be an adornment to overfed societies, but they would get short shrift if their skeletal appearance were a result of kwashiorkor or rickets. And however those who condemn the poor might think an absence of health care, nourishment or shelter a positively abrasive experience, a great deal of economic activity, on which the well-being of the economy—that anthropomorphised entity—depends, would simply cease to take place.

9

MODERNISED POVERTY

Poverty—the great survivor

One of the uncelebrated wonders of the modern world has been the survival of poverty, in the face of the vast productive power of globalism. It seems more care has been bestowed upon protecting the poor than upon the conservation of any endangered species, even as biodiversity is reduced, ancient jungles uprooted, cultures perish and the last speakers of ancient languages make their final utterances into the recording machines of ethnographers. But the poor are essential to the doctrines of wealth-creationism; for without their spectral presence, we might be in danger of declaring ourselves satisfied with what we have; a calamity not to be borne by the boundless expansionism of capital. It is also necessary that the poor, indispensable to the mythology of perpetual growth, have excited no great love in the breasts of those whose business it is to scourge them, while ensuring they remain where they are, subject to a judicious mixture of protection and punishment.

In a time of continuous change, it is inevitable that poverty, an opportunistic survivor, should be transformed to face the modern world. 'Primitive' poverty exposed most of humankind to hunger, pestilence and the arbitrary rule of the powerful, even though most religions exalted the poor, and many embraced poverty voluntarily, for spiritual reasons. The Church frequently fell short in its proclaimed devotion to the poor, but tending their neglected needs remained a holy task. In the medieval world, wealth was social: it was the—often unfulfilled—duty of feudal overlords to ensure the livelihood of, or to extend charity to, those who depended upon them. The decay of feudalism, which set people free from such bondage, at the same time rendered them responsible for their own fate: the freedom to be poor being one of the less trumpeted virtues of liberation. Labour, emancipated from servitude, had to make its own way, and with time came to be seen as the author of its own prosperity or misery. After suppression of the monasteries, vagabonds and idlers appeared in the world, inspiring such apprehension that laws had to be formulated for their control and management. The poor, tenacious, sometimes self-effacing, often assertive and clamorous, occupy the haunted house of history, impervious to eviction and exorcism.

With industrial society the poor merged, and became indistinguishable to outsiders from the mass of the labouring class. If they became an object of interest to government, this was as much because of the threat they posed to order as because of the pitiable condition in which they lived. Slowly, as prosperity became more general, the defiant and the alienated, those who, it had once seemed, were destined to remain forever excluded from the benefits of civilisation, were tamed: attached by the small comforts of life to the system that had created them, softened by the products of empire—tea and tobacco, sugar, snuff, coffee, spices, chocolate—as well as by their own organisation and efforts by reformers to legislate for housing, nutrition, health care, sanitation. In the process the poorest became more exposed: they were now isolated from those who had sheltered them, who had offered solace to the inadequate, had borne up the unquiet, and had protected the weak from the mistreatment of landlords, employers and moneylenders.

With the general affluence of the Western world from the mid-twentieth century, it seemed poverty was a residual problem; and soon, it was assumed, the poor would be included in the embrace of widely diffused wealth. It would take time, but poverty would, in due course, become a distant memory, a curiosity like slavery, child labour, penal servitude, abolished by the inevitable march of progress.

This is not what happened. It became plain that poverty would not be banished by plenty, but would turn into a condition quite different from poverty in a world of scarcity. Poverty, amid material well-being, became something else, non-participation in what everyone else took for granted, a punitive exclusion that condemned the poor to wander like souls permanently exiled from Elysium, the inhabitants of a limbo, which even the Church that invented it, saw fit to abolish. The majority, newly arrived at the banquet, swiftly took credit for their good fortune; and by the same token, did not hesitate to blame the unfortunates who had not attained that happiness for their failure to do so.

Poverty, in such a society is bound to differ from poverty thrown into relief by the opulence of a minority—and largely hereditary—elite. The poor in a society of widespread, if unequally distributed, wealth are what Jeremy Bentham called 'the refuse of the population', and Marx referred to as the 'social scum'. This group, in rich Western societies, has been the victim of an even more brutal re-naming: called 'underclass' in 1980s USA, a word which has ugly echoes of the *untermenschen* of Nazi ideology. These are sometimes described as the 'hard to reach', 'problem families', the 'excluded', those who have 'no stake in society'.

The rhetoric was much in evidence in Britain during the riots of August 2011, as earlier disturbances in 2003 in northern towns and in 1980 in Brixton, Toxteth and elsewhere. These are, as it were, the product of a society so accustomed to throwing away all that serves no obvious purpose that it cannot resist the temptation to see a portion of humanity in the same light. If there has not yet been a call to 'bring back the workhouse', this is because the 'sink estates', 'ghettos' and 'dumping grounds', where most of the poor live, are of eligibility no greater than that of the grim structures of 1834, which enfolded in stone flesh and blood which could not provide for itself. It is a deterrent in reverse: rather than forced into them by destitution, all who can get out of the slum estates do so; with the result that it is mainly the defeated, the wretched and the demoralised who remain. Although it requires costly administration to keep them where they belong, no overseers, parish officials or beadles are required to judge whether this is an appropriate place for them, or to bear the costs of dispatching them there.

In a society of aggressive plenty, excitability and distraction, where new products, experiences and objects for sale constantly appear, it is not to be expected that the poor will meekly acquiesce in their destiny as the wasted and unwanted, non-workers and negligible consumers in the global bazaar. They reject their role as a twenty-first-century version of 'the superfluous population' of the early nineteenth century. If poor estates and derelict inner city areas are scenes of violence, disturbance, substance-abuse, broken relationships and crime, this is because opportunities for escape open to the people who live there are few; unlike the expensive diversions available to the majority. An obvious feature of the August riots of 2011 was that it resembled an anarchic jail-break (and many people refer to the places where they live by the names of jails, foreign jails at that—Alcatraz, Sing-Sing, even Colditz.) For a few nights, people took a freedom denied them in the 'normal' course of events; and spontaneously expressed rage, the management of which is the work of numberless functionaries in public and private sectors of the economy. To these, the captive poor, has been entrusted the task of demonstrating the continuing penury of wealthy societies: they are the living embodiment of the need for more economic growth, fed by the strident neediness of their assertive hungers.

It is important to remember that the 'troublesome' poor, the picaresque and noisy, have always existed, but constitute only a minority of poor people. In the 1890s, Charles Booth estimated this group constituted no more than 15 per cent of the poor;[1] although they created more disturbance and unsettled the respectable majority to a disproportionate extent, and became—as they have remained—of continuing interest to all agencies of the state that deal with poverty, law and order and welfare. It is no new thing for the present government to wish to pursue this class into invisibility, and if possible, into non-existence.

Mutation of poverty

The contemporary poor are orphans of the market, outcasts of the fat of the land, without whom the general striving beyond sufficiency and satiation would be seen for what it is, a project of gilded nihilism and ornamental despair. The purpose of the poor is to show what happens to economic dissidents in rich societies. While political and intellectual pluralism are the fairest attributes of such societies, no such latitude is permitted in the economic arena. These undeserving are doomed to play out lives of self-harm, destructiveness, wrecking and robbing their own community, stealing from 'their own kind', dealing in forbidden substances, cheating and cozening, an illegal mimicry of approved entrepreneurial activity.

As victims of a re-shaping of what it means to be poor, the young would normally be the principal focus of resistance. But since these regard their exclusion from the market as aberrant, their youthful radical-

---

[1] Booth, C., *Life and Labour of the People in London*, 17 vols., London: Macmillan, 1902–1903.

ism concentrates on finding a way into the forbidden territories of wealth. This turns their anger into a deeply conservative force, since they want nothing more than to belong; their poverty, dependent because fed by desire for what everyone else has, can conceive of no alternative; no self-reliance, no collective sharing of resources, no modest adequacy, no thoughtful frugality. The closing of this possibility is an immeasurable loss to them, however it may serve the security of an unstable society.

This is 'modernised' poverty, and it has transformed the poor. The poor were the last representatives of humanity who contrived a living outside the market. These have now been subject to economic violence, since they have been coerced into the market system, and then denied the income required to live in it. The poor have, like everyone else, been thrust into market-dependency, but must live out this version of human freedom without the purchasing power required to satisfy it.

Perhaps this is why something is wanting in most accounts of present-day poverty in rich societies. Privation is accompanied by powerlessness; and the latter may be the more telling component of this kind of poverty. In other parts of the world recent migrants to the city, the slumdwellers of Asia and Africa, have memories of self-provisioning—capacity to build a shelter, a remembrance of famine-foods and of herbs and plants with healing or nutritious properties. All such knowledge has been erased from the mental storehouse of the poor in 'advanced' societies; an advance which has progressed deeply into paralysis and impotence.

All human resourcefulness, in this context, is reduced to inventiveness in getting the money that will answer needs: these await fulfilment in the same way that beggars solicit alms. Deprivation of the ability to provide for one's own needs and those of others is characteristic of this poverty; people handicapped by social, not existential, disability. If people live off the dregs of the consumer market, this is because they are also the dregs of a labour market, descendants of those wounded by the injuries of industrialisation, urbanisation, slavery, imperialism and the re-making of an old rural sensibility in the shape of industrialised humanity. We should not imagine such traumas cease to work their evil, simply because those who were never victims of them prefer to forget. The inheritors of loss perpetuate that legacy, which survives the most dramatic periods of change and prosperity.

There are powerful correspondences between the undeserving poor of pre-industrial Britain and the feckless poor of what is sometimes—wrongly—called post-industrial society.

In the pre-industrial world, critics complained that the improvident poor shirked, coupled indiscriminately, spent their money in the ale-house, evaded an honest day's labour, were indolent and imprudent, unless prodded by hunger. They gathered in gangs, in the words of the Poor Law Commission Report, 'discussing their grievances', threatening employers and taking subsistence from the parish as of right. Rough able-bodied young men seized their parish money and spent the rest of their time stealing firewood, turnips, wooden poles or pheasants from the farms. They lived in lodgings at 6d a week, terrorised the countryside, preferring 'the bread of idleness to the meat of industry.' It was com-plained they were paid to live in vicious inactivity, contracted early mar-riages and produced more and more children, a superfluous population, each of whom was allowed 1s.6d a week; sometimes they advised the overseer of their expectation of future 'reward' as soon as their wife became pregnant. Paupers said 'Blast work' or 'Damn me if I work'; and so far in excess of independent labour was parish pay, that in some places, wives were said devoutly to wish their husbands were paupers. Whole families applied for relief, so that three generations of paupers would stand before the parish pay-table. There was, according to overseers, no limit to the mischief created by these hereditary or fraudulent paupers; and their practices showed every sign of spreading to the once-respect-able mechanic or the small master bricklayer; one woman in receipt of a pension from the East India Company presented herself as in need of relief. They expected meat every day, something beyond the reach of the independent labourer. In the industrial areas, the same individual appeared before the relieving officer in five or six different parishes a week. And as for women, they knew no shame, vying with each other to give birth to bastards, for they were sure the parish would look after them, not only with necessaries but with the comforts they thought indispensable to their condition. A woman with four or five illegitimate children received a greater income than a wife or an unfortunate widow. Paupers, characterised by cupidity and fraud, thieved, wenched and wheedled their way through life, avoiding work and delighting in out-rages in the neighbourhood, making their noisy way from ale-house to cottage where they lay abed until necessity moved them to bestir them-selves for yet another day of striking fear into the hearts of the respect-able classes.

The activities of these poor, menacing as they may have seemed to contemporaries, are pallid compared with the opportunities open to their industrial successors. Cheating the overseer and deluding the magistrate were child's play, against the freedoms available to the poor of a more enlightened age and a more ample market.

And yet, there are echoes in the lives which the poor construct for themselves out of the leftovers of the market economy, not only an overflow of affluence, which scatters money far more freely than the curmudgeonly custodians of the poors' rate, but also shreds and scraps of culture which embellish their lives; not the least of which are the cultural products of TV, films, the internet, the mobile phone, the promiscuous debris of a vast entertainment industry. The fallout of consumerism has replaced the dim inventiveness of the rustic world of their forebears, colonised the imagination and nourished dreams that cannot be contained, as dreams have been, within the head and heart, but must now be lived.

Re-shaping poverty

The contemporary poor do not lead a life apart, or inhabit a separate culture from the rich, but live out a debased version of that culture. While the rich buy in all the pleasures and consolations their money can procure, that of the poor is a world of surviving and scavenging, for affection as well as for material things. If they have vigorous fantasy lives, this is because fantasy costs little: it is an insubstantial emanation of the colonised imagination; and if the heart is worn on the sleeve, this is because emotions are also close to the surface: the instant relationship, a chance encounter and swift rejection, serial loves and irrational hatreds, jealousies and resentments, prompted by perpetual drama of TV and film, a continuous stream of murderous loves and obsessive attachments. These intensive products of entertainment conglomerates are created for the purpose of a restless pacification; disturbed but fatalistic lives, in which silence and continence have no place. Passion, lust and revenge are the staple of an existence nourished by cheap alcohol, drugs, speed, dreams of escape, heroism and an iconography of luxury borrowed from a different class of betters than those who sought to regulate the passions and constrict the desires of the eighteenth century poor. Their models are not ladies of taste and breeding, but haunted skinny models and images of brooding machismo, who live in ostentatious kitsch and bling, a degraded variant of aristocratic grandeur. Their religion is black magic, Satanism, the occult, re-incarnation, astrology, mysticism and ghosts, Ouija boards, signs from the beyond, vampires and monsters, creatures from outer space. People desperately need to make something happen, in lives unfurnished by amenities supplied by the purchasing power of the majority. If they show aggression, it is because they are victims of violence: in a world which could easily provide a decent sufficiency for everyone on earth, what is it, if not violence, that arbitrarily refuses to grant sections of the people what is essential for life? What are the poor, if not people segregated for ideological purposes, to demonstrate the fate of losers, no-hopers, failures? Just as corpses dangled on gibbets in the eighteenth century, and the workhouse loomed over nineteenth century suburbs of industry, the no-go areas, sink estates and ghettos of misery are our equivalents; the warning to abandon hope is not written up on the entrances to these places, because it is self-evident, in the purple and silver graffiti of territorial markings, shabby street corners where lean tracksuited couriers dance and go-betweens wait, the occasional flash of blade against flesh, the echo of the gunshot in the afternoon traffic, the belonging of gangs, which mocks defunct solidarities of neighbourhood, kin and work.

It is difficult to encapsulate the sensibility of this poverty which, to the poor of the 'developing' world, looks like luxury. I have spent fifty years as a social worker, reporter, researcher with the homeless, unemployed and poor; yet the affective life, its spirit and shape are elusive. Perhaps this is because we are so accustomed to money-measurements of poverty that we cannot count other costs of life spent in the waste products of affluence, junk culture, the humiliation of the reach-me-down and off-cuts, the remainder of wealth.

The neglected interiors of the houses reflect the ragged psychic interiors, raided by what the modern world—quite correctly—calls 'deprivation'; because to be deprived means to have something knowingly taken away or held back. If it is 'relative' poverty, it is relative, not to the pleasures enjoyed by their peers or to those above them, as told by sober social scientists of an extensive academy specialising in the poverty of others: it is relative to an unlimited capacity of the world to produce; a vast abundance, of which the poor are outcasts, dependants of forbidden luxuriance.

The psyche of the poor assumed the shape it now presents only slowly. In the 1950s and 1960s, poverty was still concentrated in the old industrial housing, terraces and tenements of inner-cities—crumbling alleys littered with waste paper, cigarette bottles, broken glass and discarded mattresses a flower of nocturnal incontinence in the middle. Later, its habitat was 1930s and early post-war estates: red-brick wastelands, neglected gardens and grey-slate trapezium roofs, rank grass, dogs tethered to a post, gardens full of rusty perambulators and stained carpets, yards overgrown with briars, green hearts and white bells of convolvulus engulfing sheds and broken pigeon-houses; streets strewn with burnt-out cars, smashed glass and crumbled kerbstones. This, in turn, gave way to tower blocks, desolate walkways, lifts out of order, smelling of piss and fear, the draughty echo and clouded breath, graffiti, grilles to deter intruders; women stranded with babies on the eleventh floor, overflowing bins smelling of rotten food, nappies and decay, oil on the concrete, restless children playing football on an overtrodden square of grass; kids in dim light outside betting-shop and takeaway, telling each other stories of escape, thanks to temazepam and vodka, the stolen car, the lighted rag through the letterbox, the smashed window and the blackened opening of the charred front-room. By the end of the twentieth century, planners' regrets were inscribed in new villages of low-rise houses which gestured to the streets they had replaced, people thrust away the memory of industrial life; berberis and cotoneaster catching at plastic bags in their thorny branches; while inside, the second-hand furniture from the Salvation Army or Social Services gave way to flammable furniture of foam and plastic, TV became a basic necessity, without which raising children would be unthinkable; coffee, food, spilt beer, blood and piss wearing away the pattern on the carpet. On the walls, scraps of philosophy 'Live Hard, Die Young' or 'She offered her honour, He Honoured her offer, And all the night long, It was Honour and Offer'; pictures of Satanic figures with bat wings holding naked maidens against an orange setting sun, the words of a pop song, *Lonely this Christmas*, in careful handwriting. Mobile phones, hard porn and dating sites on the net ousted pub and Citizens Band radio, the note in the papershop window and the pick-up on the corner; relationships disposable as the foil containers of takeaway meals, emotional bingeing that barely survives the night, impulsive attachments and jealous possessiveness.

In Michelle's house

Last week, somebody shoved a petrol-soaked rag through Michelle's letterbox and tried to set fire to the house. Her world is full of enemies;

people looking for revenge, paying her back for something she did or said;
somebody has threatened to scar her for life or is out to get her for money
they say she owes them. One minute, Michelle says she cannot cope with
her children, and wants them taken into care; the next, she is hugging
them with a fierce tearfulness, saying she will do anything to give them a
better life. She cut her wrists and then hammered for help on a neighbour's door, leaving bloodstains on the paint. She is twenty-five.

You would know nothing of the chaos within from looking at her,
except perhaps the fugitive pain in her eyes, and scars on her wrists from
an earlier attempt to kill herself. Her arms are tattooed, a snake and a
flower. Her hair is white-blonde. Michelle wears her vulnerability like a
garment that tells the world that she is a victim; and the world responds
accordingly.

The street where she lives was respectable, but it is now awaiting
demolition. Most tenants are transients, but some older people act as a
chorus, lamenting the decline of the area in the corner shop, where the
shopkeeper has impounded Michelle's social security book as a guarantee
that she won't flit, leaving debts behind.

The house is damp, and even on a warm September day, inside, a
delayed and different climate prevails. The furniture is a museum of
junk-shop pieces from different decades of the century. A shiny, convex
sideboard from the 1930s, half-open drawers overflowing with linen,
crumpled clothing, hair-curlers, scraps of material. A spindly cabinet
from the 1950s, working-top lowered on metal struts is covered with
packets of tea and sugar, bread, jam, margarine, milk-bottles. A table
topped with plastic marble is the only modern item in the house. The
kitchen floor is covered with lino in crimson, yellow and emerald. A
1970s three-piece suite covered with rexine and foam-rubber cushions
covered with yellow nylon. The pattern on the carpet, once 1940s Utility,
has been effaced. On shelves there are scavenged fragments of orna-
ments—Capodimonte covered with dust, a tarnished brass clock, a red
glass goblet with a white rat climbing up the side, a storm-lantern, a
teddy bear. Over the chimney-breast an arrangement of daggers and
swords and what look like imitation pistols.

Danny is Michelle's boyfriend, father of three of her four children. He
has long fair hair, and is dressed in worn jeans and a denim jacket, lapels
covered with badges. His hands are dirty from mending his motorbike.
Restless, uncommunicative, he walks round the room. Stephen, two, cries

to be picked up by his father. Danny does so, and the little boy clings to him. Michelle says, 'He's all for his Dad, and so is Kelly. If I can't give her what she wants, she says, "Daddy will buy it for me." That hurts.' Danny wants a cigarette. He puts the child down, and Stephen starts crying again.

Michelle says, 'The trouble is we can't live without each other, but we can't live with each other either.' Danny says, 'I don't need this,' and he goes into the kitchen to find something to eat. 'Since he left, I've had a lot of boyfriends. I just sent the last one away. He used to beat me up, but when I told him I couldn't take any more, he left without a fuss.' She was surprised not to get another good hiding as a parting present. Most of Michelle's friends are bikers. 'I know two who got killed in accidents, and another had to have his leg amputated. I was going out with one guy, and he wanted to commit suicide on the bike with me on the back. He said he was going to drive into the back of a lorry. He said he felt like committing harry-karry, whatever. He wanted me and him to buried in the same grave.' I said, 'No thanks.' He said, 'I thought you were fed up with life.' I said, 'On my own terms. If I do it, it's gonna be my decision.' Michelle says a lot of bikers are like that. 'Danny is the same. They don't care about living.' 'Course I do,' Danny contradicts her, coming back into the room with half a dozen slices of bread and jam stuck together and marked with oily fingerprints. 'But if it's your time to go, it's your time. At least when I go, I'll have a smile on my face. And it won't matter to anybody else.'

This is a reproach to Michelle. He steals a quick glance at her as he speaks. I say, 'You've got Michelle and your lovely kids.' 'If she cared for me that much, we'd be together, wouldn't we?' 'You can love somebody too much,' says Michelle wisely. 'Whenever we're together, we can't stop quarrelling.'

'You can't trust anybody,' she says. 'There was a murder in the next street, a girl left dead after an ex-boyfriend beat her up.' She looks at Danny. He says, 'I'm not going to beat you up.' 'No, you're scared,' is her provocative response. One night last week the police came to the door. 'Somebody had phoned and said I'd left two young children in the house. I was in bed. I told them, "For your information, it's three children." They're always knocking at the door, looking for Danny.'

The front door of the house is open. This tells the neighbourhood anybody is welcome. People come and go during the afternoon. A middle-aged man, separated from his wife, sits drinking bottles of cider in the corner by himself. A former neighbour who is gay has just finished with his boyfriend. 'He put a load of pills in my tea. I didn't drink it. It tasted funny so I tipped it away.'

In the kitchen, meals are a perpetual picnic: sliced loaf, sterilised milk, biscuits and sweets, silver trays of take-aways, processed cheese, beans and potatoes, bottles of cider, Coke and vodka. The bedrooms are chaotic, mattresses on the floor, pink and yellow nylon sheets, discarded clothing, magazines, cosmetics, cigarette packets, tobacco tins, blouses and short skirts, garments made by the poor of Bangladesh for the poor of Britain. The men do not stay long: mending motorbikes and old bangers in shirtsleeves, indifferent to the cold; then a few weeks on the building, or driving, while the women take relationships apart: who is trying to split you up, take your boyfriend away, set out to get him just to prove she can? Who lied to wind you up, who is deliberately spreading syph so everybody knows whose bloke she's been with?

An economy of barter and exchange; money lost in the post, forged signatures, loans and swappings, a windblown randomness; all-night partying, staying high for a week, followed by times of reflectiveness and sadness. What does it all mean? Why was I put here? I've got so much love to give, why can't I hold anybody? I wish it was all different. I'm going to start over in a new town. The woman I was is dead, tomorrow is a new beginning.

Love is power, and sex is affection; but puritanical limits are set: I'd never hit an old woman. People who interfere with kids should be castrated. I wouldn't take from anybody in a wheelchair. Yet bullying, terrorising the helpless is also be lucrative. I do her shopping, she gives me ten quid; sometimes I keep the change, she thinks she's lost it.

Constant changes and makeovers—hair colour, dress, tattoos, body-piercings: a list of names, Clive, Ian, Doug and Clem, so every time Babe holds out her arm she sees a biography of former boyfriends; he's dead, he's inside, he done a runner, he married a Paki. Impulsiveness and spontaneity represent freedom. Why don't we, let's go and, what about, get out of our skulls, legless, wasted, party hard, only one life....

Danger runs through daily incident, a precarious reach-me-down survivalism. Curtains are closed all day; a pit-bull sleeps under the table. A Colt 45 is kept under the sofa; on the wall, a Zulu spear, a samurai sword. Self-protection, nobody else is going to look after you. I was in court, but jumped from the dock and ran. I hid out of town, came back at night. Police cars everywhere. I hid in the dustbin. Men, proud of their physical strength, wiry, shaved head, intensely physical, always on the move. Discipline—weight training, body-building, working out, not the gym, it's pooffy. I don't mind a fight, but you get more satisfaction with fists. The damage they have done to others—cut off my brother's ear with an open razor; glassed this bloke, his own mother didn't recognise him. I'm a hard bastard. I don't feel pain. I was brought up hard, I mean hard. My father broke my arm when I was a baby. I don't hate him. He brought me up to stand on my own feet. I don't hit first and think afterwards, I hit first and don't think at all. I can't cry. I did all my crying as a kid, there's nothing left.

I like serious talk. The purpose of life. You're born to die. I believe in reincarnation. When somebody dies, their soul enters a baby that's just conceived, I don't know. My Nan died the night my youngest was born, almost exactly the same time. Her soul passed into that child. I know I've been here before. I've been to places I recognise. We've all been on earth, perhaps lots of times. I think you come back; otherwise, there's no point to it. That's why I'm not scared of dying. Live dangerously. When your time comes, that's it. I like motorbikes, racing, taking risks. There's no point in being too careful. I could walk outside, slip on the pavement and break my skull. When your time comes, that's it. And if you know you're coming back, it's no big deal.

We live in debt. Everybody does. It's out of control. I took a loan, then another. Just to get through the week. How can you work, when living is a full-time job? I owe more money than I'll ever have in my whole life. The only people who come to this door want money.

He asked me to marry him, I said yes, and he went off and stayed out all night. He slept with some brass he picked up. Why would he do that? I never knew his real name. Called himself Dale. Said he was in the army. He had his own business. He bought a van to go round the coast for the summer. When he went, he took part of me and my daughter with him. She loved him, called him Daddy. I said, 'Don't call any man Daddy, there's no such thing.'

They took my kids away, I was in the street, I seen this woman wheeling a baby in a buggy. I looked down at him, and he smiled at me. She was wheeling my bleeding baby, and I didn't even know him. But he knew me.

If you haven't been loved, you want a baby, because you'll get someone of your own, give them all the love you've got; but you find out you haven't got as much as you thought; or you don't know how to show it. A baby stops being a part of you the day it's born.

In the houses, pictures of family and friends form shrines; a young man on his wedding day (to someone else, the picture of the bride cut away), a man with copper-coloured hair, dazzling teeth, a snow of confetti on his blue suit. 'He's Alice's Dad, I think. That's my Mum before she had cancer. She's bald now. My sister, I don't see her, but I still love her. That's Kyle, looks hard, but he's soft as shit. He went in the army, they threw him out because he had sex with a bloke. He tried to kill himself. When I met him, he was sleeping rough, dirty and neglected. I gave him back his self-respect, but when I thought we'd settled down, he pissed off to London with his best mate.'

'When I moved into this house, it wasn't a happy place. There were bad feelings. You can tell with houses. A man lived here, knocked his girl down the stairs and she suffered brain damage. A friend of mine has psychic powers, she did an exorcism. The evil has gone now, but there's one room I still won't go into, the front bedroom, because that's where the worst of it happened. I have dreams, I know what's going to happen. I get it from my Mum. It scares me sometimes. I look in people's faces and I can see death or suffering. I don't say anything, unless people want to have their fortune told. If they come to me, I might, but otherwise you have to keep it to yourself, knowledge is danger.'

This is another poverty. Material resources are thin, but the people do not suffer hunger and destitution. It is a different pain, an emaciated sense of trust, love spread too thin, a depleted faith in each other, an under-nourishment of the heart. Empty, gutted, broken-up inside— these are the words Michelle uses; a humanity injured in a way unfamiliar to the old people lodges now in these inimical impermanent streets, scheduled, like the lives of many of their occupants, for demolition.

If these, the apparently unrepentant poor, cause trouble to society, this is nothing compared to the troubles society causes them. The moral judgement of majorities does nothing to relieve their pain, and it certainly fails to acknowledge their often heroic efforts to survive.

In Mike and Karen's house the electricity has been off for three years. Stella, their daughter, is two. She has never seen electricity in her own home; and since she has never been outside it, she hasn't seen it anywhere else. A single butane flame lights one corner of the living room, and candles light them to bed and to the lavatory in the yard. Bedtime for her and her two older sisters is a time of shadows and fears; candlelight dances in the draughts in the echoing staircase. They have nightmares, wet the beds. One night a candle fell over in its saucer and started a fire. A few seconds after Stella had been lifted from her bed, heat from the fire shattered the window and a sliver of glass pierced the mattress where she had been lying. There had been a conflict with the electricity board (as it then was). Karen had lived there with her previous man, and when Mike moved in, arrears were so high, at the rate of paying he could afford, it would be eighteen years before the light was turned on again. They are known by the occupants of the short-life housing in the street as 'the family without electricity', as though missing some fundamental characteristic. Nobody in the neighbourhood mentions it, but people watch. When Karen goes into local shops, conversation stops, and she can feel people's eyes on her. Other children are not allowed to come and play in the house.

The glass in the front door is broken. In its place a square of hardboard with Merry Xmas painted on it. They occupy one room downstairs; floorboards covered with strips of old carpet, battered cupboards, sideboards, kitchen cabinets around the edge of the room, taken from builders' skips; a three-piece suite in grey moquette. The plaster is held on the walls only by the paper. Over the chimney breast Mike and Karen have pasted pictures of their children, old Christmas cards and Mothers' Day mementoes; a little altar to a fragile family which soon dispersed, when Mike left. He said he wasn't worthy to be a father. He couldn't get a job. Nobody owed him a living. It was his own fault. They would be better off without him.

The carer

Most people in poverty are not conspicuous. They lead lives of often heroic self-denial and devotion to others. Many of the six million unpaid carers, despite Attendance Allowance, struggle to survive, not only materially, but psychologically. Of Britain's carers 1.5 million are over sixty, and almost 60 per cent are women.

Violet looked after her mother until she died at the age of ninety-three. By that time, Violet was in her seventies. They lived in a small terraced house close to the centre of town, where, by a process of profane conversion, chapels have become wine bars and churches furniture depositories. The houses are mostly 'short-life', an irony not lost on Violet who has spent lengthy years in the same rented property, which fell into ruin during her long vigil at her mother's side in her slow decline.

The house was never modernised. There was a plaster sink, with a geyser that must have been added in the 1940s, still functioning in the early 1990s. The only heating was a gas fire, one that ought to have been removed years ago, with a bare element that burned with a blue flame and filled the room with head-aching fumes. Wooden cupboards built into the walls, bursting with long-paid bills, birth, marriage and death certificates, and family photographs; a chenille drape at the door to keep out draughts; rag rugs on scuffed linoleum, the pattern of which had become barely discernible. Minnie, Violet's mother, spent much of her day sitting on the horsehair sofa, reading the paper with a magnifying glass. There was a china cabinet, with rose-patterned cups that had not been used for decades, some Victorian plates and a few objects from her mother's house—a silver thimble, a delicate cream jug and a set of silver-gilt spoons set in a blue velvet box. Everything in the house spoke of a pinched privacy and proud self-reliance; but Minnie's daughter bore the burden.

'My father worked in a factory. He was a sensitive man, intelligent; too good for this life. He died in 1957, still in his fifties. She lived thirty-five years after him; but her whole life revolved around her being on the brink of the grave, waiting to join him. She only really found her identity as a widow.

'We didn't see many people the last years,' she says. 'I was exhausted most of the time. Mother wanted to go into a home, but I wouldn't. "No," I said, "you looked after me when I was helpless, now it's my turn." "Ah yes," she said, "but what'll happen to you when I'm gone?" I used to say, "I can look after myself." "That's what I thought,", she said.

'We never had money for luxuries. We often had to go without. Of course, the pension was a blessing, and in the last few years, we had two pensions coming in. If we hadn't I don't know how we would have managed. I'm not complaining. I am thankful I was spared to close my mother's eyes for her. But the last years, for about seven of them, I didn't know what a night's sleep was. I used to lie awake, listening for her. If she needed the commode, or if she cried out in her sleep, I used to get up and comfort her, and sometimes I'd get into bed with her till she fell asleep. Only I was wide awake. She wouldn't ask for help, social services. She thought it was charity. But I had to pay the price for her pride.

'The neighbours were nice enough. They said, "If you need anything, you know where to find us." But that was another way of saying we shan't offer to help. You learn to read between the lines of what people say.

'When you're living in this reduced way, you lose perspective on the world. Mother used to wake up earlier and earlier, so our whole day was out of shape. We'd have breakfast sometimes at three thirty in the morning, and by half past ten, we'd have lunch, and our last meal about four o' clock. We went to bed at six, especially in winter. It's almost as if you're wishing time away, urging the next day here, even though you know time can't bring anything good.

'It's all over now. I feel I shared her widowhood; I was a widow but never a bride. I'm not lonely. I go to church, and I have friends there. There's not many of us. I live frugally, because I was brought up poor, and what you've never had you don't grieve for. I've got one thing most people don't, and that's the knowledge that I did my duty; to me that's my most valuable possession.'

The poor in winter

How did poor people pass from scarcity into this penurious modernity? Had it already happened when I was in Glasgow twenty years ago?

For the man separated from his wife, last night's meal was potatoes mashed with half an onion and a tin of peas. In the fridge, there is a can of lager and some long-life milk. On a spindly kitchen table a sliced loaf, a tub of margarine and a bottle of hot-pepper sauce.

He can afford to heat only one room in the flat, so the bedroom is closed. He sleeps on the sofa under a foam duvet, his coat as pillow. In any case, he sleeps very little. Unhappiness is insomniac; a rancid smell of male misery. TV plays all night. At five in the morning, he falls asleep in front of women's golf or motor-cycle racing from Florida. He doesn't even get undressed. There is no hot water: an icy splash in a bathroom where each breath creates a fog of vapour.

Winter briefly refurbishes the landscape. Last night, a fall of snow muted the grey housing blocks, softened the hard edges. The trees are black polyps in the wind; a flock of crows black holes on a white cloth.

The cold gets inside the houses. A powder of snow crystals comes through unsealed window-frames. In bedrooms, the only warmth is from the breath of sleepers. Silver rivulets collect in puddles on the sills, and mould blossoms on the thin wallpaper.

Sometimes, it seems, the chill has penetrated the inner spaces, and the affections have become wintry. Separated. Gone away. Split up. Deserted. Abandoned. Left. Abused. A language of disengagement. I used to be a nice guy, but I'm all right now. My life is full of less: I've been jobless, homeless and penniless; now I'm hopeless.

Poverty? Using the same tea-bag till the tea comes out pale as piss. The flat was furnished by the corporation, fit for a separated man: serviceable cord carpet, brushed nylon curtains, plastic nets, a plain suite and beds for when the children come at weekends. They've even stopped providing furniture: too many people were selling the contents and leaving. The buildings are low-rise, three storey, stairways of chipped concrete, painted brown and pale yellow. Windows protected by wire mesh: some flats have been burnt out—black scorchmarks on grey stone, the empty socket of a window.

One flat was vandalised while the family was out. They wrecked everything. Like a bomb had hit it. Everybody knows who it was. Kids, twelve or thirteen. The family has split up, while the father redecorates another derelict flat at the other end of the Scheme.

The children watch images of war on TV. The same pictures repeated: B52s give birth to a litter of bombs in the sky. Children are war-victims too, crying out in the night, their heads a jumble of craters and rubble. In the morning the beds are wet. Fathers in The Gulf: a disproportionate number of men in the army come from the sometime industrial belt of Scotland. If there is resistance to the war here, it is because this is also the front line of a war that has gone on for ever, a war against the poor.

Cracking up, breaking up, falling apart, breaking down; images of disintegration. You hurt those close to you, who else gives a fuck? Why put your fist into the face of a stranger? Those you love, or loved, or thought you loved. Next morning, at least there is evidence that you're still alive, eyes bruised, congealed blood, the sour breath of drink, the self-wounding anger.

In austere pubs, with their squares of coloured glass at the window, men drink, their own pain their companion. Jokes are hard. Why did God make piss yellow and spunk white? So the Irish can tell if they're coming or going. Why do Iraqis carry shit in their wallets? For identification. But after a few drinks, it is they who are victims. I'm an arsehole. I'm a drunken bum. Don't listen to me, I'm useless. Look at me, what have I got? Who am I?

MODERNISED POVERTY

If people are ashamed to admit they are poor, this is because images of luxury are so pervasive that anybody unable to lay hands on all the good things must be stupid. They collude with the denial that they even exist. No wonder they're invisible.

These are places to get out of. A transfer. An exchange. A runner. A woman is forced out of her flat by neighbours complaining about the wains. They didn't just complain, they beat up the children's father, cracked his ribs. Neighbours. You dread who's going to move in. Shit-heads. Pakis.

In the end all you've got is your own flesh and blood. The bonds are stretched but they don't break. Mothers especially. 'She wouldna let the wind blow on me.' 'She'd give me the top brick of the chimney.' 'She'll never close her door on me, no matter what I do.' A twenty-four year-old wins her battle with the Housing Department for a warm dry house for her baby, born three months prematurely, weighing twenty-three ounces. Twenty-three ounces of humanity, how much is that a pound? She wants her children to be brought up where there are values as well as prices.

Now they are losing the jobs they priced themselves into during the last recession: the real jobs which replaced shipbuilding, steel and coal, prove light as thistledown in the economic wind. Security is the only growth industry: locks and bolts at doors and windows; what's the point, everything has gone. There is a double padlock on the community hall, barbed wire over the fanlight. Boys join the army for the sake of security, certainly not their own. Security: you come home one night and there is a torn piece of paper on the kitchen table telling you the person you thought was your refuge has gone.

The last good job I had? On the buses, fourteen years ago. Since then, work has been an insult: bribe the security man in the supermarket so you can take a few jars of coffee to sell. How do I live? He crooks one arm, draws the other hand to and fro, miming a fiddle.

What kind of a world are the wains going to inherit? My windows were put in three nights in a row. I had them mended, said nothing. You pray they'll get bored and leave you alone. The young are not afraid of anything. I see them playing 'chicken' in front of the buses, or riding their bikes the wrong way up the motorway. They're not even scared of death; once they've lost that, what are you going to tell them?

I was jumped by a gang of kids, left for dead. Since then, I'm scared, I get headaches, I can't work. A neighbour's brother was killed after a

Rangers/Celtic match. He tried to take a knife from somebody who was threatening people. He didn't know this guy had just stabbed somebody; the knife ran straight through him.

I'm glad to be alive. I took LSD, smack; a lot of the kids I was at school with are dead now. At that time, the city was full of old hippies. They'd been in Goa. They told us the pigs there had got addicted to the shit of addicts. I spent ten years of my life strung out. Too many lives thrown away.

In the bitter evening the snow swirls around the lights from the mobile shop. Some of the men are in shirt sleeves. Aren't you cold? We've pure alcohol in our veins. The man buys a tin of frankfurters in baked beans. Separated from my wife and kids. Separated from my money; the only thing I've left to be separated from is life; and that won't be long.

Vales of tears—after the pit closures

The vale of Merthyr has been transformed: sheep graze on the human-made mountains of clinker and ash, which have been re-moulded and grassed over, so that they blend with the natural contours of the hills. Many industrial wounds have been healed: ferns and foxgloves, cerise tapers of willow-herb have reclaimed the lower slopes. It looks like an official conspiracy, to cover up all evidence that the industrial era ever happened.

One result of this is that the social experience of young and old has been separated by something even more impermeable than the passage of time, which does its work of estrangement well enough. The transmission of a culture of work, chapel and trade union has faltered in the re-arranged décor. A new generation is articulated to a life from elsewhere; no longer anchored in this sometime site of coal, steel and heavy manual labour.

The division is reflected in the domestic scene. The old-fashioned interiors of retired miners are brightened by fires heavily banked up against a chill July day; worn hearthrug covered with dog-hairs, upright Windsor chairs, flagstones and bare linoleum occupy a quite different culture from the central heating and wall-to-wall carpets in the homes of younger people, outsize suites of plastic and foam and an electric-blue picture of wild horses, or image of a cute child crying glycerine tears, music centre and video. The young do not want to hear how they dug pits in the garden to get coal during the 1926 General Strike, nor how their grandparents considered themselves lucky to get the top of a boiled egg for their tea; nor of the old ironmaster who, when jobs were scarce, 'told you to send your missis to see him, and if he liked her and she'd pull down her pants for him you were in'. The experience of distant industrial accidents cannot be transmitted, says the miner who lost a father and two uncles in separate incidents in the space of fourteen months. The triumphs, too, are not easily communicated, like that of the eighty-one year-old who was the first individual in the valleys to get the verdict of a coroner changed. 'They said my father died of natural causes. The coroner asked, "Is there anything you want to say?" I said, "Are his lungs still available? I want them analysed in the laboratory." They discovered he had died of silicosis. They said "natural causes" to avoid paying compensation. They were bloody unnatural causes, and I wanted it known.'

The young have other preoccupations, although they, too, are concerned with survival. On the Gurnos estate on the edge of Merthyr, in grey geometrical maisonettes from the 1960s, Louisa lives with her daughters, Nicola, two and Michelle, three months. She lives apart from the children's father, an estrangement that has nothing to do with their relationship, and everything to do with finance. She is on income support, while he is working in a factory that produces Christmas decorations. He stays with them two nights a week—any more would represent cohabitation. Louise says, 'The children's father is reduced to an occasional visitor. Nobody in their right mind gets married round here. You're worse off if you do.'

There is a story on the Gurnos that you make a living out of betraying people who are 'on the banjo' ('fiddling') by denouncing them to the Department of Health and Social Security. 'They say you get a bounty of £50 for every conviction. There's enterprise for you.'

Gareth is sixteen. He wonders if he'll get compensation for the accident that kept him for a month in the Burns Unit at Chepstow. He was doing car maintenance on a youth employment scheme, when the cleaning fluid he was using blew up in his face. He has burns on the cheek, neck, hand and leg. 'It was bad enough working for a pittance without getting scarred for life for the privilege.' Gareth's brother works as a taxi-driver, long hours, but earning enough to keep a family whose father walked out on them five years ago.

'We're bored,' say the young people who lean over the concrete balcony of Merthyr's exiguous shopping centre. 'I've got a drink problem,'
says a seventeen-year-old boy, 'I can't get enough.' 'This is a rough town.
Friday and Saturday nights, stay off the streets if you don't wanna get
hurt,' There is, in the valleys, a redundant male energy that does not
disappear as a consequence of closed pits and abandoned steelworks. 'For
generations,' I was told, 'young bodies have been grown like crops for
work or war. Now there's neither.'

Wealth has flowed out of these valleys ever since the ironmasters set
up in the eighteenth century. Later, coal streamed out through the great
Brunel station at Merthyr, now demolished. In the later twentieth century, it was the export of people that continued the drain of wealth—the
unemployed who walked to Birmingham, families migrating to Canada,
teachers and preachers who went all over the world. One old woman
said, 'We vowed our sons would not go down the pits. It broke our hearts
to see them leave, but we'd rather that than see their bodies broken by
the mines.'

In our time, the vast technical expertise of the valleys has perished
through lack of use, skills and knowledge have fallen from the hands and
brains of people, and have been embalmed in heritage centres, like the
blast engine house at Dowlais, where, after 250 years, metal is no longer
produced. Merthyr was the biggest iron town in Europe. Dowlais supplied the rails for the system in India, Russia and parts of South America.
Trevithick's first steam engine ran here in 1804. Cannon for the Crimea
were made in Merthyr. 'In India during the War, if I felt homesick,' one
former soldier said, 'I only had to go and look at the railway track—
"Rolled in Dowlais"—and I felt better.'

Some of the skilled men—and they were men—are bitter about their
subsequent career—the craftsman turned petrol-pump attendant, the
miner working as night-club bouncer. A manager at a textile firm making
silk stockings lost his job when the works were taken over by Courtauld's.
He then worked on the assembly line at Hoover. 'I was putting two
screws into a piece of metal. They'd 've had monkeys on the job, if
bananas had been cheaper.'

As the old chapel culture of the valleys decayed, the radical secular
alternative of the labour movement, which grew in such ambivalent sym-
biosis with it, is also in retreat. At a Labour Party meeting in Rhymney,
people say the meetings are as empty as the chapels. The story of religious

survival—the saving remnant, the faithful few—is one of a melancholy eventide of faith; and so it is with the dwindling membership of the Labour Party. People talk more readily of the past than of the future. 'We never used to lock our door, day or night; I wouldn't leave the lavatory door open now, somebody'd take the bloody seat.' They remember the 'monkey parade' along the High Street after chapel, all the young people in their best clothes, where many met their future marriage partners. The old women are defensive now about the drudgery they endured. They say they had no choice but to service men, whose bodily strength 'was the only protection you had against destitution'. 'We were always indoors,' mused one woman. 'When the kids came in, their first question was "Where's Mam?" But at least,' she said, 'they didn't grow up into hooligans.'

If the past has more savour than the present, this is because 'you knew where you stood'. The main talking point on the days I was there was whether the perfume factory has polluted the river. All the fish have been killed. 'That's three times we've re-stocked the river,' says one man fishing. 'I caught a trout last week, cooked it for supper. Couldn't eat it, it tasted of diesel.' The local newsagent's shop has been sold to an Indian family, the first in Rhymney; even before they move in 115 people have cancelled their paper. The grandfather of the present owner was Italian; interned in 1939, he was released following a petition signed by a majority of the townspeople.

If men feel the loss of their labour as an insult, women have been the primary beneficiaries of the extinction of heavy industry. Rowena and Gill had worked in factories, making furniture, telephones, toys and bras. 'You're made to believe that because you work in a factory, that's all you're fit for. I never knew there was so much work to be done, such crying human need.' They have been released by their husbands' unemployment to work full time, as a care worker and in an old people's home respectively. Although much of the work for women is an extension of their domestic caring role, it gives a strong sense of independence. A woman whose husband has leukaemia says, 'It means I've taken over his role. He's very happy the work is there for me. And I know he may not have long, but I have to get out of the house sometimes.' A woman widowed last year says that work has been her salvation.

The women look back now on the tyranny of men with an incredulity that their mothers and grandmothers accepted it for so long. 'Everybody said my grandfather was a lovely man. Well, he might have been—outside the house. Inside, he was a tyrant. He gave his wife thirteen children; but he was the biggest baby of all.'

The feelings are ambivalent. Work scarred the people of the valleys, but its removal scarred them also, in a different way. Industrial life was a savage visitation; it was made more bearable by women, who had no choice but to sacrifice themselves for the children, and indeed, the men who depended upon them. But they had no choice either. No one chose industrial society. No one ever voted for the conditions in which they lived and worked. No one asked for constant child-bearing and high child mortality, for breathing and lung disorders that abridged lives and sent the bereaved to the parish and the workhouse. The men, too, were powerless. They submitted to humiliation and affronts to their dignity every day; it is a great sadness, and the tragedy for women, that the men were not wise—or instructed or perceptive enough—to forbear to take out their powerlessness on those with even less power than theirs. It was a joint tragedy. When pit disasters occurred, and women gathered at the pit-head, there was little sign of any jubilation that they were to be delivered from drudgery by the death of the tyrant; only the dread and terror that comes from loss, and for most, that also meant the loss of love, and not simply the slender income that buffeted them and their children from absolute dereliction.

In the late evening in Rhymney, the great cauliflower shower-clouds subside and a cold wind ripples the grass in the valley. In a pub, an unadorned drinking place, to the clatter of glasses and the rhythmic sound of darts puncturing the board, a former miner, now in his eighties, says, 'Thatcher should have done to her what she did to this country— have her bloody heart cut out.'

Discipline and its discontents

If the unsuspecting paupers of the early nineteenth century were unaware they were about to be disciplined by the rigours of mill, factory, workhouse and the hundreds of lunatic asylums under construction, those emerging from the ruins of manufacturing industry had as little idea of the meaning of the shining decor of plenty, that stage in which they had walk-on parts.

The relaxation of the rhythms of industrial life coincided with the decline of imperialism; shortage of labour in the post-war economy led to recruitment in the Caribbean and South Asia; people subject to the rigid laws of a colonial power, its racist ideology and supremacist view of its mission in the world. They arrived in a country where punitive restraints were being lifted in the interests of economic expansion and the widening reach of affluence. Transplanted into an unfamiliar environment, they found universal provision for the poor, health care, unemployment and disability benefit, old age pension and allowances for children—accepted as basic rights; the rules of industrial discipline fallen away.

It was not long before the costs to the poor of the abrupt transition from the most stringent social control to an absence of boundaries (the social analogue of an expanding economy) became apparent. Many migrants, who were among the most adventurous and enterprising in their country of origin—for who else would make such journeys?—discovered they were doing labour disdained by a newly emancipated working class: keeping textile mills open twenty-four hours a day; working as cleaners, auxiliaries in the health service, driving buses and trains, working as janitors, maintenance personnel, security guards in a low-paid service sector. If discrimination, prejudice and xenophobia proved to be part of the meagre reward for which they had left home, this did nothing to conciliate their children, who were also exposed to the contradiction of relaxed social restrictions and unofficial hostility and rejection.

The consequences for community and family continuity among the most disadvantaged were catastrophic; a dereliction of parenting disproportionately affected lives ravaged by discrimination, segregation or simply generations of exclusion. In the functionless void into which a generation has grown, young women have children as an affirmation of identity and gender, while young men flee—much as they did in the eighteenth century, when they left their offspring to the mercy of the parish. Characteristic was the twenty-five-year-old I met who left his wife with three children under five, because he felt his highest duty was 'to find himself', 'to hang loose' and seek out the life of which he felt he had been cheated.

No one knows how many young men in Britain are starved of what are called 'male role-models', except figures of fantasy projected into their lives by the media as celebrities—footballers, heroes and stars. These icons of masculinity, however, remain shadows to their youthful votaries. They are an inadequate substitute for flesh and blood, for loving hands to hold and to guide within the boundless confines of kinship and love.

Fathers, whose power—both in the working class community and in the colonial family structure—was arbitrary and unlimited, whose word was law and whose capacity to command went unchallenged, were preparing their young for industrial discipline, unemployed frugality or regimented colonial servitude. The softer, less coercive face of capitalism banished the mask of harsh austerity, replacing it with the benign smile of universal provider, bringer of sweet indulgence.

The ache left by absconding men is soon filled. The older image of the patriarch has not gone away, any more than raw male power has ceased to exist. That violence is now institutionalised in what are called 'cultural products', video games, fast cars, the glamour of the outlaw, the hero who acknowledges no equal, a media iconography of warfare, futuristic and intergalactic fighting, as well as a nostalgia without end for the Second World War, and an ambiguous fascination with Nazism. These totems of brute force are also modified by more decorative androgynes of pop and fashion, a more acceptable face of masculinity and its ambivalences in the contemporary world; but these have far from displaced the idea of dominant masculinity.

A powerful after-image of male power pervades the culture. It serves many young men starved of actual contact with adult males. In order for this to be effective, it requires the mediation of the peer-group, which selects, adapts and re-interprets for its members the meaning of being a man. It is absorbed osmotically by groups, which impose their norms of moral order as inflexibly as the most ferocious patriarch, when he threatened his boys with his trouser-belt, strap, stair-rod and other domestic articles of correction he could lay his hands on.

The peer-group has its own codes, loyalties and sense of honour; and performs a do-it-yourself masculinisation, a powerful, highly conservative version of maleness, through which young men acquire characteristics and assume behaviours which do not reach them through personal relationships of loving care, but are confected independently of the missing individuals, nominal occupants of a father-role.

With the loosening of family bonds, the semi-compulsory entry into the labour force of more single parents, boys are left increasingly to fend for themselves. This opens the door for a strange free-enterprise and extra-familial parenting: for heroes, stars and adventurers, the applauded 'role-models' serve the privatisation of fatherhood, albeit in a very public way. This has nothing to do with the 'private life' in the sanctuary of the home, beloved by traditionalists, or indeed with the claustrophobic confinement painted by sometime radicals. Although the images are public, they remain the property of entertainment, sporting and fantasy conglomerates. In this way, group or gang culture is in the vanguard of industrialised parenting, which is more efficient than leaving it to mere birth-parents, whose skills have, in any case, decayed, and can be accomplished only with the intervention of professionals, bringers of 'parenting classes' to those who, it seems, have been so dispossessed they are no longer competent to bring up those whom they love as much as they ever did. Here is an impoverishment familiar to Dickens and Mayhew, which has survived into an era of unequalled wealth.

The sanctity of family life has long been coveted by free-market buccaneers, whose eye is always on the alert for new territories to open up, areas ripe for development, in the truly imperial spirit of their forebears. The promotion of 'family values' has become mere ideological window-dressing. The family of political cliché is a figment, its personnel embalmed lay-figures. The reality is of parents deprived of their social function in the raising of children, reduced to providing them with money to buy in what is necessary for the passage of a child from infancy to childhood to adulthood; wondering where they are at night, what they are doing, dreading the knock on the door, the midnight visit from the police, the wail of a siren, the report of a stabbing, blood on the pavement, at worst, cards, flowers and teddy-bears at the improvised wayside shrine...

As in the early industrial era, the extended family was disrupted, so its nuclear successor is now under pressure from this next stage of industrial society. The nuclear family has become a depleted, depopulated place, where the intensity of emotion is hard to contain, since so few people are there to absorb it; and the family collapses in acrimony and anger.

Whatever freedoms these breakages confer on adults, they bring anxiety and confusion to the young; boys who find in the media the trappings of a powerful machismo, girls who seek identity in two-dimensional silhouettes of desirability projected onto the internal screens of colonised fantasy.

When young men return to the 'real world', outrage follows the expression of values that have nourished their starveling lives. That real world turns upon them, criminalises their distorted heroics, despises them for the caricature of belonging created by peer-groups, through which angry waifs have proved themselves men. And these express only contempt for missing flesh and blood. He was never there. Father is a dirty word. I went to see him and he didn't recognise me. If I saw him in the street I wouldn't know him. He was a bastard. If he was on fire I wouldn't piss on him.

The knifing in the takeaway, a fight in the car park, joyriding, the supermarket robbery, the assignation with rivals from the neighbouring postcode, avenging a slight, the restoration of 'honour'—who can say on what shadowy figures they work out their fury when a stranger challenges them, someone looks at them the wrong way, a word out of place unleashes the desolate anger accumulated over years?

The Generations

The house is on an estate built in the 1980s; a flimsy structure, apparently of red plastic and Perspex, in a landscape of grassy slopes, struggling saplings and a stream already choked with old mattresses and supermarket trolleys. The houses are terraced, and face a dual carriage-way. At the back, spiky pyrocanthus shrubs and thin silver birch trees.

Three generations live here: the grandmother is thirty-six, the mother sixteen and the baby a few weeks old. The child is a beautiful girl, with dark hair. She sleeps in a plain box-shaped cot, her face pink against the white blanket, her arms outstretched. The grandmother says 'Put her bootees on.' 'She's warm as toast' her mother says sharply. The older woman sighs. It's going to be hard for her not to interfere. She loves babies; just looking at the child makes her cry. 'When I think of the world she's growing up in. I'd like to take her away where nothing can harm hurt her.'

While the mother prepares the baby's feed, the grandmother picks her up. She holds her to her face, and the baby sucks vigorously at her lower lip. Grandmother says 'You've given me bee-sting lips, sexy.' The little girl has the fragile vigour of the new-born; she expresses herself with her whole body, but her movements are held fast by the grandmother's strong arms. By the time her mother comes in with the bottle, the baby is asleep again.

The grandmother is a big woman, whose hard life has left her looking older than her years. She wears a pink floral dressing-gown and fleecy slippers. 'I want to pick her up all the while. I love the smell of babies. Last night I looked after her, gave her two feeds, took her into my bed. I wish things could stay like this for ever.'

The baby's mother is unwell. She had a kidney infection and now has a persistent cough. She hated being pregnant. Somebody told her she was ugly, and she feels she still is; but as she leans back on the sofa in a pink tracksuit, the baby sprawled on her breast and stomach, they are a beautiful and touching sight. She shows some photographs of the child taken only six hours after birth, mounted on little cards, with details of her name, weight and time of arrival. In the space on the card where it says 'Parents', she has deleted the 's' carefully in biro, before inserting her own name.

She was frightened of giving birth. The pain lasted forty-eight hours, and the epidural was not very effective. She was given a drug to delay labour, which allowed her a few hours sleep. She had sixteen stitches. The grandmother says, not without satisfaction 'She won't get her figure back, she's got terrible stretchmarks. We've all been there. A bloke tells a girl he loves her and that's her life fixed. But I wouldn't be without the baby for the world', then looking at her daughter, 'any more than I would ever have been without you'.

The grandmother's own mother is still in her fifties; and she lived until recently with *her* mother on the other side of town. Five generations of women; families, not extended laterally, but vertically through time, a long filament of kinship on which people are threaded; a new kind of family structure, providing continuity and knowledge transmitted down the years. Although this child just missed knowing her great-great-grand-mother, there is every chance that this relationship will be known to her own children.

Grandmother says that she and her family have always lived in poverty. There has never been enough of anything—food, warmth, decent cloth-ing, a home of their own. She says 'I have stolen for my kids, and I'd do it again. I never had a chance for an education. My father came and went. My Mum used to say "Hello stranger" when he walked in. He'd stay for a couple of days, leave a few quid and then off again. She used to say no woman could hold him, he was a wanderer. In the end, he wandered out of his own mind. He worked, only he didn't think it was his job to look after his kids. He always swore I wasn't his, so that gave him the excuse.'

The mother of the new baby says she would have been lost without her own mother. 'Social Services asked me if I wanted her put up for adop-tion within a couple of days of her being born. My Mum went mad at them. 'Just because we're poor', she said, 'doesn't mean we don't know how to love each other.' I wish I'd stayed at school. I'd like to work, but what is there for somebody like me, I've got no qualifications. A baby needs so much. I'm never going to know what it's like to go into shops to buy other things people get every day.'

Her brother comes home. He is fourteen. Awkward, he feels left out in the house of women. Laconic and self-conscious, he moves with spare gestures learned from older boys on the estate. He practices martial arts, especially kung-fu. When asked how good he is, he says solemnly he is not allowed to boast of his prowess. It is part of the art to be disciplined. Keep control of yourself at all times, even when threatened and have to put your skill to the test in self-defence. Otherwise, you could kill. You have to learn to handle yourself. I don't start fights, but if anybody tangles with me, they'll wish they hadn't.

The grandmother talks about the neighbourhood. Until recently, a woman had been lodging with them. She is a lesbian, and has now gone to live with a friend, whose husband is doing a long stretch in the nick. He was in the Hell's Angels. Before you can rise above a certain level, you have to do three tasks—rob a grave, commit a violent crime and I can't remember what the other is. She says 'I've got a lot of friends on this estate, mostly women. We talk. We have therapy sessions. You think you have problems until you hear about other people's lives. One girl, her husband made her have threesomes—sometimes another bloke, sometimes a woman. The trouble with men, all they think about is football, sex, drink, sex, cars, sex, fighting, sex.... I mean, women think about sex as well, but they know things men don't, they know much more than men. A lot of men can't stand it, and that's what makes them violent.

Sometimes my Mum comes to stay. She was widowed last year. She wants to come and live with us. She was looking after her mother and her husband while they were both terminally ill. I mean, she drives me crazy sometimes, she belongs to a generation that worked in the mills, and she can't understand why the world isn't like it was when she was young. But she's done more than her duty, so I suppose in the end, that's it isn't it? You have to look after them the way they looked after you. She's got problems with her neighbours, they play loud music all summer long, all-night parties. She asked them to turn it down and was told to fuck off. My Mum's frightened. When you get old, the world is a scarier place. I expect we'll find room for her.

The grandmother would like to move from the estate. 'I've offered a refuge to a lot of women, a place where they can get sympathy and shelter. But I'm fed up with them saying they're finished with men, and then they meet a new bloke and it's all going to be wonderful, a new life is beginning and goodbye for ever; and there they are, two weeks later on the doorstep, crying their eyes out and showing their bruises. I know I'm not the world's greatest innocent, I can tea-leaf, but I know there's other things in life.

The grandmother speaks of the tenderness of generations of women. When she says—as she does repeatedly—'The only thing we've got is each other', she appears to speak deprecatingly, but she knows in that simple avowal there is a world of resourcefulness, commitment and loyalty, without which they would be far, far poorer than they are with the grudging—and decreasing—subsistence the State allows.

The poor and the working class

Owen Jones in his book *Chavs*, claims the whole working class is stigmatised by the word.[2] He may exaggerate, but it is certainly applied to many poor people, some of whom are working, others unemployed. A large proportion of the poor have always been in work. The point was made by Charles Booth and B. Seebohm Rowntree—about half of those in poverty were working, although their labour was low-paid, casual, or intermittent. The high point of the 'working class' came after the Second World War, when the penitents of capitalism became loud in their declarations of inclusiveness and affection for those who had been called— sometimes with distasteful irony—hewers of wood and drawers of water, toiling masses, the salt of the earth, the labouring poor. Frightened by the menace of socialism, power and wealth hugged the working class to their bosom in so tight an embrace that they all but suffocated, showered with welfare (now repudiated) rose-hip syrup, malt, vitamin C, milk and cradle-to-grave security; an affection that proved, like so many in the post-war world, no lasting relationship.

The second feature about both loathing for the poor and class hatred is that they pre-date industrial society and existed long before the appearance of Karl Marx, and other warriors of working-class supremacy. A far more ancient dislike of the poor by the rich precedes class society. This may have lapsed during the democratic era, when the powerful

[2] Jones, Owen, *Chavs: The Demonization of the Working Class*, London: Verso, 2012.

realised that extending the franchise might offer the majority who were poor an opportunity to vote away their privilege, and they assumed a showy concern for the people, and a commitment to their uplift.

The third element is that the appearance of 'chavs' is a consequence of the new confidence of the rich in the world, transformed from suckers of the blood of the poor into the universal providers of everything we need. Chavs are assertive, and in their mimicry of branded clothes, bling and sportswear (whether fake goods or real), they pay homage to wealth and power, even if, (or perhaps because) they have so little of it. Chavs are a reincarnation of the lower orders, the masses, Burke's swinish multitude, the great unwashed, the proles—a changing nomenclature, which groups together several sets of people——those dependent on benefit, pensioners of the welfare state, the working poor and the assertive former working class who throw their new-found wealth around, exciting a mixture of snobbery and contempt in those who cannot quite stop thinking of themselves as their 'betters'. Chavs also embody another ancient feature of the poor—the homage they pay to the rich by their efforts to imitate them.

Embedded in these older habits of thought is a vibrant contemporary issue. For what is seen—by Owen Jones and others—as the defection of Labour from those it regarded as its 'own people' is also a reflection of the altered sensibility of the working class, and the consequent modification of the meaning of poverty: dismantling industry also demolished the psychic structures of an industrial working class, reduced now to a remnant of the great industrial population which endured until after the Second World War. The undermining of the industrial base and the industrial mentality was not caused by Thatcher: it was part of a wider process of globalisation, which saw the whole world integrated into a single division of labour; few national entities were untouched by it. That no political party or group has been able to speak directly to the new sensibility (apart from the BNP which found a way into the hearts of some of its more alienated people) is not the fault of an archaic Labour party: it is that the market has ousted politics as a primary determinant on identity, or rather, the market has become politics. Participation now means having the money to buy in the necessaries of life. It is in this context that the new poor should be placed.

There are other groups of alienated and excluded—an older generation of survivors of the old working class; young Muslims who take their faith seriously, and who are regarded by those in power as potential destabilisers of the peace; radicals of the Left and Green movements, who make up the Occupy and other anti-capitalist movements, and those, mostly young and vigorous people who are prepared, not to organise, but to protest, in the form of riot, burning and looting, prominent in the events of August 2011. These appear the greatest threat to power. They follow a recognisable tradition of unrest, disturbances, unruliness and rioting, from eighteenth-century bread riots, to the Luddites, the Swing riots, Rebecca riots, the Plug riots, the physical force faction of the Chartists, down to the disturbances in Brixton, Toxteth, the northern towns and most recently, London and the Midlands in 2011. These are the truly disaffected; and the response of Authority and indeed, of the majority, whose voice the popular press claims to represent, has been as virulent as that of governments facing the mob in the early industrial period.

For when the poor have been reduced to a minority, it is only to be expected that the majority—even if they are also struggling—should turn upon them and their alleged predations on the public purse, with hostility and anger; a development wholly to the benefit of the truly rich and powerful. This is why the events of August 2011 provoked such a vehement reaction: the killing of Mark Duggan by the police in Tottenham was the trigger for an outburst of repressed anger by a section of the young working class, unemployed, poor and their sometimes well-off sympathisers. When the wildfire rioting spread, it mutated, and concentrated itself on acquisitive crimes and attacks on property. It demonstrated the fragility of social peace, the presence of profound dissatisfaction beneath a surface of civility and order, and worsening social injustice, an apparently unbridgeable gulf between rich and poor. The response to these outbreaks of violence followed another long tradition, namely, disproportionate sentences, and the determination to 'make an example' of offenders. Thus it was that, according to a study by *The Guardian*, the sentences passed on convicted rioters were longer than those normally incurred by the same offences. Two young men charged with inciting a riot on Facebook—which never took place—were sentenced to four years in prison. A student was jailed for six months for stealing a bottle of water from a supermarket. A man was charged with the theft of two scoops of ice-cream and an ice-cream cone. One man was jailed for four years eight months for throwing a brick, stealing alcohol, chocolate and cigarettes; another was given thirteen months for stealing a television; a man found with a bag of clothes worth £500 was sentenced to sixteen months for 'theft by finding'. Another received eighteen months for receiving stolen goods. A majority appearing in court were under the age of twenty, and about a quarter juveniles.

Lee Bridges in an analysis of the riots observes that six months after the events of August 2011, of the 2,710 persons brought to court across the country, just under 1,800 cases had been completed.[3] Of these, 1,483 had led to conviction and 945 (64 per cent) sentenced to immediate custody, with the average length of the prison sentence being 14.2 months. These figures indicate that riot-related offenders received immediate custody at approximately three times the rate as those normally sentenced for similar offences, and that the average length of their sentences was nearly four times longer.'

The Vice-Chair of the Criminal Bar Association said it was not the job of judges 'to deliver a message on behalf of the government', when passing sentence, but it was part of their role to identify 'serious aggravating features that elevate the crime beyond the ordinary'. Eric Pickles, Secretary of State for Communities said, 'These kind of exemplary sentences are necessary. I think people would be rightly alarmed if that incitement to riot got off with just a slap on the wrist.' Atavistic fear of the poor was roused. A Crown Court judge said, 'The principal purpose is that the courts should show that outbursts of criminal behaviour like this will be and must be met with sentences longer than they would be if the offences had been committed in isolation. For these reasons, I consider that the sentencing guidelines for specific offences are of much less weight in the context of the current case, and can properly be departed from.'

Some judges even reached for language reminiscent of the eighteenth century in their pronouncements. Rejecting the appeal of the Facebook incitement charge, the Lord Chief Justice said, 'It's very simple. Those who deliberately participate in disturbances of this magnitude, causing injury and damage and fear to even the most stout-hearted of citizens, and who individually commit further crimes during the course of the riots are committing aggravated crimes. They must be punished accordingly and the sentences should be designed to deter others.' Although sentences available to the judiciary are far less severe than anything open to them in the eighteenth and nineteenth centuries, the distinct class tones

---

[3] Bridges, Lee, 'Four days in August: the UK riots', *Race and Class*, Vol. 54, No. 1, London, 2012.

are heard of those who, for generations, passed severe sentences on the poor for petty offences; the descendants of those same people still occupy positions of power, and although they discreetly camouflage their distaste for those who appear before them, the relationship remains unchanged. What is more, they have widespread popular support: according to *The Guardian*, 70 per cent of people thought sentences should be harsher than would be customary for crimes committed during disturbances.

Politicians quickly called the riots 'pure criminality'; this was calculated to deny that society had any role in the creation of such disorder. Discrimination against young people, especially non-white youngsters, by the police (no policeman has ever been found guilty of the death of any of the 333 people who died in their custody over eleven years), unemployment, low-paid work, jobs without careers, an absence of social function, all played out in a context of conspicuously flaunted wealth, have no part to play in the production of the guilty individuals: society and its multiple injustices are not determinants in the conduct of the people; a belief which, however comforting, and however often repeated by power, guarantees one certain outcome; and that is a repeat of what it deplores with such indignant and high-minded complacency. Perhaps the saddest comment came from the MP for Tottenham, David Lammy, who, spoke of the limitations of the world of many young men, the, 'countless young boys and young men I have met who cannot remember the last time they left Haringey. Their lives are needlessly parochial. They have no idea of the opportunities that lie elsewhere in London, let alone the rest of the country.' There is bitter irony, of which he can scarcely be unaware, in his denunciation of a parochialism that was, for hundreds of years, enforced upon the poor in Britain, and the forced epic journeys of the forbears of many of his constituents, first of all to occupy the plantations of the Caribbean, and then to fulfil low-paid labour in the country that had originally enslaved them.

A bus stop in south London. A young woman gets on with a little girl of about three. She carries plastic bags of shopping, some packets of Pampers and her child's scooter. Encumbered and bad-tempered, she sits down beside me and calls to the girl. 'Portia, come here.' Thinking how touching it is to hear the names of Shakespeare's characters on the lips of the people, I say to her 'That's a pretty name'. 'Yeh,' she says, 'she's got lots of pretty names—Porsche, Lamborghini, Ferrari. Her father loved fast cars. He pissed off in one, and left me all his debts.'

The most troublesome poor defy all attempts to defeat, punish, soften, placate or abolish them. If deterrents are set up to prevent their abuse of the welfare system, it is the timid and fearful who suffer, while they continue their predations upon the world, or fill prisons, which engenders further mischief. It is time to consider a different approach to such people, for the casualties of industrialism are not so much wilful destroyers of the well-being of others, as victims, whose need for compensation for the injuries they have suffered may be greater than the vengeful desire of the righteous to add to the already considerable disadvantages that beset them.

Rather than punishing those who show an understandable distaste for humiliating—and usually ill-paid—work, a different conception of such work, and those expected to perform it, is required. Instead of refusing relief, reducing the income of poor people unwilling to fulfil the most menial labour, we should consider compensating those who undertake the least attractive labour when they assume tasks which a majority consider beneath their dignity. It is not unthinkable that a civilised society could offer people who face dead-end work, poorly remunerated jobs, numbing repetitive actions, not chastisement, but an acknowledgement that theirs is indeed an undesirable fate. Their sacrifice should be made good, either by extended time off, by sabbaticals from labour, by something other than meagre wages which reflect the value the market—and not humanity—places upon them and their contribution to necessary work. It is a much commented irony of the economistic ideology that the rich must be given more to 'incentivise' them, while the poor must receive less to achieve the same end.

Through all economic vicissitudes, individuals attribute their good fortune and success to personal merit. This has the agreeable corollary of allowing them to see in the failure or poverty of others a moral defect. This is probably the greatest temptation of the well-to-do; and is reflected in responses, both official and popular, to the poor. It is as live an issue today as it has been in the history of the Poor Laws; and is exploited to great effect by politicians and moralists. With what avidity we take personal responsibility for the good times; and with what reluctance we accept it as our own fault, when we fall into poverty, unemployment or loss!

THE IMPOVERISHMENT OF RICHES

The nineteenth-century debate

There was much discussion about the standard of living of the people in the early industrial era, the period from 1780 to 1840. Debate focused largely on whether the income of the labouring classes rose or fell during that transformative age. Cultural critics argue that, even if it can be shown that purchasing power rose, the loss of rural livelihoods, migrations into slum cities, the disorientation and discipline of industrial production and forcible adaptation to a bewildering world the people never made, turned the experience into a social and spiritual catastrophe. The question of whether tea and potatoes were more nourishing than bread and beer is eclipsed by the great sorrow of the unchosen transhumance to the long season of industry. Whatever material gains were registered, it was felt as a time of grief; akin to that of indigenous peoples in the wider world, when their way of life was laid waste by invasion, and their culture contaminated by those more powerful than they. Echoes of this are heard today, wherever people have thrust upon them, whether they demand it or not, the benefits of modernity; even if this involves the shattering of their cosmos, the ruin of custom and tradition, the destruction of the known forest, river, grassland or mountainside. That industrialism scarred the people of Britain in a similar way has rarely been conceded.

No one captured the sense of depletion of the countryside in eighteenth century Britain more poignantly than Oliver Goldsmith in the fresh wave of enclosures of the later eighteenth century. His poem, *The Deserted Village* dates from 1770.[1]

> Sweet smiling village, loveliest of the lawn
> Thy sports are fled, and all thy charms withdrawn;
> Amidst thy bowers the tyrant's hand is seen,
> And Desolation saddens all the green:
> Only one master grasps the whole domain,
> And half a tillage stints thy smiling plain.
> No more thy glassy brook reflects the day,
> But, choked with sedges, works its weedy way;
> Along thy glades, a solitary guest,
> The hollow-sounding bittern guards its nest;
> Amidst thy desert walks the lapwing flies,
> And tires their echoes with unvaried cries:
> Sunk are thy bowers in shapeless ruin all,
> And the long grass o'ertops the mouldering wall
> And trembling, shrinking from the spoiler's hand,
> Far, far away, thy children leave the land.
> Ill fares the land, to hastening ills a prey,
> Where wealth accumulates and men decay.
> Princes and lords may flourish, or may fade:
> But a bold peasantry, their country's pride,
> When once destroy'd, can never be supplied.
> A time there was, ere England's griefs began,
> When every rood of ground maintained its man;
> For him light Labour spread her wholesome store,
> Just gave what life required, but gave no more:
> His best companions, Innocence and Health;
> And his best riches, ignorance of wealth.

A number of themes in Goldsmith's poem have accompanied industrial society ever since; not the least being a memory (false, some argue) of better times, although this is an understandable response to moments of involuntary upheaval. Perhaps the time remembered was not wonderful, but it was familiar, and the dissolution of the way of life to which people had long accommodated themselves was in a state of dissolution. Nostalgia is a sentiment, not only for those who grow old, but also for

[1] Goldsmith, Oliver, *The Deserted Village*, 1770.

survivors of social and psychological dislocation. That it has recurred regularly for at least the 250 years since Goldsmith wrote, suggests a certain popular obduracy, a desire to conserve by people constrained into changes not of their making and not to their advantage.

The 'ignorance of wealth', helpful to the limited life of an agricultural labourer, may be read partly as a justification for the lower orders knowing their station, for they could scarcely be unaware of the style of living—far from penurious—of local gentry. That they made few demands of luxury for themselves may indicate the poet's approval of the power of rural hierarchy, but it also hints that 'the poor' were not yet the highly conspicuous social problem they were on the threshold of becoming: what sufficed for the labouring poor had not begun to torment commentators and trouble the spirit of reformers in the generations to come.

That the sense of loss was stronger than mere passing regret is clear in the writing of William Cobbett, who pursued his *Rural Rides* in the late 1820s, more than half a century after Goldsmith's poem.[2] Cobbett was a great doubter and denier of 'progress', in both country and industrial areas. Bigoted, prejudiced, he nevertheless registered with elegiac passion the passing of a world. Of a farmhouse in the Weald of Surrey, he notes, 'Every thing about this farm-house was formerly the scene of plain manners and plentiful living. Oak clothes-chests, oak bedsteads, oak chests of drawers, and oak tables to eat on, long, strong and well supplied with joint stools. Some of the things were many hundreds of years old. But all appeared to be in a state of decay and nearly of disuse. There appeared to have been hardly any family in that house, where formerly there were in all probability, from ten to fifteen men, boys and maids; and, which was the worst of all, there was a parlour! Aye, and a carpet and a bell-pull too! One end of the front of this once plain and substantial house had been moulded into a parlour; and there was the mahogany table, and the fine chairs, and the fine glass, and all as bare-faced upstart as any stock-jobber in the kingdom can boast of... And I dare say it has been Squire Charrington and the Miss Charringtons; and not plain Master Charrington and his son Hodge and his daughter Betty Charrington, all of whom this accursed system has, in all likelihood, transmuted into a species of mock gentlefolks, while it has ground the labourers down into real slaves. Why do farmers not feed and lodge their work-people, as they did formerly?

[2] Cobbett, William, *Rural Rides*, London: Penguin, 1967.

Because they cannot keep them upon so little as they give them in wages. This is the real cause of the change. There needs no more to prove that the lot of the working classes has become worse than it formerly was... Judge then, of the change that has taken place in the condition of these labourers! And, be astonished, if you can, at the pauperism and crimes that now disgrace this once happy and moral England.' The question of nostalgia is not so much for things of value that have been lost (although they are often perceived as such), but the disorientation brought on by the unfamiliar.

At the time when Cobbett was expressing his spleen against the plight of rural England, Sir James Kay-Shutleworth, in a pamphlet of 1832 on the *Moral and Physical Condition of the Working Classes* (that 'moral' precedes 'physical' suggests a strangely archaic order of priorities), describes the urban experience of those who sought refuge from rural poverty in the new mill towns of the north of England.[3] He evokes the scene from Ducie Bridge overlooking the River Irk in Manchester (later elaborated by Engels): 'The Irk, black with refuse of dye works erected on its banks, receives excrementitious matters from some sewers in this portion of the town—the drainage from the gas works, and filth of the most pernicious character from bone works, tanneries, size-manufacturers &c. Immediately beneath Ducie Bridge, in a deep hollow between two high banks, it sweeps round a large cluster of some of the most wretched and dilapidated buildings of the town. The course of the river is here impeded by a weir, and a large tannery, eight stories high (three of which stories are filled with skins exposed to the atmosphere, in some stage of the processes to which they are subjected, towers close to this crazy labyrinth of pauper dwellings).' Of the cotton operative, he observes, 'prolonged and exhausting labour, continued from day to day, and from year to year, is not calculated to develop the intellectual or moral faculties of man...The population employed in the cotton factories rises at five o'clock in the morning, works in the mills from six to eight, and returns home for half an hour or forty minutes for breakfast. This meal generally consists of tea or coffee with a little bread. Oatmeal porridge is sometimes, but of late rarely, used, and chiefly by the men; but the stimulus of tea is preferred, especially by the women. The tea is almost always of a bad, and some-

---

[3] Kay-Shuttleworth, Sir James, *Moral and Physical Condition of the Working Classes*, pamphlet, London: Ridgway, 1832.

times of a deleterious quality; the infusion is weak, and little or no milk is added. The operatives return to the mills and workshops until twelve o'clock, when an hour is allowed for dinner. Amongst those who obtain the lower rates of wages this meal generally consists of boiled potatoes. The mess of potatoes is put into one large dish; melted lard and butter are poured upon them, and a few pieces of fried fat bacon are sometimes mingled with them, and but seldom a little meat. ... At the expiration of the hour, they are all again employed in the workshops or mills, where they continue until seven o'clock or a later hour, when they generally again indulge in the use of tea, often mingled with spirits accompanied by a little bread.'

The passage from the faltering paternalism of a decayed moral economy into the ambiguous liberties of political economy brought new poverties—working hours of an intensity unknown in agriculture, adulterated foodstuffs, industrial diseases, pollution, insanitary dwellings, the attentions of bailiff, moneylender and magistrate.

That it is possible for people to become better off economically, even if culturally and psychologically they feel worse, is accepted in connection with the first industrial epoch. Gertrude Himmelfarb says, 'Historians on both sides of the controversy have been at fault: the "optimists", as they are known, who argue so strenuously that the standard of living was rising that they pay little heed to contemporaries who believed otherwise and acted on that belief; and the "pessimists" who maintain that whatever the truth about the material standard of living, the important fact was the decline of the "quality" of life, and who define that quality in terms more appropriate to the sensibilities of a late twentieth-century professor than of an early nineteenth-century labourer.'[4]

Efforts to 'balance' the argument underestimate the disequilibrium of the lives of the early industrial workers, forced from the pinched predictability of country life into chill jerry-built tenements of industry around mills, manufactories and pit towns of the nineteenth century; a process familiar all over the world now, disarmingly expressed by the professionals of other people's uprooting as 'rural-urban migration'. Then, it was a time for sorrowing departures, even though journeys were often only ten or fifteen miles; for people moved into an unknown environment, in pursuit of unfamiliar livelihoods on terms not fully revealed to them.

[4] Himmelfarb, Gertrude, *The Idea of Poverty*, New York: Alfred A. Knopf, 1984.

They sought in squalid exile a precarious sufficiency, undermined by fever, pollution and hunger. And such was the grim harvest of humanity in the northern towns, and so high infant mortality, that life expectancy in Leeds and Manchester in the early nineteenth century was less than twenty years.

E. P. Thompson expresses the common experience: the 'average' working man remained very close to subsistence level at a time when he was surrounded by the evidence of the increase of national wealth, much of it transparently the product of his own labour, and passing, by equally transparent means, into the hands of his employers.[5] In psychological terms, this felt very much like a decline in standards. His own share in the 'benefits of economic progress consisted of more potatoes, a few articles of cotton clothing for his family, soap and candles, some tea and sugar, and a great many articles in the *Economic History Review*.'

There was considerable uncertainty as to the advantages to the people of industrialisation, especially to the labouring poor. (This category lapsed in the mid-twentieth century, although it has made something of a comeback recently, in discussions about a 'living wage')

Karl Polanyi blames 'economistic prejudice' for the judgement that the industrial revolution was no disaster.[6] 'For how could there be social catastrophe where there was undoubtedly economic improvement?' He observes, 'Actually, of course, a social calamity is primarily a cultural and not an economic phenomenon that can be measured by income figures or population statistics. Cultural catastrophes involving broad strata of the common people can naturally not be frequent; but neither are cataclysmic events like the Industrial Revolution—an economic earthquake which transformed within less than half a century vast masses of the English countryside from settled folk into shiftless migrants.' Likening the process to that which colonial powers practised on the cultures of empire, Polanyi believes that, although the economy may be the vehicle of destruction, 'the lethal injury [is] to the institutions in which social existence is embodied. ... The condition of some native tribes in Africa today carries an unmistakable resemblance to that of the English labouring classes during the early years of the nineteenth century.'

[5] Thompson. E. P., *The Making of the English Working Class*, London: Victor Gollancz, 1963.
[6] Polanyi, *The Great Transformation*, op. cit.

Raising economic judgements over and above all others negates any plausible assessment of gain and loss to society, to culture, to civilisation. The triumph of this ideological measure over all others makes it difficult for us to judge both the advantages and the damage to humanity of the coercive change that came with industrialism.

Gain and loss in the present

The doubts and questions over 'progress' in the late eighteenth and early nineteenth centuries have not accompanied more recent social and economic transformation in the western world. These have been exempt from any such interrogation, since it is obvious that everything that has happened since the Second World War has been of unequivocal benefit to all the people. The triumph of economic judgement is no longer contested. In contemporary experience, the relinquishment of those industries, which brought forced change two hundred years earlier, has coincided with such self-evident improvement in the standard of living of the people, that it would be churlish and eccentric to challenge such a development.

One of the questions this book asks is whether, if in the early industrial era, people became better off economically and yet felt this as impoverishment, in our time, an impression of continuous advance and betterment may not also have been accompanied by other kinds of dispossession, the loss of other resources, qualities and attributes essential for a decent life?

If the evidence for this is less clear than for the earlier period, the complaint persists that it is indeed so. If Cobbett and others lamented losses to a declining peasantry amid agricultural 'improvements', consolidation of land ownership in the early nineteenth century, in popular experience, the dramatic advance in the lives of the people in the period since the 1940s, has also been attended by an undertow, a murmur of loss and resentment; a feeling unrecorded by monitors that evaluate only economic improvement—growing incomes and the 'power' to purchase which these bestow upon their possessors. This 'power' lies only in an (admittedly) widening range of goods, services and sensations to which they have access. The instruments that measure this are too crude to record the feeling of powerlessness, the absence of any consultation with the people over whether they wanted the industries, in which their lives had become rooted, and which gave them meaning and function in society, to be swept away. These were abolished with the same indifference towards those who laboured in them, with which they had been established in the first place. There was no sense that the people had any part to play in such decisions; they were onlookers, bystanders of their own fate; and 'democracy' had no role, either in the coming of industry or in its departure. Political slogans of 'people power' freeze on the lips of 'activists' and politicians alike. That the material way of life of people is much improved is not in dispute; only they were never asked about the removal of the reasons for existence of the industrial towns and cities in which they had, in the old journey from country to town, been obliged to make a home.

The question of contemporary nostalgia

What has often been described, emphatically and dismissively, as nostalgia or perverseness, has deep roots. The lament for a golden age—even when such ages were distinctly tarnished or burnished with the gold of fools—is as heritable a feature of British life as an eager yearning for the future. It persists through scenes of change, whether for good or ill—periods of economic boom, years of distress, times of war and want, intervals of expansive hope, moments when people have seen old skills struck from their hands and been forced to acquire new ones, when settled values have been overthrown, and even the perception of good and evil has been modified from one generation to another, almost from one moment to the next.

In our time, popular regret winds itself around the social aspects of economic change, loss of a purpose and social function, as well as of the disintegration of the organisations, institutions and defences of the Labour Movement—the restorative practices initiated by the people themselves against the ravages of industrialism. For these—the solidarities, the consciousness of a shared destiny—have been demolished, along with the mills and factories, forges and mines which gave urgency to the creation of such instruments of resistance. Just as the making of necessities had given people dignity, the certainty that what they made was of use and worth, even if they remained inadequately rewarded for their work, so networks of kinship, neighbourhood and labour had also developed, which, in the absence of any official provision in the early industrial era, offered protection against want, destitution and loss. This, what some economists refer to as 'social capital' had to be demolished, in order to make way for the feelings of insufficiency that created demand—often for the very things people had surrendered—in the marketplace.

The advantages that have accrued to a majority of people—especially women—with the decline of heavy industry are indeed spectacular. The deliverance of women from drudgery, relentless childbearing and repression of the intellect is expressed eloquently by Margaret Forster in her memoir *Hidden Lives*.[7] At the end of her chronicle of women's wasted energies and thwarted intelligence, she writes, 'All the women whose lives and times I have touched upon, would have been able to fulfil themselves in an entirely different and much more gratifying way if they could have benefited from the radical changes in the last half century from which I have benefited ...Everything for a woman is better now, even if it is still not as good as it could be. To forget or deny that is an insult to the women who have gone before, women like my grandmother and mother.'

This is not to be disputed. But it fell to women, whose lives were shadowed by a domestic labour without end—keeping at bay the flakes of soot in the air, boiling the washing in a copper, scrubbing and scouring, a penitential work that atoned for nothing, and subject to the arbitrary caprice of fathers, husbands, brothers and sons—to bring their humanising strengths to what would otherwise have been an unbearable existence without their wisdom and self-sacrifice. It does not do to judge too severely the actions of people in societies where they act under duress. We may be appalled and revolted that men did not practise more of what they preached in the workplace and the trade union, in terms of solidarity and collective responsibility in their own household.

The gains are great, and to suggest that any forfeit outbalances or cancels them is an enterprise that appears as vain as it is doomed.

In spite of this, it should not be thought that the end of any way of life—no matter how oppressive—to which people have given their strength, energy and substance is a matter solely for celebration. Industrial life lasted three or four generations in the towns and cities whose names were synonymous with the making of some necessary article of daily use. It had taken root, and its landscapes shaped—scarred—the mental and moral view of the people. Workers had no say in determining

---

[7] Forster, Margaret, *Hidden Lives*, London: Viking, 1995.

those conditions; but the softening of its hardships by women, its material want and psychic cruelty, especially for children and elders was an incalculable contribution to the maintenance of human decency in brutal times. The figure of the woman, to whom everyone turned in times of suffering, perplexity and grief was neither caricature nor sentimentality; she did not refuse to touch the dead, to clean the incontinent, to console the bereaved and did not judge the wrongdoer. She did not wait to be asked, 'Send for Mrs So-and-So' was the first reaction whenever trouble—that companion of impoverishment, folly and ignorance—appeared. Women acted out of a sense of what was right and just in a world where so much was wrong and unfair.

The values and beliefs that formed the sub-culture of the working class, the sense of shared predicament that ran through all the industrial areas of Britain, simply dissolved when the curse of industrialism was lifted. They ceased to be relevant with the establishment of the welfare state, although in summoning women into paid economic activity, it is significant that disproportionate numbers were absorbed into what became known as the 'caring professions'.

In the heyday of its buccaneering imperialism, Britain has casually shattered other societies in the name of Christianity, improvement, progress, development and all the other high ideals of the self-interested. Colonial subjects were prevented from enacting their rituals, customs and traditions; and went to mourn the loss of meaning in city slums with the consolations of drugs and alcohol

The pit villages and factory towns that fell into ruin in the second half of the twentieth century underwent something of the same removal of purpose. It gave a grievous blow to the sense that people had made of lives which were poor and depleted enough; for posterity to rob it of meaning is to heap further humiliation on those broken by this process.

There is another story concealed by this triumphal narrative of progress; perhaps because it has been told so often, there is no room for any other tale in the overcrowded imagination. The fable confuses deliverance from poverty with the destruction of the industrial base of Britain. There was no other pathway to attain a modest level of prosperity and well-being. Poverty which, for centuries, had been declared by politicians, philosophers and all the wisdom of the ages to be God-given, immutable and inevitable, was suddenly abridged by the system which had told these stories, not because it had changed, but because it was threatened by the socialist alternative; however unreal that threat now appears to have been, it was under this impulse that the better world was summoned into existence after 1945.

And yet, this good fortune was not greeted with jubilation; perhaps because it has been attended by social evils which have no place in the earthly paradise which such an access of riches might have brought about. A morbid desire for more, chronic discontent and a nagging worry that enough is insufficient for our needs; addictions, emotional and mental distress, depression, violence, the desire for perpetual escape from the nihilism that lies behind the altered décor of a capitalist plenty—these are some of the malign attendants of our improved lives. These are, of course, all attributed to human nature, unregenerate and irremediably fallen; an antique plague-pit for all that cannot be accounted for within the narrow compass of economic reason.

Wealth, vitiated by fear of neighbour, distrust of friend and competition of kin; wealth, jealous, vigilant and self-regarding; wealth that lacks generosity of spirit, does not deserve to be called wealth at all, for it impoverishes people within, as well as preying on a shrinking, wasting world.

Mutations of industrialism

If it is now accepted that the social turmoil of the industrial revolution detracted severely from monetary improvements that came with it, the possibility that something similar occurred in recent decades, at the time of the explosion of affluence, has more rarely been broached. Any claim that there may have been sacrifices, forfeits and losses with the coming of general prosperity, has been scorned, since in the presence of the 'opulence' we have seen, such an assertion is preposterous, contrary to common sense, that multi-purpose weapon of the self-interested. But in a world of appearances become reality, the preposterous often lurks beneath the smooth presentation of the obvious. Because the gains have been so spectacular, any loss incurred would have to be fairly dramatic. Whether or not this is the case deserves closer attention.

Does a common thread run through both the imposition of industrial manufacturing in Britain, and the removal of it; that thread being that whatever was being won, gained or conceded to the people, occurred simultaneously with something being taken away, the yielding of some capacity or quality, the perishing of some custom or tradition, the elision of something treasured? Such a view not only calls into question the transference to the modern world of the old Whig version of progress, but might hint at a more sombre reality; that beneath the hymns and sunshine, the mantras and universal chanting of the merits of goods and services available to the people, fraud and expropriation were also taking place. In other words, can economic gains ever compensate for social, psychological and spiritual losses, if such intangibles are not simply the imaginings of the deranged?

Has something been removed by stealth, despite the shining splendour of our good fortune? If so, it was certainly not in the material realm, where all has been so benign that a whole world has to be kept out of the sites of privilege, and 'No Trespassing' signs have been hung with polyglot clarity, for the benefit of those who would still 'vote with their feet', who sometimes forfeit their life in an attempt to circumvent obstacles that are to keep the global poor out of fortresses of wealth and power. Indeed, privilege has been so busy exporting itself to sites of desolation all over the planet, that the model which originated here is now seen as the universal, the only possible, way to grow rich. And even countries whose economic prowess is now so admired, China, Brazil, India, the praise heaped upon them is because they are 'beating us at our own game'. Whether, if the game is truly ours, we can be defeated or not, is another matter.

If anything was cast aside by the fortunate of the earth, as redundant to their new prosperity, what could this have been, and since it was no material thing, does it count; and if so, how is it to be counted?

The fallibility of economic reason

The weakness lies with 'economic reason', a form of rationalisation that seized the minds of privilege in the early nineteenth century, and has exercised a fateful influence ever since. Because humanity has always been haunted by poverty, insecurity, lean seasons, hunger and spoiled harvests, any promise of an end to these ancient threats was bound to be seen as deliverance. What more welcome title could any work bear than that which dwelt upon the *Wealth of Nations*; and how readily the sense it contained hardened into cold wisdom, and subsequently, into dogma, after it had been augmented by all that avarice and egotism could devise. The self-regulating market had not become a revelation in Adam Smith's time, but became so when elaborated by the inheritors of political economy, who had small difficulty in persuading themselves that they had discovered a natural process, a reflection of the workings of Divine Providence on earth.

The calculus of classical economics was always based upon a selective set of values, which measured limited aspects of human interaction, and eliminated everything that did not fit categories that had fixed themselves obsessively in the minds of its practitioners. Much that was omitted was attributed to that 'invisible hand', the guiding extremity of the Creator. Once accepted, this established for all time, as it were, the presence of the god (or God) in the machine; and the act of faith, installed in the realm of reason, was extended there, as though it were commentary on scripture.

Having passed through industrial manufacture and its extinction; having seen the spread of capitalism to virtually the whole world, scything down, crushing or absorbing whole cultures and civilisations, we can perceive more clearly how partial and reductive this ideology was; but its working out in the world was so dazzling and dynamic that, for a long time, it easily concealed the flaws in its theory. We now face the dissolution of that ideology: it survived the onslaughts of socialism and communism, but is now decaying from within, a far more potent work of self-destruction. For a generation, the vanquishing of Communism only strengthened the Western way; indeed, it obscured the fact that we were living through a crisis, not simply of the heresy that was socialism, but of the industrial paradigm itself.

It now appears extraordinary, that humanity should ever have been diminished to the pitifully reduced concept of 'labour', even in the interests of something so momentous as a revolution, industrial or otherwise. Of course, this was admirably suited to the stunted idea which the ruling castes then had of the labouring poor; but its persistence over the generations has been remarkable. Even more bizarre was the formulation by opponents of capitalism of an alternative future based upon the supremacy of this same narrow version of what it means to be human.

The creation of a 'labour market' in the early nineteenth century must stand as one of the most perverse distortions of human purposes ever recorded: humanity, in all its diversity, richness and splendour, re-shaped in the guise of commodity, a factor of production, no different from cabbages or chairs, only more abstract; and hunger was to be the spur that would compel people to offer the work of hands, heart or brain at a price the market would accept; a prompting to which more inert commodities were resistant.

We know what denial this was of the capacities and inclinations of people, what cruel disregard for the mind and spirit (as well as the body), when they were expected to insert themselves into a crude division of labour, in which each town and city in Britain was built upon a single industry. This was justified, not only by the necessities of political economy, but also by the scriptural imperative that, 'in the sweat of your face shall you eat bread, till you return to the ground; for out of the ground you were taken: for dust you are and to dust shall you return' (*Genesis* 3; 19).

So powerful have these beliefs been, that their diversion of human energies still echoes in the pitiful political rhetoric of our time: the 'reform' of an education system that will prepare a new generation for an unknown 'labour market of tomorrow', the urgency of getting consumers into the shops to 'rescue' falling sales, the anthropomorphising of 'the economy', the 'health' of which takes priority over the health of the people, the desire by government to 're-balance' the economy, no matter what other loss of equilibrium may be incurred.

The 'environment' or the life-support system of humanity?

The re-shaping of humanity was not the only derangement required by the making of industrial society. Equally brutal was the transformation of the natural world into 'raw materials' to feed industry. In the early twenty-first century, we can also see the damage caused by false commodities other than labour: the 'products' of the biosphere, the resource-base on which all economic systems depend. This part of the ideological construct was also sanctioned by scripture. 'And God said, let us make man in our image, and after our likeness, and let him have dominion over the fish of the sea and over the fowl of the air, over the cattle, over all the earth; over every creeping thing that creepeth upon the earth.' (*Genesis* 1; 26). What greater licence was needed to justify the use of the earth and its treasures, not so much for human aggrandisement, as for the elevation of a privileged fraction of humanity?

The euphemism, 'the environment', has been invented, in a gesture of secular piety, to register our discovery that the resources of the world are finite; even though all humankind has been pressed into the dissipation of these treasures, in order to fulfil the ideology-become-prophecy of political economy.

We are now dispelling the fiction that nature and humanity are commodities, changed through the savage alchemy of political economy into labour and materials, the rawness of which could only ever have been cooked up by a half-baked creed which has now set a whole planet in ebullition.

The growth of cultures, civilisations, patterns of kinship, affection and community, the necessary labour of survival, as well as the work of celebrating and lamenting our brief sojourn on earth, are indivisible. What have been described as 'externalities' of the economic system—the perishable beauties of the world, the values of belonging, the unbidden gifts and the spontaneous charity of people to one another, in sum, the most precious aspects of our being—are the most vital parts of our life. Yet they have no place in the political arithmetic of the balance sheet and the bottom line; but have been excluded, interlopers with no right to raise their heads in the sublime feasting of money.

Clearly, the areas of human experience ripe for plunder have been as extensive in recent times as at the dawn of industrial society; that they are not necessarily located in those places where a watchful tradition has understandably been accustomed to observe them—in oppressive workplaces and humiliating labour—does not mean they are less real than the violence imposed upon the new manufacturing classes who, unaware still of what historian Eric Hobsbawm called 'the rules of the game', found themselves in an inferno of clattering machinery, which caught them up—sometimes literally—in its hostile workings, often with fatal results. Those who called themselves friends of the people, defenders of the workers, have been largely unaware that the attrition of intangibles—ties of kinship, the ability to act together, sharing of resources—can be as wounding to flesh and blood, to heart and spirit as the physical labour of an earlier industrial era. This myopia has disabled enduring effective action against an economic system, the malign workings of which continue more or less unchecked by the somnolent vigilantes of labour.

Material security was beyond most of the people in the first industrial era: a reasonable sustenance was to be had, only intermittently, following the seasons of trade and money, which proved even less predictable than those of seed-time and harvest. Lack of an assured survival at that time was the urgent preoccupation of trade unions and the politics of labour:

but what were then living, urgent necessities ossified with time, became ritualised, embalmed in phrases like 'the aspirations of the people', while the 'standard of living' was calculated principally in monetary terms, since opposition to capitalism accepted its own evaluation of money as the sole measure of well-being and security; while all the time, like a thief in the night, under cover of rising incomes, people were robbed of things no less indispensable to survival than food or drink—the need for a social function, a sense of meaning and purpose, the recognition of a shared destiny with others, not only neighbours and kin, but also with those in distant places, particularly when their lives were damaged so that we might experience rising income on which our dependency on the market was built. Many of the small comforts that softened industrial life in the nineteenth century were won at the costs of others, largely invisible to the modest beneficiaries of the violence done to them. This has become institutionalised, more intense and extensive in our time, so that there is scarcely anything in daily consumption, a child's toy, a garment, a tropical fruit, a piece of jewellery, uncontaminated by the suffering of people whose existence is unknown to us. This is only a fraction of our unwitting forfeits, the modest privilege won at incalculable, and now apparently irreversible, costs.

The deepest loss

The propaganda of constant material progress—publicity industries, manufactured joys, excitable promises of rewards, prizes and free gifts, offers and giveaways, above all the continuous music, the soundtrack of our lives, as it is sometimes referred to, and the kaleidoscopic images which dazzle the eye and sometimes deceive the heart—have all focused on confirming the evidence of people's senses, that everything is getting better, and must continue to do so indefinitely, despite economic recessions and downturns; interruptions which only emphasise the importance of restoring the status quo, the rising graph, expectations of better tomorrows, which will pursue one another until the last judgement, an adjudication deferred *sine die*.

And here we are close to a more profound loss to all humanity in the modern world, scarcely observed by the clamorous forward march of industrialism; and this loss is the most difficult of retrieval. The idea of perpetual improvement has been so beguiling and plausible, accompanied by such paeans of praise to the productive power of a system become global, that the discarding of alternatives has appeared as trivial as the junking of any other kinds of waste which litter the planet. The claim by Mrs Thatcher in the 1980s that 'there is no alternative'— a propos, at that time, of the continuing de-industrialisation of Britain— was then derided and treated with scorn. But like many enunciations of revelation, over time, it has taken on the allure of common sense, and in its turn, that common sense has been elevated into wisdom, and that wisdom into truth.

The vast majority of countries on earth, even those which, in theory, uphold some form of socialism, have been enticed into obedience to the laws of political economy. Only a few outlaws still defy the consensus, and these are regularly chastised by a right-thinking, recently conceived, 'international community', whose only unifying idea is to hunt down all who deny the monumental orthodoxies of global capital; that these include such unattractive entities as Iran, North Korea, Zimbabwe, and a few of the remaining kleptocracies of Africa—Eritrea, Congo (Brazzaville) and Cameroon—only enhances the zeal of the constituents of that fragile community.

If it is true, as the enthusiasts and defenders of the existing order (and who is not now among them?), that all other ways of answering human need than through the vast conglomerates, by whose grace we now receive our daily bread, rice or corn, have been annulled, this has implications so serious that they are scarcely adverted to by the lovers of pluralism and diversity. If there is no possibility of change (which is to be inferred from the constant insistence of all politicians upon 'change', virtually all of it vacuous and trivial); if we have indeed forfeited our ability to depend on any other method of responding to the basic requirements of humanity than the global market, we have—almost casually, it seems—thrown away a most fundamental freedom. For the capacity to change is no marginal liberty, particularly in the presence of global warming, resource-depletion, reduction of biodiversity and an inequality which no country on earth appears capable of reducing: it has become an urgent imperative at the very point when it has been declared both redundant and unobtainable. The right to choose how to answer age-old questions about the purpose of life, as well as more practical questions of how to provide for seven billion people on the planet, are not abstruse academic questions, for they go to the heart of the deep dependency, produced by an unbiddable market which, if it is self-regulating, is so in defiance of, and inimical to any human agency: like the impenetrable forest, the crashing waterfall or the rocky promontory, it has become a force of nature, and as such, has been made sacred to the artificial indigenes who live in its shadow. Even governments which have voluntarily given up control, believing their intervention could only damage its delicate mechanism, are now incapacitated by their own surrender, and can no longer carry out the democratic desire of their own peoples, if this runs counter to the higher law of the universal market; a market that, like God, can chastise and correct, reward and punish according to a morality against which our conduct offends by its very humanity.

The need for systemic change (not the miserable mantras of 'reform', 'radical new ideas' or 'blue skies' and 'out-of-the-box thinking'), when humanity is confronted by circumstances and dilemmas undreamed of by early industrialism, is essential to survival; and if this has been closed down in the future foretold by the savants of determinist economics, we have been impoverished more profoundly than anything known to even the most wretched farm labourer who, in 1810, with his wife and children, moved his scanty bundle from the wasted hovel of his native village, and set out for the grimmest environment ever known to humankind, the unwholesome tenements of Manchester, the sunless courts and alleys of Sheffield and Leeds, the cellar-dwellings of Liverpool and the rookeries of St Giles.

Something vital, perhaps irreplaceable, has been spirited away from the people, which makes us poorer in ways uncounted by the tellers of wealth and the auditors of bottom lines, which, in any case, threaten to collapse beneath the weight of their fictive figures. That the powers of the world recognise this is heard in the defiant triumphalism of the words they address to the critics, protesters, anti-globalisers and radicals of this generation. 'What would you put in its place?' they ask of those who would change the world; as though this were a vindication of their felling of forests and jungles, exhaustion of resources, pollution of ancient watercourses, vitiation of the air and soil, adulteration of food and the effect of all this on the climate systems of the world. In their challenge lies an acknowledgement of their own responsibility for voiding the earth of its treasures and the evictions of humanity from stability and belonging. The question is to be thrown back at those who pose it: what do they propose to put in place of the used-up elements necessary to sustain the biosphere?

THE IMPOVERISHMENT OF RICHES

It appears that all the indicators calculated to show the resistless advance of humanity through time suggest a far darker progression; and a more just assessment of gain and loss, and indeed, of wealth and poverty, is overdue. We have beguiled ourselves with fantastic stories of 'win-win situations', of something-for-nothing, of painless change, even of more-for-less. But when we weigh the profusion of the world which, according to the economic reckoning, was worth $70 trillion in 2011, against, not only the formidable poverties unanswered by such a sum (3.25 billion people living on less than $2 a day), but the poverties excavated in the heart and psyche of even the richest (the ten million millionaires, perhaps), against the apparent impossibility of finding a way out of a construct which presses each year with greater pressure on the face of the earth, who can tell whether the resources of humanity, like those of the planet, are not becoming visibly more depleted? We may have grown rich individually, but we have been impoverished collectively.

The erosion of cultures

One of the grimmest consequences of global monoculture is its power to extinguish other forms of life and other human ways of living. Biodiversity, linguistic variety and cultural diversity are also victims of the reductive gauge, which measures poverty by the money people do not have, no matter what other abundance, material and spiritual, they may enjoy. Twenty years ago, Wolfgang Sachs pointed out that once it was established that 'poverty' was interpreted as per capita income, and all cultures and societies were subjected to this restricted standard,[8] 'such different worlds as those of the *Zapotec* people of Mexico, the *Tuareg* of North Africa, and the *Rajasthani* of India could be classed together'; a comparison to the 'rich' nations relegating them to a position of almost immeasurable inferiority. In this way, 'poverty' was used to define whole peoples, not according to what they are and want to be, but according to what they lack.

Wolfgang Sachs says, 'Frugality is a mark of culture free from the frenzy of accumulation... Instead of cash wealth, everyone usually has access to fields, rivers and woods, while kinship and community duties guarantee services that elsewhere must be paid for in hard cash....' Sachs

---

[8] Sachs, Wolfgang, in *Context*, Winter 1993, http://www.context.org/ICLIB/IC34Sachs.html

says, 'destitution becomes rampant as soon as frugality is deprived of its foundation—community ties, land, forest and water'. He uses the word 'scarcity' as deriving from modernised poverty. 'It affects mostly urban groups caught up in the money economy as workers and consumers whose spending power is so low that they fall by the wayside. Their capacity to achieve through their own efforts fades, while at the same time, their desires, fuelled by glimpses of high society, spiral towards infinity. This scissor-like effect of want is what characterises modern poverty.'

The cry of indigenous cultures, that they are being forced to enter into the developmental paradigm which, despite its advertised pluralism and tolerance, is cruelly uniform, since it is a forge, in which all the wealth of the world is forged indeed, reduced to money. Bushmen, Penan, Inuit, Yanomami—all have been 'integrated' into a shrinking universalism, in the name of freedom; a freedom which, for many, means the liberty to exist in urban squalor and violence, conditions of which their allegedly 'primitive' society of origin had no conception. It is a cruel paradox, that the values of restraint, modest resource use and respect for the planet— not as expensive add-ons, but as an integral part of conserving cultures— are being trashed, at the moment when they are needed as never before. The best hope for humanity lies, not in mimicking ancient cultures, but in taking from them lessons in moderation and a conserving spirit. The ancient knowledge of cultures which have survived for millennia is not only disregarded, but is extinguished by a civilisation which can tolerate no rival to its piratical wealth-production.

The wasting within

There are other destructive forces concealed by progress and prosperity. They are not made visible, as the wasted stumps of blighted forests are, or the shelters torn by thorn-bushes of that growing group with nowhere to go, the refugees of globalism. The wasting disease of the world not only wears away the fabric of the world, it also consumes human resourcefulness from within. Constant expansion of the market under-mines the ability of human beings to provide for themselves and for others. This affects rich and poor alike. If the rich have the compensa-tory money to buy back all they want, such losses may, for a time, go unobserved. Ivan Illich was one of the first to draw attention to this development, when he described the encroachment of market-provided goods upon the power of human beings to act autonomously in answering their own needs.[9] The need to make, in the active sense, is as great as the need to be provided for, in the passive voice. In 1978 he wrote, 'The peculiarly modern inability to use personal endowments, communal life and environmental resources in an autonomous way infects every aspect of life where a professionally engineered commodity has succeeded in replacing a culturally-shaped use-value. The opportunity to experience personal and social satisfaction outside the market is thus destroyed ... This new impotence-producing poverty must not be confused with the widening gap between the consumption of rich and poor in a world where basic needs are increasingly shaped by basic commodities. That gap is the form traditional poverty assumes in an industrial society ... Where this kind of poverty reigns, life without addictive access to commodities is rendered either impossible or criminal. Making do without consumption becomes impossible, not just for the average consumer, but even for the poor.'

Illich's argument is that, 'beyond a certain threshold, the multiplication of commodities induces impotence, the incapacity to grow food, to sing or to build ... An addiction to paralysing affluence, once it becomes ingrained in a culture, generates "modernised poverty".' Each new item that appears in the market represents a substitute for our own capacity to satisfy the needs of ourselves and those we love; and that capacity falls into a deep slumber, from which only dire necessity will awaken it once more.

In the contemporary ideology of globalism, what the Chilean economist Manfred Max-Neef describes as pseudo-satisfiers of need dominate;[10] that is to say, ways of answering need that only partially fulfil their purpose, or destroy the answering of other needs in the process. Needs are, in any case, re-shaped at source, as it were, so that they appear to be answered by some marketed commodity; and the elusiveness of satisfactions comes, not from the non-availability—or unaffordability—of this or that product, but from the falsification that takes place between need and the object or service that claims to answer it. Constantly renewed desire, which is essential to the function of its continuous disappointment in the encounter with whatever is designed to appease it; and

9 Illich, Ivan, *Towards a History of Needs*, Berkeley, CA: Heyday Books, 1982.
10 Max-Neef, Manfred, *Human Scale Development, Application and Further Development*, New York: The Apex Press, 1991.

William Leiss' 'culture of wanting' is set in train.[11] Among the examples Illich gives of this process of deformation is 'the translation of thirst into the need for a Coke'.

The criticism of market dependency is that it impoverishes in two ways. It robs us of abilities which are part of the basic human patrimony of transmitted competences. That agencies, government or private, must set up classes for parenting, or life skills, or anger management, for dietary counselling, for the conduct of our relationships, suggests levels of basic ineptitude that never affected even the most elementary societies. A requirement to replace lost—or neglected—capacities with expensive and value-added substitutes, indicates a cultural primitivism which would be considered intolerable in any traditional indigenous society. These wasted skills have not been discarded through inadvertence, but have been thrown away; consequences of which are not confined to the poorest, but affect, in varying degrees, all society, which must increasingly 'buy in' what is usually considered the freely conveyed heritage of all members of any human society. Secondly, deeper market penetration of our lives (and the invasive imagery is taken from classic economic discourse) leads to a growing reliance upon material resources, and a propensity to use them up all the faster; for even the former abstractions of appetite, desire and yearning are re-formed by the esoteric recombinant experiments of the market, and transformed into monetary transactions; which can only aggravate the ecological crisis.

The losses associated with this debilitating affluence are usually treated as discrete 'issues', with specialists assigned to the solution of each, whereas they are interlinked and mutually reinforcing, and represent a cumulative and increasingly oppressive impoverishment. So it is that the forfeit of solidarity with neighbours, kin and friends, merges with the loss of function in a widening dispersal of labour, which estranges the doer from the mystifying work which is the object of his or her labour. Instinctive knowledge of how to assuage the sufferings of others, to celebrate our own lives, to relieve the pains and troubles of our existence, to deal with bereavement, grief and separation, is replaced by intense specialisms, profound but narrow qualifications, the expertise of strangers. These are won at the expense of a general knowing of what it

[11] Leiss, William, *The Limits to Satisfaction*, McGill-Queen's University Press, Montreal, 1988.

means to console, heal, amuse, delight and enchant one another; the human reservoirs are emptied of their richness and plenitude, and frozen in the ownership of those whose professional status uniquely entitles them to judge, and even lead, the lives of others.

The appearance in the market of every new wonder, haloed by its must-have desirability, represents in some measure the loss of some neglected or abandoned power. It is inevitable that the succession of objects of novelty and distraction should be accompanied by various forms of forgetting; a feature which pervades much of contemporary life; not only erasure of historical memory by a ubiquitous present tense, but the amnesias of hyperactive media, and the sad and partly-socially induced dementia of the elderly, who collude with a culture that requires forgetting, so that the same old things may be introduced afresh, shining with a patina of newness and perhaps branded as somebody else's intellectual property. It also wipes out memory of other ways of doing things and answering need, and causes all alternatives to fall into the abyss of irretrievable or utopian ideas, unfitted for the sadly fanciful construct of the 'real world'. And finally, it contributes towards the obliteration of that same real world, beloved by economists, politicians and other respecters of a reality which has annulled all others, since that world, in all its beauty and diversity, is being laid waste.

Impoverishment has many guises, other than the ragged neediness of the early industrial period, and there are other roads to serfdom than the over-mighty governments dreaded by Frederick Hayek. Is it because that poverty was so overwhelming and disabling, that it closed our minds to other forms of dispossession, the abstraction of other qualities indispensable to human autonomy and belonging? To be consoled for our lost liberties by deepening market dependency is a sorry comfort, since each step into the glittering caverns of abundance takes us further from the daylight of self-reliance.

Michael J. Sandel writes that, 'Economists often assume that markets are inert, that they do not affect the goods they exchange. But this is untrue. Markets leave their mark. Sometimes markets crowd out non-market values worth caring about.' He shows how commodifying certain precious human attributes diminishes or degrades them ... So to decide where the market belongs, and where it should be kept at a distance, we have to decide how to value the goods in question—health, education, family life, nature, art, civic duties and so on. These are moral and political questions, not merely economic ones.'[12] As more and more aspects of our lives are transformed into market transactions, this process sets these vital experiences out of reach of the poor, and at the same time, damages the values they embody. He considers the marketing of body-parts, the loss of the gift relationship in the donation—or selling—of blood, the ability of companies to take out life insurance on their employees without informing them; and suggests the extension of market relationships destroys the value of things on which no price has previously been set.

The greatest gift to the poor would be the release of wealth from the captivity of money; much as it seemed to the early apologists of capitalism that they were called to free wealth from the constraints of religious faith. Illich understood that while the forms of wealth are many and varied, as long as these are locked up in money, their utility is impaired and their value distorted. While the great truth remains, that the absence of the means to procure survival dooms human beings, it is an even greater falsehood to claim that the amassing of those means leads to a corresponding heightening of well-being. It does not; it is, as it always has been, a form of idolatry, and one that takes on a peculiar malignity in a world that has forsworn religion.

The pathological society

Most who have sought sincerely to attend to the necessities of the poor have done so without seriously interrogating the monetary measures which are believed to secure sufficiency or exclude people from it. Amartya Sen in *Development as Freedom*,[13] following the path travelled by Peter Townsend in his *Poverty in the United Kingdom* in 1979,[14] defines poverty as the inability to function and fully participate in society; on the face of it, an apparently humane and unexceptionable judgement.

Townsend says, 'Poverty can be defined objectively and applied consistently only in terms of the concept of relative deprivation.' For him, relative deprivation has a double meaning: it is relative, not only to other groups in society in relation to which the individual feels relatively

[12] Sandel, Michael J., *What Money Can't Buy: The Moral Limits of Markets*, New York: Farrar, Straus and Giroux, 2012
[13] Sen, Amartya, *Development As Freedom*, Oxford: Oxford University Press, 1999.
[14] Townsend, Peter, *Poverty in the United Kingdom*, Berkeley and London: University of California Press, 1979.

deprived, but it is also relative to the changing patterns of living and consumption in the same society. He gives, as an example of the latter, the changing nature of clothing. 'Who would lay down a scale of necessities for the 1970s for young women in Britain,' he asks, 'consisting of one pair of boots, two aprons, one second-hand dress, one short skirt made from an old dress, one-third of the cost of a new hat, one-third of the cost of a shawl and jacket, two pairs of stockings, a few unspecified underclothes, one pair of stays and one pair of old boots worn as slippers, as Rowntree did in his survey of York in 1899?'

Yet underlying this common sense are implications which Townsend, even as late as 1979, could not perhaps have foreseen. For instance, with change, which may or may not represent 'progress' and 'development', if a decline in nutritional standards should occur, would one who clings to archaic notions of an austere diet which actually sustains health, be poorer than one who crams him or herself with denutrified but more expensive foodstuffs? If Townsend could not have been expected to anticipate this, Sen certainly might have done so. For if the very customs and norms of societies from which people are excluded, become pathological, who can measure the poverties which affect those favoured by being among the included and participating? Societies whose consumption patterns appear to betray, as one of their principal motivations, a morbid desire to find out what lies on the other side of their own destructiveness, cannot be said to be balanced or rational.

In this context, if the ability to function socially is the measure of fully taking part, then whatever is needed to bring people to the required level must be provided, even if this means a continuing assault upon their own power to answer need and upon what remains for future generations. That human inventiveness may permit us to evade the consequences of our actions remains a possibility, however slim; promises to mine precious metal from asteroids or colonise outer space are gambles which have taken on disproportionate significance in the rapid depletion of the only planet we—so far—have, upon which to practise our already advanced skills of sabotage. Simply because the many prophets of apocalypse, from the *Book of Revelation* to Malthus, turned out to be wrong, this does not guarantee permanent immunity from collapse, as the history of even the most enduring and impregnable empires shows.

If the psalms and hymns in praise of the achievements of capitalism are so loud and relentless, this is because they conceal more effectively the disruption within. Beneath the display and showy appearances, something is always being removed from our possession; and as fast as it is reclaimed, the requisitions and appropriations move on elsewhere. Because relief from the most basic want has haunted the desires of humanity, the gift of abundance has been used, not to satisfy need, but to mask the filtering away of things no less precious than those vital for our sustenance. The celebration of wealth serves as the occasion for almost all the festivals in the western world; and the spirit of perpetual carnival only shrouds the curtailment of freedoms, the narrowing range of choices, a growing powerlessness over our fate.

The slogan 'what the people want' has been the cry of the immobilists of permanent progress. What the people do not want, but what they must have if they are to enjoy the sometimes damaging luxuries of industrial society, is less loudly heard; but all the grim attendants of wealth—crime, violence, drugs, waste, impotence, fear—follow in its train, an inseparable part of the evils that accompany the goods that capitalism has famously delivered.

Why are the undeniable advantages that have been placed at our disposal by our productive power believed to be inseparable from the ruinous penalties that spoil contentment? Where is it written that it is not possible to enjoy all that is necessary for a decent and dignified sustenance, without the excess and exorbitance, and without the co-existence of what Carlyle called 'idle luxury alternating with mean scarcity and inability'? The idea that if the evils were abolished, the goods, too, would instantly vanish, is an empty but potent threat. This sense of menace that hangs over our fragile well-being is essential to the maintenance of insecurity, which will feed our continued striving for more and our search for an elusive, unattainable place to rest and to savour the fullness of life.

This is the blackmail of the rich. It is the corollary of the one-sided bargain, that if the rich become much richer, the poor may become a little less poor; with the implication that if anyone lays a hand on our wealth, interferes with our capacity for accumulation, all the slender prosperity and flimsy comforts will be destroyed and brought to nothing.

Who can believe that in a world without the excesses of those prepared to dismantle the planet in pursuit of their megalomaniac dreams, life would be pallid, grey and worthless? To rid society of this trauma would be, not privation but liberation. How has it come about, that livelihood, survival and happiness of everyone depends upon the caprice of the rich, and their willingness to create the wealth which alone will permit us to survive, never mind to live well? How did the colonisers of sufficiency, the enclosers of the public commons, the land-grabbers of the necessities of others, come to rule the world? Even the words for their misdeeds have lapsed in the language—the engrossers and regraters, the usurers and simonists, along with the bestiary of a vanished population of sharks, wolves, vultures and jackals, have not ceased to exist, but the vocabulary that denotes their activities has died, so that the dominance of the world does not appear to have passed into the hands of sinners, or malefactors, but is in the control of those re-branded as entrepreneurial heroes, philanthropists, benefactors and humanitarians.

New Poverties

The emergence of new forms of poverty, sometimes only glimpsed, rarely more than partially visible, does not conform to predictions made by Marx, since not only are the areas in which they occur not material, but it is the very material abundance of capitalism which has been the source of these other, less palpable, but equally harmful, poverties. Since the desire for security and sufficiency is one of the most persistent dreams of humanity, it is difficult to conceive of a social and economic system that could effortlessly fulfil that dream without dreadful costs, including the ruin of many other human satisfactions. It may appear perverse to posterity that the price of plenty should have proved beyond the means of a system that could have achieved it, but failed to do so for arcane doctrinal purposes, which are as relevant to the contemporary world as Luther's denunciations of interests on loans, since these were 'invented by the devil and sanctioned by the Pope'.

It is now possible to judge the extent of the poverties that have accompanied the conspicuous enrichment of late industrialism. Not only the ruin of belonging, towns and cities whose reason for existence has been abolished; but, far more compelling, the cancellation of alternatives to the dynamic that devours the earth and calls it development. The death of socialism, and complicity in its funeral rites by social democracy, have left a single, apparently incontestable system, to which deepest liberties are forfeit, if there are indeed no other ways of answering human need than through its approved and inescapable mechanisms. For the cost of this is the price of the planet and the future generations who were to have been

its inhabitants. All this adds up to an overwhelming experience of collective impoverishment; but since the world has concentrated solely on
individual enrichment, wider depowerment goes largely uncounted. If
ever radical solutions were required, it is now, in this most conservative,
most fearful, time. Such thinking would demand a more critical analysis
of wealth and its implications; in a reminder of the blame which people
attached to the Poor Laws for creating the poverty they sought to heal,
the 'answer' to human dilemmas—wealth—would appear as the principal
cause of the evil it claims to remedy.

The fate of rich and poor is inseparable, despite efforts to keep them
apart—gated communities, exclusive clubs, the appropriation of the best
locations, privatised spaces, secret gatherings in 'playgrounds', unspoilt
paradises of privilege. The simultaneous existence of the extremes to
which the world is host impairs the well-being of the rich no less than it
jeopardises the survival of the poor.

The right to life is the most fundamental of all human rights. But an
economic and social system which boasts its global reach and its power to
deliver trivial commodities to what were, until yesterday, the most remote
places on earth, nevertheless believes it 'natural' that millions of women
each year give birth over a grave, even while, elsewhere in the same global
order, purposeless wealth accumulates to serve nothing more than vanity
or greed. The right to life should not be a distant 'millennium goal', when
the objective of delivering fizzy drinks or hamburgers to sites where life is
extinguished for want of clean water, can be realised without effort.

Thomas Carlyle tells a parable from an Edinburgh doctor about the
connectedness of human destinies.[15] 'A poor Irish Widow, her husband
having died in one of the Lanes of Edinburgh, went forth with her three
children, bare of all resource, to solicit help from the Charitable Establishments of the City. At this Charitable Establishment, and then at that,
she was refused; referred from one to the other, helped by none;—till she
had exhausted them all; till her strength and heart failed her, she sank
down in a typhus-fever; died, and infected her Lane with fever, so that
seventeen other persons died of the fever there in consequence. The
humane Physician asks thereupon, as with a heart too full for speaking,
"Would it not have been economy to help this poor Widow? She took
typhus-fever and killed seventeen of you!—Very curious. The forlorn

[15] Carlyle, Thomas, *Past and Present*, London, 1843.

Irish Widow applies to her fellow-creatures, as if saying 'Behold, I am sinking, bare of help; ye must help me! I am your sister, bone of your bone, one God made us, ye must help me!' They answer, 'No; impossible; thou art no sister of ours!'; But she proves her sisterhood; her typhus-fever kills them; they actually were her brothers, though denying it!'"

Because the privations of our abundance do not have the tangibility of physical poverty, our response is not straightforward. It often expresses itself in ways that bear little apparent relation to the experience of loss. The cult of immoderate consumption is one of these: a denial of limits by flaunting their absence, an obsessive fascination with the agents of disassembling Creation; reverence for the lords of the world, whose inventiveness in the making of wealth grants them licence for irresponsible destructiveness.

There are many historical precedents for irrational behaviour in reaction to dispossession: the apocalyptic ghost-dance of the defeated culture of the Plains Indians, the Canudos of Brazil who built their sacred city under the influence of Antonio Consilheiro in 1893 (the story told by Mario Vargas Llosa in the *War of the End of the World*), the visionaries who told their followers to divest themselves of all they possess on a date revealed by their prophet, and to await the end of the world on a mountain top; the followers of the cultists who preferred to die in the Branch Davidian siege at Waco in 1993, the Jonestown massacre in Guyana in 1978 or the 600 deaths in 2000, in Kanganu in Uganda, all members of the Restoration of the Ten Commandments cult founded by Joseph Kibwetere. The early industrial era in Britain was characterised by the intense devotional feeling of Methodism, or Karl Mannheim's 'mass frenzy and a despiritualised fury',[16] which E.P. Thompson[17] also saw in the cult of the prophetess, Joanna Southcott.

Our own time has also been characterised by chiliastic cults, but the spiritual and emotional disorientation of recent upheavals in the West has been effectively recuperated within the system that generates that confusion. Movements like Scientology and the Moonies have prospered in the past half-century, but the fastest-growing cult in the world is sometimes described by the still faintly ironic term 'consumerism.' This institutionalised aberration is not necessarily seen in its most characteristic form in

---

[16] Mannheim, Karl, *Ideology and Utopia*, New York: Harcourt Brace, 1936.
[17] Thompson, *The Making of the English Working Class*, op. cit.

the queues outside department stores on winter nights, and the bursting through the doors of what are called 'bargain-hunters' in a disorderly rush when the doors open at 4am, although that is one of its festive rituals. It is observable daily, in what is described by attentive economists, as the 'footfall' in the ex-urban malls and vending galleries of the modern world; and in the wonder provoked by each new object of merchandise that appears there is also a sense of astonishment that such things should be available, that we should have survived until now without them and that we have been unable to answer the delight they furnish from within the fast-depleting treasury of our own creative imagination.

The raising of 'the consumer' into human identity has been a fateful development. It demonstrates the power of an economic system to sustain its growth by expanding the capacity of humanity to ingest whatever it produces: without a voracious appetite for all available goods, that system would perish. As it is, people grow obese as the world shrinks. It is the mirror-image of what, in another era, made people into one-dimensional labour; it has the same reductive quality, isolating as it does, a single aspect of our being, and making of it the crucial component of who we are.

Its power to work through the subjectivity of people has nothing to do with a human nature, to a deep understanding of which it lays claim: it is the nature of capitalism, and if it knows how to render itself indistinguishable from human yearning, this is a tribute to its artful ingenuity, its capacity to insinuate itself into the heart and spirit. In a curious after-echo of the first industrial epoch, it, too is an industrial project, in its mining of desire, its manufacture of wants, its weaving of dreams on the less substantial looms of fantasy, its forging of needs and its fabrication of answers to wants never yet formulated. This culture of wanting threatens to engulf the planet; the exigencies to which it responds have little to do with the objects, services or experiences actually purchased, which are almost arbitrary; but the formidable output of the great engines of production must be subject to a swift and wasteful trashing by devotees of the cult. Schumpeter's 'creative destruction' is alive and well, and we are eager apprentices to the mystery, ready to devour the commodities that arise as variants of our obdurately scanty needs, needs that must be worked, re-worked and worked-over again, in order to fashion new items to squander and turn to the dust to which we shall also return.

THE IMPOVERISHMENT OF RICHES

The paradox of wealth

Is it coincidence, that as humanity is chastened by its own destructive power, and driven to the penitent imperative of conserving the planetary heritage, the individuals who command most respect are those who can requisition for their consumption the largest proportion of global resources? The growing divergence between rewards received and contributions to society is one thing—as in the self-administered emoluments of bankers and Chief Executives of corporations and transnational companies; but it is quite another, that people should be admired, not for any accomplishment, but simply for being rich. These find themselves objects of emulation, 'role-models', simply because they have wealth or celebrity (usually both), rather than as the result of any valuable skill or meritorious proficiency. To be rich is now regarded as a fitting ambition for the young; a compensation, perhaps, for coming into a world which cannot be changed, since it was already brought to a state of high perfection long before they were born. This inheritance of despair is to be redeemed only by the heaping up of compensatory treasures, all too corruptible by moth and rust, since rapid disintegration is built into their flimsy composition.

What might puzzle impartial observers (should any be found in this best of all possible worlds), is why the rhetoric about more careful resource-use, safeguarding the natural riches of the world, and passing them on, intact, to future generations, is accompanied by greater paroxysms of destruction by people feted for their heroic capacity to consume. Why are the agents of planetary demolition so noisily applauded?

'Imagine no possessions,' sang John Lennon (echoing *Matthew* 19:21)— the only line in his remarkable career for which he was ridiculed. It might be expected that chronicling the lives and loves of the rich, their extravagant passions and expensive sorrows, the caprice of fame, the grandiose expenditures of power, would be, in a wasting, wanting world, not a cause for celebration, but a social disgrace. Those who live with reckless disregard for the well-being of the poor, in both the present and the future, might have expected to be regarded, not as champions of liberty, but as trampling the freedoms of others. The pieties enunciated about poverty remain sterile cant until the issue of wealth is addressed, even though any assault on the acquisitions of the rich is regarded as a secular sacrilege. If the legions of people dedicated to 'poverty-abatement' were to turn a portion of their fractious energies to the extenuation of wealth, some small contribution to equity might be achieved.

For this is the 'secret' of poverty; and despite the passionate efforts devoted to its 'abatement', its 'mitigation', even its 'abolition'; despite poverty-reduction goals and aspirations, its relationship with wealth remains, like an adulterous union between some archaic monarch and favourite, clandestine, an object of careful concealment and profound official silence.

The remedy for poverty lies in the cure for wealth

The sickness of rich societies is not caused by poverty. Poverty is merely an aspect of what we, perhaps mistakenly, call wealth. However unpopular the figures of the banker-as-conjuror, financial regulators with their softness of touch, the dexterous drivers of investment vehicles and wise managers of hedge funds have become, this has done nothing to impair the exaltation of wealth, a feature as old as humanity, but intensified since the invention of political economy, and reaching its zenith in the contemporary world, where high 'net-worth' individuals, celebrities and those whose turbo-charged life-styles serve as example to more humble aspirants to majestic consumption. No longer oppressors of the poor, the rich, perceived by the religious of an archaic age as extortioners, and by more recent socialists as appropriators of the necessities of the people, have been transformed into their emancipators; since it is thanks to their wealth and power that we enjoy amenities apparently indispensable for our survival.

At the same time, the sweat and tears of the poor have become exudations of shame; the sucked blood and exploited substance have ceased to be objects of pity, and are now regarded as a necessary price to pay for the treasures which the rich, the makers of the weather, make to rain down upon us. They appear frequently on TV screens as 'philanthropists' and benefactors, categories, the principal qualification for which is an ample fortune. Whoever heard of a poor philanthropist?

This makeover of the rich, so they now appear in the world as bringers of harmony and peace, is a direct consequence of the 'failure' of the oppressed and the poor to justify hopes vested in them by now-nullified ideologies of liberation. The redemptive 'destiny' of a working class, despite the 'scientific' dreams of Marx, showed itself to be illusion; but the rich, well aware of the value of such a role, have picked it up and assumed the restitutive mantle, since they have been able to promote their dauntless labour in the vineyards of wealth as the salvation of humankind.

Not only have the representatives of the poor been proved incapable of fulfilling their exciting, if menacing, role as dispossessors of privilege, they have also showed themselves to be as unjust and corruptible as those they were to have overthrown. This has been a double calamity for the emancipatory doctrines of socialism which, unrealised, now occupy a limbo akin to that of Christianity (ah yes, say its dwindling band of devotees, but 'true' socialism, like 'real' Christianity, has never been given a fair chance, betrayed, as it has been, by its prophets and leaders). The liberators of humanity looked to the labouring poor as 'agents' of social transformation. They allied themselves with the political vanguard in the march of progress, which would wrest power from its unworthy holders and employ it in the interests of the exploited and humiliated; even if the exploited and humiliated perversely chose new forms of exploitation and humiliation over promises of emancipation.

The prophets and visionaries of new dawns, better tomorrows and other worlds, were confounded. Their project was subject to the most audacious takeover bid in history, as the rich presented themselves, full of new-found virtue, to realise dreams which the labouring poor had ceded to them. Former plutocrats, grinders of the faces of the poor, vampires and capitalists, have been rehabilitated, not only by their own powers, but also by the dismal neglect of the workers to play the part allotted to them, whose supporters had guilelessly imagined that history—the fickle opportunist—was on their side.

The ascent of the rich to the high places they occupy has been effortless; they have taken over the task of rescuing humanity from the coarse toiling hands of its would-be liberators. They did not have to free themselves from the toils of a faith which regarded them with the circumspection due to those who set at risk their immortal soul. They didn't have to convince the people that they were not plutocrats, or that they had not bilked widows and orphans of their charitable pence. They have been wafted upwards by virtue (the supreme virtue) of money, unencumbered by whether it is inherited, meritoriously gained, acquired through the marketing of some talent or a win on the lottery. Money is the equivalent in a secular society of divine grace, and it lights upon the elect who are answerable to no one.

The rich occupy a supraterrestrial space, which scorns national boundaries and the limitations of geography. Their talent for the generation of wealth will bring the whole world into capitalism's realm of freedom, that *pays de cocagne*, utopia, a never-never land, far more material than any of the castles in the air constructed by the myopic seers of socialism.

Billions of anxious faces turn towards the healing light of the countenance of the rich; no wonder we are watchful in our service: we dance attendance on their whims, observe with unconcealed envy the mansions of the blest where they dwell, the fleet conveyances that facilitate their busy mobility, the tireless labour of their exceptional talents, the aura of magical luxury which spangles their passage through the world. We cannot get enough of their multiple homes, guarded islands, exquisite taste and enviable possessions, their celestial loves and epic tragedies; even their failed relationships and expensive divorces, public detox and private rehab, showy suicide attempts and premature deaths do nothing to impair our wonder at their superior station; their sufferings only make us weep the more in sympathy with a lofty existence which we can only mimic, hoping for a visitation of the same transforming power which our small skills and the blessing of Lady Luck may conceivably bring.

It is natural that the bankruptcy of ideologies of popular empowerment should have shifted trust once more from the collective power of the poor onto the mighty; a re-affirmation of older forms of deference. Few now admit to having believed in the virtues of the poor, and recantation is in the air; it has, after all, been the historic function of wealth to command the labour, allegiance and respect of the people. What distracted ideologues repine for promises of revolution in a world returned to its sense, in resumption of control by its rightful owners?

Revolutions, moral and material

Thus the ideology of political economy has been made material. And just as theory has been frozen, as it were, in the pyramids of marble and glass, cascades and hanging gardens, sacred groves of a paradise regained by an economic cunning that has outwitted the gods, there is no poverty in this world that is not an artificial fabrication, the shadow of wealth. While attention is turned towards the 'problem' of the poor, and the abolitionists of poverty seek to enhance their miserable income and raise their depressed purchasing power, the true progenitors of poverty continue their baleful course unhindered and untouchable.

THE IMPOVERISHMENT OF RICHES

The medieval world, dark, backward and superstitious, did possess one piece of knowledge denied to modernity. It distrusted the temptations of wealth because it saw these as more destructive than a near-universal poverty. The poor never looked to economic growth for succour. When what they wanted became readily attainable in the industrial era; it was withheld, and if this was for reasons of scarcity, this was a scarcity of the heart and a want of the imagination.

Tawney wrote about an economy no longer embedded in a wider culture, but liberated from the constraints of religion.[18] Even he could not have foreseen the extent to which wealth would become the object of veneration, not merely taken out of society, but elevated over and above it, source of the abjection of a humanity which magnifies its own creation.

But Tawney showed how ancient sins could be changed into virtues essential for accumulation. There is, therefore, no reason why, in a depleted world of want and waste, an equally significant reversal might not take place. Why should avarice and greed not once more be recognised for what they are—a subversion, not only of the right of the poor to subsistence, but also the zealous assistants of the malign work of dissolution of a whole planet? The direct connection between the reverence for wealth and the destruction of the human habitat has been elided, so these appear to exist independently of each other; and an impermeable barrier seems to separate the accumulations of riches on the one hand, and the erosion of the resource-base on the other; the world gutted of its treasures that can no longer sustain or heal has nothing to do with the predations of the rich. The awkwardness of this is often eased by the recruitment of celebrities, who ally themselves with the defence by indigenous people of their sacred lands against mining conglomerates, become 'goodwill ambassadors' to the starving, 'speak out' against wars over diamonds, precious metals and stones, deplore the hunters to extinction of ancient forms of life, for the sake of ivory, aphrodisiacs, medicines and pelts, lead campaigns against drugs that have, in many countries, claimed as many lives as a medium-sized war, support resistance to the alienation of land from subsistence farmers, herders and nomadic cultivators, even deplore the criminal economy of Mafiosi, gangs and organised fraud that mocks and mimics official enterprise. What more effective camouflage could be imagined for combatants on the side of such destructive justice?

---

[18] Tawney, *Religion and the Rise of Capitalism*, op. cit.

Of course, nothing would be more senseless than adding to the woes of the world, in countering this deformed notion of riches. Neither force nor violence is likely to be effective, since the superior weaponry, not all of it physical, is in their hands. If the sins of Christianity could be surreptitiously transformed into virtues under the magic touch of economic dynamism, what would it require for the virtues associated with economic growth in a perishing world to appear, not as heroic and worthy of applause, but as shame and disgrace? What this needs is a change of perception, perhaps the most subtle revolution of all. It would be vain to think that the existing order is going to be overthrown by physical force and disturbance, of which there is always more than enough. But the power of human vision, the ability to see the same things in a different light, animated the apostles of modernity, energetic individuals impatient with inhibitions imposed by religious custom and archaic law upon their talent and prowess; why should such capacities be beyond us under the burden of the doom-laden orthodoxies of our time not be available to us?

It would be good to think it unnecessary to turn upon wealth the insolence it adopts towards poverty—the contempt in which it holds the losers, no-hopers, failures and no-account trash. If only it were enough to see wealth as the ashes of prodigality; the used up waste of greed; the futile heaping-up of demolitionists of the earth. Is it possible to imagine the mansions of the wealthy mouldering unregarded; the gaze of indifference wandering over their exorbitance; the exhausted iconography of jewels, furs, yachts and private islands become emblems, not of self-glorification, but of dishonour and betrayal; their inert beauty being met, not with adulation, but with the careless glance and neutral shrug.

There is, perhaps, no need for animosity against those who believe they have 'made it', have 'got it all'. The withdrawal of public approval from the prodigies of the market, the favourites of fortune, whose measureless appetites have become a strange object of admiration, would shrivel the boastful vanity. Let wealth be left to pursue its lonely course in the world, while the rest of us devote ourselves to what matters, our own lives, no longer impoverished by the prestige of those who claim deference only for their adroit manipulation of money.

An indolent habit of admiration for all that money can buy, and the dull aspiration to pursue it, are hard to break. But when an increasing proportion of the price we pay for everything goes into dismantling the future, it is as perverse as it is irrational to revere those who wield the most hefty hammers in this labour of destruction.

THE IMPOVERISHMENT OF RICHES

Remedies for poverty that blame the poor demonstrate the changeless antiquity of prejudice, despite our faith in 'progress'. That poverty is irremediable is an integral part of the mysterious dogmas of wealth-creationism. To this end, symptoms of being poor—addiction, idleness, demoralisation—are described as causes; and these can be safely located in the moral failings of poor people. Assessments of poverty that measure only its distance from wealth are a re-hash of the work by older cartographers of Maps of Pauperland. Policies that renounce efforts to define sufficiency are grounded in despair. To abandon redistribution is to acknowledge that have-nots merit the nothing they possess, while those who imagine a 'cure' to be found in economic growth, defy the ability of people to endure humiliation without protest. Above all, the incapacity to admit the impoverishments which have accompanied our accumulation of riches make us all poor.

The retrieval of another version of wealth is something we practise daily, since it lies in the freely given, the acts of mercy and charity, the performance of duty, the endurance and patience of those who care for the infirm, sick and old, all the gifts of humanity not subject to the transaction or the exchange, all that is shared voluntarily, the pooled resources and the recognition of a common vulnerability, the ability to see ourselves in others, a validation of the homely and familiar, the capacious storehouse of inner human resources, to which the material treasures of the world are ancillary, the simplicity of our needs and the ease with which they can be satisfied outside of the market. Poverty-reduction requires first and foremost a diminution of the wealth that makes poor. Wealth-abatement is a slogan unlikely to be hung in the marble halls of merchandise, the human-made hanging gardens with their harvest of inedible fruit, the assembly lines of the factories of China, the drug-processing laboratories of Mexico, the bauxite mines deep in the ancestral lands of indigenous people, nor even not in the collecting boxes shaken at the somnolent conscience, with their image of an emaciated child, the white aid vehicles disappearing in a cloud of the red dust of Africa. Without some mitigation of this sickly parody of what it means to be rich, poverty remains, not merely a comfortable associate of wealth, but its indispensable, most cherished companion.

CONCLUSION

It was believed by the medieval world that 'natural law', that is, the law of God, forbade usury and demanded a just price and a fair day's wage. With the coming of the industrial era, political economy discovered that the laws of nature did not conform to the simple understanding of antiquity. The laws of nature were in reality the laws of commerce, and these were the laws of God. If such a dramatic inversion can occur, no matter over how long a period, there is no reason why such another revolution in ideas should not take place, even though there may not be centuries at our disposal for its accomplishment. Greed, covetousness and avarice have shown themselves as destructive of human happiness in our late, wise, age as they ever were; yet the greedy and covetous are everywhere regarded with emulous awe. The dangers of wealth have become apparent once more, not because they threaten our chances of a happy afterlife, but because they plunder the natural world, at the risk of threatening this life for future generations. We have come full circle. Poverty is merely a by-product of the vast wealth we have known: it does not depend upon wealth for its easement, but upon sufficiency and security, accomplishments well within our capacity.

If any change in our perception of human behaviour is unlikely to occur for the sake of our immortal soul, that is all the more reason why it should occur for the sake of our mortal existence, and our enduring sense of human justice.

Jeremy Seabrook   London, July 2013

INDEX

INDEX

INDEX

INDEX

development in, 26; Keighley, 145; Leeds, 145, 194, 206; Liverpool, 206; living wage in, 40; London, 69, 72, 96, 132, 146, 166, 185, 187; Manchester, 112, 137, 192, 194, 206; migrant communities in, 144–6, 176–7; Parliament, 22, 46, 67, 90, 109; Sheffield, 206; St Giles, 129, 206; York, 127, 131–2, 213
United States of America (USA): 123, 128–9, 155; Branch Davidian Siege (1993), 217; labour force of, 118
Unwin, Jane Cobden: 105
urbanism: 100

vagabonds: as subcategory of poor, 67–8; beggars described as, 44–6, 48

wealth: 24, 148, 212, 222, 224–5; accumulation of, 25–6, 214, 223; as ambition, 219–20; celebration of, 214; creation of, 8, 17, 86; 'ignorance of wealth', 191; religious view of, 15–16
wealth-creationism: 8, 17; role of the poor in, 153
Webb, Beatrice: co-founder of Fabian

Society, 132; role in Poor Law Commission (1906), 132–3
Webb, Sidney: co-founder of Fabian Society, 132; role in Poor Law Commission (1906), 132–3
welfare state (UK): 23–4, 148, 188; creation of (1945), 23, 35–6; opposition to, 150–1; structures of, 149
West, Rebecca: 125
Wilberforce, William: 73
William Senior, Nassau: 90, 92
Wilson, Harold: background of, 27
Winstanley, Gerard: *True Levellers' Standard Advanced* (1649), 51
workhouses: 31–2, 64, 66, 72, 102, 128–9; conditions in, 67, 103; creation of, 62–3; infant and child mortality rate in, 72–3; opposition to, 58, 74; proposed regulation of, 103
World Bank: 18
Wycliffe, John: 42

Young, R.: *Poor's Advocate, The*, 57–8
youth population: shift in motivation of, 156–7

Zimbabwe: 205